New Directions in the Study of Policy Transfer

Policy transfer analysis seeks to make sense of the cross-cultural transfer of knowledge about institutions, policies or delivery systems in an era of globalization. The purpose of this volume is to evaluate how useful policy transfer analysis is as a descriptive, explanatory and prescriptive theory of policy change. It provides both a response to its critics and it presents a variety of new directions for studying processes of policy transfer. The chapters proceed from an underlying assumption about the field of enquiry; that policy transfer analysis alone cannot provide a general explanatory theory of policy change but when combined with other approaches an empirically grounded account of policy change can be developed. Hence each of the chapters adopt a methodological pluralism in which complementary theories of policy development are combined in order to develop a theory of policy change that accounts for the role of particular agents of policy transfer in forging policy change. This is an important contribution to our understanding of the impact of globalization on domestic policy formulation.

This book was previously published as a special issue of *Policy Studies*.

Mark Evans is Director of the Australia-New Zealand School of Government's Institute for Governance at the University of Canberra. Mark's published research focuses on four areas of concern: public administration and public policy; policy analysis; evaluating the impact of processes of globalisation on domestic policy formation; and, post-war reconstruction and development. The research theme that binds all of these areas together is his interest in institution-building and processes of governance.

New Directions in the Study of Policy Transfer

Edited by Mark Evans

Routledge
Taylor & Francis Group

LONDON AND NEW YORK

First published 2010
by Routledge
2 Park Square, Milton Park, Abingdon, Oxfordshire OX14 4RN

Simultaneously published in the USA and Canada
by Routledge
711 Third Avenue, New York, NY 10017

Routledge is an imprint of the Taylor and Francis Group, an informa business

First issued in paperback 2015

This book is a reproduction of *Policy Studies*, vol. 30, issue 3. The Publisher requests to those authors who may be citing this book to state, also, the bibliographical details of the special issue on which the book was based.

Typeset in Times New Roman by Value Chain, India

British Library Cataloguing in Publication Data
A catalogue record for this book is available from the British Library

ISBN 978-0-415-58400-5 (hbk)
ISBN 978-1-138-97706-8 (pbk)

Contents

Notes on contributors

Bossman E. Asare is in the Division of Social Science, Graceland University, Lamoni, IA, USA.

Claire A. Dunlop is a lecturer in the Department of Politics, University of Exeter, Exeter, UK.

Mark Evans is Professor of Governance, Australia–New Zealand School of Government, Director, Institute of Governance, University of Canberra.

Chris Holden is Lecturer in Global Health, Centre on Global Change and Health, London School of Hygiene and Tropical Medicine, Keppel Street, London WC1E 7HT, UK.

Claudia Landwehr is Schumpeter Fellow at the Institute for Political Science at the Goethe-University Frankfurt am Main. She is currently leading a research project on the distribution of health care in OECD-countries. Her most recent publications include Political conflict and political preference. Communicative interaction between facts, norms and interests (Colchester: ECPR Press 2009) and 'Deciding how to decide. The case of health care rationing', forthcoming in Public Administration.

David Marsh is Professor of Politics, Director of the Research School of Social Sciences, Australian National University; Research School of Social Sciences, ANU College Of Arts And Social Sciences; Room: 1110 Coombs Bldg 9; Canberra, Australia.

Andrew Massey is Professor of Politics, Department of Politics, University of Exeter, Amory Building, Rennes Drive, Exeter EX4 4RJ, UK.

Sucheen Patel is affiliated to the Department of Politics, Queen Mary College, University of London, Mile End, London E1 4NS, UK.

J.C. Sharman is a Professor and Queen Elizabeth II Fellow in the Centre for Governance and Public Policy at Griffiths University, Australia; Centre for Governance and Public Policy, 170 Kessels Road, Nathan, QLD 4111, Australia.

Donley T. Studlar is in the Department of Political Science, West Virginia University, Morgantown, WV 26506-6317, USA.

Katrin Toens is an assistant professor at the Institute for Political Science at the University of Hamburg. She is currently working on a book about the implementation of European higher education reforms in Germany. Her most recent articles include 'The dilemma of regress. Justice and democracy in recent critical theory' (European Journal of Political Theory 2007, (6) 2, 160_179) and 'Lobbying for justice. Welfare associations in Europe' (European Integration Online Papers http://eiop.or.at/eiop/texte/2006-010a.htm).

INTRODUCTION

New directions in the study of policy transfer

> First, if any individual points have been well made by previous writers, let us try to follow them up; then from the collection of constitutions we must examine what sort of thing preserves and what sort of thing destroys cities and particular constitutions, and for what reasons some are well administered and others are not (Aristotle, 384 to 322 BCE, *Nicomachean Ethics*, X, 1181b).

Studying policy transfer

There is nothing new about the concept of policy transfer or its application. As early as 315BC, Aristotle in his *Nicomachean Ethics* advised fellow citizens of the rationality of engaging in lesson-drawing from positive and negative experiences in the development of great city states. Yet although policy transfer has been habitual practice since the dawn of civilization, it has become increasingly common to observe that there has been an upsurge in the scope and intensity of policy transfer activity as a consequence of changes to the field of action in public policy-making (see Dolowitz and Marsh 2000, Common 2001, Evans and Cerny 2004). It is claimed that this is largely the function of the world of public policy becoming smaller due to dramatic changes in global political and economic institutional structures and to nation states themselves as an outcome or response to various processes of globalization.

At the same time, these structural changes have precipitated a range of problems at the organizational level such as: issues of cost containment; increased pressure on public organizations to engage in income generating activities; the need for more effective coordination of policy systems across sectors and levels of governance; new patterns of need caused by the widening gap between rich and poor, changing social and demographic patterns (e.g. longer life expectancy, smaller sized families); greater ethnic diversity and conflict within urban areas; the formation of stronger regional identities; and rising expectations of public services due to the pervasiveness of quality management. As public organizations do not always possess the expertise to tackle these problems, they increasingly look outside the organization to other governments or non-governmental organizations for the answers. Richard Rose (1991, p. 3) observes that:

> Every country has problems, and each thinks that its problems are unique ... However, problems that are unique to one country ... are abnormal ... confronted with a common problem, policy makers in cities, regional governments and nations can learn from how their counterparts elsewhere responded.

Moreover, the public demands more from government than ever before and this form of pressure politics has been mediated through politicians to civil servants:

> This government expects more of policy-makers. More new ideas, more willingness to question inherited ways of doing things, better use of evidence and research in

policy-making and better focus on policies that will deliver long-term goals (Blair 1999).

Given the complexity of public policy-making and operational delivery and the emphasis on evidence-based, risk averse decision-making, policy transfer has increasingly become the 'rational choice' for policy-makers (see Davies *et al.* 2000, Pawson 2002) and different forms of policy transfer such as bandwagoning (Ikenberry 1990), convergence (Bennett 1991), diffusion (Majone 1991), emulation (Howlett 2000), policy learning (May 1992), social learning (Hall 1993) and lesson-drawing (Rose 2005) have been identified in a wide ranging interdisciplinary literature.

Policy transfer analysis therefore seeks to make sense of the cross-cultural transfer of knowledge about institutions, policies or delivery systems from one sector or level of governance to another level of governance in a different country. As Harold Lasswell (1970, p. 3) said, policy transfer analysis is about providing 'knowledge of and knowledge in policy making'. Policy transfer analysts are therefore interested in: pre-decision-making processes and the key actors which shape policy-making; transfer programme management and enhancement; policy implementation and the causes of policy 'failure'; and issues involved in researching and studying policy change. Policy transfer analysis therefore focuses on one or more of three areas of study that are commonplace in normal policy analysis: description, *how policy transfer is made*; explanation, *why policy transfer occurs*; and prescription, *how policy transfer should be made*.

Critique

Policy transfer analysis, however, is not without its critics. There are four main areas in which the policy transfer approach has been subject to critique. First, it is argued that policy transfer analysis cannot be distinguished from normal forms of policy-making in general (Evans and Davies 1999) and rational approaches to policy-making in particular (James and Lodge 2003), and, by implication, it has no distinctive domain of enquiry. Second, it is further claimed that policy transfer analysts fail to advance an explanatory theory of policy development (James and Lodge 2003). Third, policy transfer analysts are also accused of failing to provide rigorous tools for evaluating whether policy transfer has occurred or not (Page 2000). Fourth, it is maintained that policy transfer analysts fail to make their research relevant to the world of practice (Evans 2006).

Purpose

The purpose of this book is to evaluate how useful policy transfer analysis is as a descriptive, explanatory and prescriptive theory of policy change. It provides both a response to its critics and it presents a variety of new directions for studying processes of policy transfer. The articles which follow proceed from an underlying assumption about the field of enquiry: that policy transfer analysis alone cannot provide a general explanatory theory of policy change but when combined with other approaches an empirically grounded account of policy change can be developed. Hence each of the following articles adopt what Rod Rhodes (1995) has termed a methodological pluralism in which complementary theories of policy development are combined in order to develop a theory of policy change that accounts for the role of particular agents of policy transfer in forging policy change. So with this purpose and assumption in mind seven new directions in the study of policy transfer are presented in this volume.

Counter critique

Mark Evans begins with a consideration of the four central research questions in the study of policy transfer. What is studied when policy transfer is studied? How is policy transfer studied? Why do public organizations engage in policy transfer? In what ways can the policy transfer approach be improved? He then presents a multi-level 'action based' approach to policy transfer analysis which has been deliberately designed to confront the central criticisms of policy transfer analysis. The purpose of this opening article is to provide readers with both a technical introduction to the study of policy transfer and a critical argument.

David Marsh and Jason Sharman then demonstrate that the policy transfer and the policy diffusion literature share a great deal in common in so far as they both observe that diffusion/transfer is an important factor in policy change and identify a similar range of mechanisms as driving transfer/diffusion. It is argued that the logical next step is for each approach to study how these mechanisms interact. Diffusion and transfer differ significantly in terms of the structural approach of the former versus the agent-centred approach of the latter. Marsh and Sharman therefore contend that we need to integrate these approaches if we are to establish patterns of diffusion and explain how and why they came about.

Claire Dunlop's contribution to improving the explanatory power of policy transfer analysis focuses on enhancing our understanding of decision-maker learning. She utilizes Peter Haas's (1997) epistemic community framework as a means of exploring the influence of experts in international policy transfer and capturing the variety of ways in which decision-makers learn from their knowledge. Dunlop suggests that variety is best captured by differentiating between the control enjoyed by decision-makers and epistemic communities over the production of substantive knowledge (or means) that informs policy from the policy objectives (or ends) to which that knowledge is directed.

Chris Holden turns his mind to the limited attention that has been paid in policy transfer analysis towards the role of strategy in policy-oriented learning. He also investigates the role of an agent of transfer which has largely been ignored in the existing literature but plays an increasingly salient role in public service production: commercial interests. He investigates these agents of transfer through a case study of an attempt to export Public Private Partnership (PPP) services. His article concludes that the attempt to export PPP services entails a strategy of trying to 'export' the policy itself, despite evidence that the technical capacity needed by the public sector to make the policy effective is often lacking in the target countries. Hence, policy transfer occurs for financial gain rather than to realize public value.

In his account of the reform of the Bank of England in the post-war era, Sucheen Patel develops a multi-level explanation of policy change which integrates policy transfer analysis with incrementalism and the policy streams approaches. The contention of this article is that the driving forces behind the two monetary decisions are analogous and can best be explained using three models of policy change.

Incrementalism is used to explain the long-term historical background to the reform processes. Policy transfer provides an account of the external influences which informed the process of policy-oriented learning. The multiple streams approach allows for a consideration of issues of monetary control and credibility that predisposed the Labour Party to adjust the institutional status of the Bank of England, thus reversing earlier policy. It employs these models to demonstrate an association between the factors that brought about the policy for nationalization and a similar set of factors that set in motion the policy to grant its independence. In sum, Patel presents a classic exposition of the use of methodological pluralism in policy analysis.

Katrin Toens and Claudia Landwehr's innovative article on cross-national and cross-sectoral policy-learning proceeds from the argument that the existing literature is characterized by the absence of a comparative assessment of the risks and potentials of different strategies of policy-learning. This sin of omission does not only have significant implications for the study of policy learning but also for its practice. The authors use the normative concept of improvement-oriented learning to assess the risks and potentials of three learning strategies: imitation, Bayesian updating and deliberation. They observe that the distribution of risks and potentials is most advantageous in deliberative learning strategies, but that imitation is the most risky learning strategy, and Bayesian updating ranges somewhere in-between.

Bossman Asare and Donley Studlar investigate the role of lesson-drawing in facilitating policy change in the context of multilevel governance. The article examines the impact of processes of lesson drawing on the adoption of restrictive secondhand smoke policies in Scotland and England in 2006 and 2007. The study finds that, in both countries, secondhand smoke policies were influenced by the adoption of similar policies in other English-speaking jurisdictions, especially the Republic of Ireland. Moreover, the adoption of a non-smoking policy in Scotland influenced policy development in England. These observations confirm existing claims of similar policies developing in the English-speaking 'family of nations' even at different levels of government (Evans 2004).

The final substantive chapter by Andrew Massey takes issue with the concept of 'policy transfer' arguing that it is more accurate to refer to *policy mimesis* (the imitation or reproduction of a policy in another context) rather than a simple transposition across geographical and political boundaries. It further argues that there are levels of isomorphism within a given public administration and in consequence both coercive and mimetic isomorphism, as well as professionaliza-tion act as intrinsic dynamics to successful policy mimesis. Massey's observation emphasizes the importance of situating policy analysis within its proper context and giving due attention to issues such as time (chronologically and historically), culture, political culture, economics and geographical location. The issue's conclusion provides an overall assessment of the utility and prospects for policy transfer analysis as a heuristic theory of remarkable forms of policy-making which emanate from cross-cultural policy-oriented learning.

Contribution

In summary then, through a combination of theoretical and empirical enquiry, this special issue attempts to advance our understanding of policy transfer in three ways.

First, the issue provides the first critical introduction to the study of policy transfer since 2000 (Dolowitz and Marsh 2000). Second, it seeks to demonstrate the value of adopting multi-level, interdisciplinary frameworks for describing and explaining processes of policy transfer. Third, it emphasizes the importance of making policy transfer analysis relevant to the world of practice (Burton 2006).

Professor Mark Evans

Director, Australia-New Zealand School of Government,
Institute for Governance, University of Canberra

References

Bennett, C., 1991. Review article: what is policy convergence and what causes it? *British journal of political science*, 21, 215–233.

Blair, T., 1999. *Modernising government*. London: HMSO.

Burton, P., 2006. Modernising the policy process: making policy research more significant. *Policy studies*, 27, 3.

Common, R., 2001. *Public management and policy transfer in Southeast Asia*. Aldershot: Ashgate.

Davies, H., Nutley, S. and Smith, P., eds., 2000. *What works? Evidence-based policy and practice in public service policy*. Bristol: Policy Press.

Dolowitz, D. and Marsh, D., 2000. Learning from abroad: the role of policy transfer in contemporary policy-making. *Governance*, 13, 5–24.

Evans, M., ed., 2004. *Policy transfer in global perspective*. Aldershot: Ashgate.

Evans, M., 2006. At the interface between theory and practice: policy transfer and lesson-drawing. *Public administration*, 84 (2), 479–489.

Evans, M. and Cerny, P.G., 2004. Globalisation and public policy under new labour. *Policy studies*, 25 (1), 84–107.

Evans, M. and Davies, J., 1999. Understanding policy transfer: a multi-level, multi-disciplinary perspective. *Public administration*, 77, 361–386.

Haas, P.M., 1997. *Knowledge, power and international policy coordination*. Columbia: University of South Carolina Press.

Hall, P., 1993. Policy paradigms, social learning and the state: the case of economic policy-making in Britain. *Comparative politics*, 25, 275–296.

Howlett, M., 2000. Beyond legalism? Policy ideas, implementation styles and emulation-based convergence in Canadian and US environmental policy. *Journal of public policy*, 20 (3), 305–329.

Ikenberry, J.G., 1990. The international spread of privatisation policies: inducements, learning and policy bandwaggoning. *In*: E. Suleiman and J. Waterbury, eds. *The political economy of public sector reform*. Boulder: Westview Press.

James, O. and Lodge, M., 2003. The limitations of 'policy transfer' and 'lesson drawing' for public policy research. *Political studies review*, 2003, 179–193.

Lasswell, H., 1970. The emerging conception of the policy sciences. *Policy sciences*, 1, 3–14.

Majone, G., 1991. Cross-national sources of regulatory policy-making in Europe and the United States. *Journal of public policy*, 11, 79–106.

May, P., 1992. Policy learning and failure. *Journal of public policy*, 12, 331–354.

Page, E.C., 2000. *Future governance and the literature on policy transfer and lesson drawing*. Paper prepared for the ESRC Future Governance Programme Workshop on Policy Transfer, 28 January 2000.

Pawson, R., 2002. Evidence and policy and naming and shaming. *Policy studies*, 23, 211–230.

Rhodes, R.A.W., 1995. The changing face of british public administration. *Politics*, 15 (2), 117–126.

Rose, R., 1991. What is lesson drawing? *Journal of public policy*, 11, 3–30.

Rose, R., 2005. *Learning from comparative public policy: a practical guide*. London & New York: Routledge.

Policy transfer in critical perspective

Mark Evans

Australia–New Zealand School of Government, Institute of Governance, University of Canberra, Australia

The world of public policy is becoming increasingly small due to dramatic changes in global communications, political and economic institutional structures, and to nation states themselves. This article evaluates the implications of these changes and challenges for both the study and the practice of policy transfer and provides an understanding of the relationship between systemic globalizing forces and the increasing scope and intensity of policy transfer activity. It provides: an explanation of policy transfer as a process of organizational learning; an insight into how and why such processes are studied by policy scientists; and an evaluation of its use by policy practitioners. The article argues that the limits of policy transfer analysis as a descriptive, explanatory and prescriptive theory of policy change can be addressed through the development of a multi-level 'action based' approach to the study of policy transfer.

Introduction

This article provides an assessment of the development and current use of the concept of policy transfer as it has evolved in the study of public policy. Its purpose is to evaluate the character of this interdisciplinary approach to cross-national policy development and to assess its strengths, weaknesses and potential theoretical and methodological development. It therefore considers: the domestic and international circumstances that are likely to bring about policy transfer; the key approaches to the study of policy transfer that have emerged over the past decade; and, the scope and dimensions of the policy transfer process. The article is organised around a consideration of four central research questions. What is studied when policy transfer is studied? How is policy transfer studied? Why do public organisations engage in policy transfer? In what ways can the policy transfer approach be improved?

What is studied when policy transfer is studied?

Policy transfer analysis is a theory of policy development that seeks to make sense of a process or set of processes in which knowledge about institutions, policies or delivery systems at one sector or level of governance is used in the development of institutions, policies or delivery systems at another sector or level of governance. Different forms of policy transfer such as bandwagoning (Ikenberry 1990), convergence (Bennett 1991), diffusion (Majone 1991), emulation (Howlett 2000), policy learning (May 1992), social learning (Hall 1993) and lesson-drawing (Rose 2005) have been identified in a wide ranging literature which has attracted significant academic attention from domestic, comparative and international political scientists.

The contemporary study of policy transfer originates from policy diffusion studies, a sub-set of the comparative politics literature. Research in this area focused on identifying trends in timing, geography and resource similarities in the diffusion of innovations between countries and, in the United States, between states in the federation (see Walker 1969). However, these studies revealed little about the process of transfer apart from its identification of mechanisms of diffusion and focused exclusively on the study of policy transfer between developed countries. The latter preoccupation continues to characterize much of the contemporary literature on policy transfer which has primarily focused on studying voluntary policy transfer between developed countries as a process in which policies implemented elsewhere are examined by rational political actors for their potential utilization within another political system (Dolowitz and Marsh 2000).[1] This article begins by describing the scope of enquiry in policy transfer analysis with regard to agents of policy transfer, forms of policy transfer, processes of policy-oriented learning, obstacles to policy-oriented learning and outputs of policy transfer.

Agents of policy transfer

The study of policy transfer analysis should be restricted to action-oriented intentional learning: that which takes place consciously and results in policy action. This definition locates policy transfer as a potential causal phenomenon: a factor leading to policy convergence. However, this article distinguishes policy transfer from policy convergence in that the latter may occur unintentionally, for example due to harmonizing macroeconomic forces or common processes. The element of intentionality in this definition of policy transfer makes an agent essential to both voluntary and coercive processes. Intentionality may be ascribed to the originating state/institution/actor, to the transferee state/institution/actor, to both or to a third party state/institution/actor. For example, if the agent of a particular transfer is the state which first developed the policy, or a third party state (Country C) seeking to make Country B adopt an approach by Country A, it is likely that there are coercive processes at work. Alternatively, there may be a series of agents at work either simultaneously, or at different points in the process. A necessary but insufficient criteria for identifying policy transfer is therefore to: (1) identify the agent(s) of transfer and the policy belief systems that they advocate; (2) distinguish the resources that they bring to the process of policy-oriented learning; (3) specify the role they play in the transfer; and (4) determine the nature of the transfer that the agent(s) is/are seeking to make. At least eight main categories of agents of transfer can be identified in the literature on policy transfer: politicians; bureaucrats; policy entrepreneurs including think-tanks; knowledge institutions (KIs), academicians and other experts; pressure groups; global financial institutions; international organizations; and supra-national institutions (see Stone 2000b).

Forms of policy transfer

Policy analysts deploy the policy transfer approach as a generic concept that encompasses quite different claims about why public organizations engage in policy learning. Typically, policy transfer analysts refer to three different processes of transfer: voluntary transfer or lesson-drawing, negotiated transfer and direct coercive transfer. The first is a rational, action-oriented approach to dealing with public policy problems that emerge from one or more of the following: the identification of public or professional dissatisfaction with existing policy as a consequence of poor performance; a new policy agenda that is introduced due to a change in government, minister or the management of a public organization; a political strategy aimed at legitimating conclusions that have already been reached; or an attempt by a political manager to upgrade items of the policy agenda to promote political allies and neutralize political enemies.[2]

The second and third processes of transfer involve varying degrees of coercion and are common in developing countries. Negotiated policy transfer refers to a process in which governments are compelled by, for example, influential donor countries, global financial institutions, supra-national institutions, international organizations or transnational corporations, to introduce policy change in order to secure grants, loans or other forms of inward investment. Although an exchange process does occur, it remains a coercive activity because the recipient country is denied freedom of choice. The political economy of most developing countries throughout the 1980s and 1990s has been characterized by the implementation of SAPs in return for investment from the IMF, or the World Bank. This is a reflection of the pervasiveness of negotiated forms of policy transfer to developing countries.[3] Another form of indirect policy transfer can be identified when governments introduce institutional or policy changes due to a fear of falling behind neighbouring countries. For example, Japan's economic miracle in East Asia proved inspirational to neighbouring countries such as Singapore, South Korea and Malaysia. John Ikenberry (1990, p. 102) terms this process 'bandwagoning'.

Direct coercive policy transfer occurs when a government is compelled by another government to introduce constitutional, social and political changes against its will and the will of its people. This form of policy transfer was widespread in periods of formal imperialism and its implications can still be seen today in contemporary Mexico, Kenya, India, Pakistan, Sri Lanka, Zimbabwe and South Africa, for example. In developed countries, however, policy transfer activity tends to focus on voluntary transfer or lesson-drawing. Negotiated processes of transfer can be identified with regard to majority decision-making in the European Union (see Wincott 1999, Padgett 2003), but such forms of transfer tend to be the exception rather than the rule.

Processes of policy-oriented learning

Four different processes of policy-oriented learning emerge from the process of transfer (Evans 2004b). The first and rarest form of policy-oriented learning is *copying* where a governmental organization adopts a policy, programme or institution without modification. For example, the former UK Chancellor of the Exchequer, Gordon Brown's working family tax credit system is a direct copy of the

American earned income tax credit system (Evans 2004a). Second, there is *emulation* where a governmental organization accepts that a policy, programme or institution overseas provides the best standard for designing a policy, programme or institution at home. For example, US policy once again proved the standard against which English crime control policy was made under New Labour (Tonry 2004). *Hybridization* is the third and most typical form of policy-oriented learning. This is where a governmental organization combines elements of programmes found in several settings to develop a policy that is culturally sensitive to the needs of the recipient. For example, New Labour's welfare programme 'New Deal for Young People' was a product of lessons drawn from initiatives in Australia ('Lone Parents and Partners', 'Working Nation' and 'single gateway/one stop shops' programmes), Sweden ('Working Nation'), the Netherlands ('single gateway/one stop shop' programmes), Canada (the 'Making Work Pay' scheme) and over 50 'Welfare to Work' schemes in the USA. In addition, institutional memory (for example, 'Job Seekers Allowance' and 'Restart' schemes from 1988 and 1996) was also influential (Evans 2004a). Fourth, there is *inspiration* where an idea inspires fresh thinking about a policy problem and helps to facilitate policy change (Common 2001). The Guardian newspaper recently reported a meeting between Bernie Ecclestone, the owner of Formula 1 Holdings and officials from the UK's Department of Health and Great Ormond Street Hospital. The subject of the meeting was to discuss the lessons that could be drawn by Accident and Emergency departments from the organization of rapid pit stops during Formula 1 Grand Prix focusing specifically on Health and Safety policy.

Obstacles to policy-oriented learning

The proof of policy transfer lies in its implementation. In other words, it is not possible to identify the content of a transfer and by implication whether transfer has occurred without adopting an implementation perspective. So what factors can constrain policy transfer and policy-oriented learning? As Figure 1 illustrates, three broad sets of variables have been identified in the British case study literature: 'cognitive' obstacles in the pre-decision phase, 'environmental' obstacles in the implementation phase and domestic and, increasingly, domestic public opinion. These variables interact in complex and often unexpected ways and inform the process of policy transfer. 'Cognitive' obstacles refer to the process by which public policy problems are recognized and defined in the pre-decision phase, the breadth and detail of the search conducted for ideas, the receptivity of existing policy actors and systems to policy alternatives and the complexity of choosing an alternative. The most significant cognitive barriers for agents of policy transfer to overcome at this stage of policy development are normally issues arising from the prevailing organizational culture and the need for effective cultural assimilation of policy alternatives.

'Environmental' obstacles refer to the absence of effective cognitive and elite mobilization strategies deployed by agents of policy transfer, the need for the development of cohesive policy transfer networks to ensure successful policy-oriented learning, the broader structural constraints (institutional, political, economic and social) that impact and shape the process of lesson-drawing and the normal technical implementation constraints that inhibit or facilitate the process of

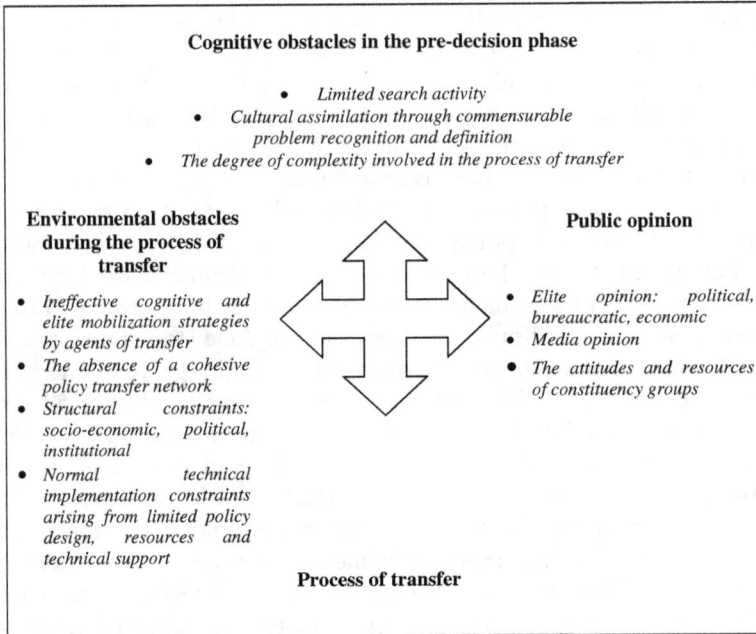

Figure 1. Mapping potential obstacles to processes of policy transfer*.
*This is an interactive model in the sense that these sets of variables do not exist in a vacuum; they interact in complex and often unexpected ways.

lesson-drawing (Sabatier 1986). The latter would include: coherent and consistent objectives; the incorporation of an adequate causal theory of policy development; the sensible allocation of financial resources; hierarchical integration within and among implementing organizations; clear decision rules underpinning the operation of implementing agencies; the recruitment of programme officers with adequate skills/training; sufficient technical support; and the use of effective monitoring and evaluation systems including formal access by outsiders.

Outputs from the process of transfer

Using Peter Hall's (1993) terminology, the outputs from processes of policy transfer can include: first order change in the precise settings of the policy instruments used to attain policy goals (marginal adjustments to the status quo); second order change to the policy instruments themselves such as the development of new institutions and delivery systems; and third order change to the actual goals that guide policy in a particular field (negative ideology, ideas, attitudes and concepts). Of course, negative lessons can be drawn in each form of policy change.

How is policy transfer studied?

The literature on policy transfer analysis may be organized into two discernible schools: one which does not use the label 'policy transfer' directly but deals with different aspects of the process using different nomenclature and one which uses the concept directly. This amorphous literature can be organized into five main approaches: process-centred approaches; ideational approaches; practice-based approaches; comparative approaches; and multi-level approaches.

While there is inevitably some overlap between these approaches (for instance, all of them engage in some form of comparison) they are all distinctive with regard to their central focus of inquiry.

Process-centred approaches

Process-centred approaches focus on the process of policy transfer directly in order to explain the voluntary or coercively negotiated importation of ideas, policies or institutions. It argues that policy learning is based largely on the interpersonal interaction between agents of transfer, bureaucrats and politicians within inter-organizational settings. In these settings there exists a pattern of common kinship expressed through culture, rules and values. Hence, an emphasis is placed on analysing the structure of decision-making through which policy transfer takes place and relationships between agents of transfer and their dependencies. These include state and non-state actors who are actively engaged in policy learning such as bureaucrats and think-tanks. Process-centred analysis also tends to be a predominantly inter-state approach that emphasizes the role of state actors as active agents seeking solutions to policy problems rather than the passive agents depicted in pluralist or corporatist decision literatures. Rose (1993, p. 6), for example, deploys the concept of lesson-drawing as a method for learning from past and/or extra organizational experiences, emphasizing the role of the bureaucrat and the programme itself in the process of policy learning.

Rose's research in the 1990s on lesson-drawing contributed to our social scientific understanding of both the role of the programme as an instrument of public policy, and the conditions under which programmes can be effective in non indigenous settings. For Rose, the important features of this process are the circumstances surrounding the learning of lessons from other sources, the extent to which they are adopted and, crucially, the impact they have on the new policy environment. His research is virtuous in its descriptive understanding of policy development and can be used to explain certain aspects of the process of transfer. The research ably demonstrates who has relationships with whom and it can describe how these relations impinge on the making of policy (e.g. why some actors are influential and others are not). However, while the approach is important to our understanding of the nature of the process of transfer, it has shortcomings in explaining why policy transfer takes place in the first place due to the limited reflection on the role of exogenous forces in processes of lesson-drawing. Rose also provides limited empirical evidence to support his main empirical assertions and focuses completely on voluntary processes of transfer between developed countries.

Practice-based approaches

Three prescriptive avenues for policy transfer analysts have emerged associated with organizational learning, evidence based policy-making and comparative public policy. The organizational learning approach is largely a product of management studies and its concern with public sector learning from the private sector. Indeed, it has superseded Total Quality Management as the key strategy for improving public sector performance (Tushman and Nadler 1996). It is based on the proposition that the quality of an organization rests on its ability to demonstrate that it can learn collectively through the application of new knowledge to the policy process or innovation in policy implementation. As Olsen and Peters (1996, p. 4) note, organizational learning involves the 'development of structures and procedures that improve the problem-solving capacity of an organization and make it better prepared for the future'. The literature distinguishes between the notions of organizational learning and the learning organization. The former is based on observing learning processes within organizations, while the latter provides an action-oriented perspective for improving the performance of public organizations.

It is noteworthy, that recent research in this area by Reschenthaler and Thompson (2001, p. 53) concludes that 'governments and organizations within government have been, and are, seriously disadvantaged as learning organizations'. This approach has only very recently been introduced in the study of policy transfer through Richard Common's (2004) study of the British government's attempt to become a learning organization. It is particularly useful in helping policy analysts to identify potential obstacles to policy transfer and in providing insights to practitioners on how to develop the type of learning organization conducive to the facilitation of successful policy transfer (see Pedler *et al.* 1991).

The second prescriptive avenue for policy transfer analysts' was largely a response to new political dynamics. The British government's 1999 *Modernising government* White Paper represented an acknowledgement of the need to modernize policy and management at the centre of government. It argued that government 'must produce policies that really deal with problems; that are forward-looking and shaped by evidence rather than a response to short-term pressures; that tackle causes not symptoms' (Cabinet Office 1999). The Blair government's aspiration was given institutional expression through the creation of the Centre for Management and Policy Studies which had a clear mandate both to establish more productive relations between government and academia in order to generate high quality evidence-based research to inform practice and to consider the broader training needs of the civil service (Cabinet Office 2002). The Cabinet Office's (2001) *Better policy-making* mapped out an evidence-based approach to policy for achieving the former based on: reviewing existing research, commissioning new research, consulting relevant experts, and/or using internal and external consultants and considering a range of properly costed and appraised options. The Cabinet Office's (2005) *Professional skills for government* programme dealt with the skills and training requirements of the civil service.[4] There has subsequently been an explosion of intellectual and discursive activity around the evidence-based practice approach, the establishment of the ESRC UK Centre for Evidence Based Policy-making and Practice at Queen Mary College, University of London and even an academic journal (*Evidence and Policy*) but little evidence as yet of improvements in government policy and operational delivery (Davies *et al.* 2000, Burton 2001, 2006).

The third prescriptive avenue has emerged from within the comparative public policy literature on lesson-drawing. Richard Rose's (2005) *Learning from comparative public policy: a practical guide* confronts, though perhaps unwittingly, two of the central problems with much of the present academic literature on public administration in general and lesson-drawing or voluntary policy transfer in particular.

First, there is the relative absence of enterprising prescription to help public organizations solve public policy problems and, second, a stark failure to engage with practice, reflected in the reluctance to make social scientific enquiry relevant to practice. This has made it all too easy for practitioners to dismiss social scientific enquiry as 'abstract' and 'impractical' at a time when academics should be helping to set the public policy agenda. The integral relationship between evidence-based practice, rational lesson-drawing and good policy-making has created a political space for comparative public policy specialists to provide a unique contribution to public policy discourses.

Learning from comparative public policy combines social scientific reflection on the domain and utility of the concept of lesson-drawing with a prescriptive enterprise aimed at providing a practical guide to learning. As Rose (2005, p. xi) asserts, it is '... not a book about explanation, for theories that specialize in explanation, such as rational choice, do not tell you how to do what is rational. This book is addressed to readers who want to learn how to draw lessons'. He defines a lesson and its domain of utility as a:

> ... distinctive type of programme, because it draws on foreign experience to propose a programme that can deal with a problem confronting national policymakers in their home environment ... It is a practical, nuts and bolts outline of the means as well as the ends of policy (Rose 2005, p. 22).

The chapters that follow in his account are organized around a detailed sequential discussion of 10 steps that Rose recommends to practitioners in order to evaluate whether or not a non-indigenous programme should be applied domestically:

(1) Learn the key concepts: what a programme is, and what a lesson is and is not.
(2) Catch the attention of policymakers.
(3) Scan alternatives and decide where to look for lessons.
(4) Learn by going abroad.
(5) Abstract from what you observe a generalized model of how a foreign programme works.
(6) Turn the model into a lesson fitting your own national context.
(7) Decide whether the lesson should be adopted.
(8) Decide whether the lesson can be applied.
(9) Simplify the means and ends of a lesson to increase its chances of success.
(10) Evaluate a lesson's outcome prospectively and, if it is adopted, as it evolves over time (Rose 2005, p. 9).

Each chapter draws on selective empirical, personal anecdotal evidence and assertions from secondary literature culminating in the observation, 'As time goes by, the ultimate achievement is that the foreign origins of a programme are forgotten. It then becomes described as no more and no less than the way we do things here' (Rose 2005, p. 139).

A critique of Rose's work would rest on the identification of four sins of omission. The first would be the lack of a discussion about the relationship between the concept of lesson-drawing and the broader literature on policy transfer. Given the salience of this literature in British political science in particular it is important for Rose to clarify his terms within this context to lend clarity to the debate for students and scholars alike. The second, is that it is difficult to discern between the concept of lesson-drawing and normal forms of policy-making in general (Evans and Davies 1999) and rational approaches to policy-making in particular (James and Lodge 2003) and, therefore, it has no distinctive domain of enquiry. However, lesson-drawing does have a distinctive domain of enquiry rooted in its cross-national character. Third, the lesson-drawing approach cannot provide a general theorization of policy change that accounts for all processes of lesson-drawing. It can only provide a partial account of policy change emanating from the relationship between the structure of the policy network and the agents operating within them and the network and the policy outcome. If applied in isolation from macro-analysis, this overlooks the potential for the existence of a causal relationship between the network and the environment in which it operates. Moreover, at the same time, the network is interpreted, reinterpreted and constrained by participating actors. Hence, the complex, interactive relationship between network (structure) and agency needs to be analysed in any study of lesson-drawing. This criticism is in keeping with Keith Dowding's (2001, p. 89) depiction of non-formal models as 'time consuming', 'expensive' and prone to 'trivial findings'. Fourth, Rose can also be accused of not providing rigorous tools for evaluating whether a lesson has been drawn or not (Evans and Davies 1999). Moreover, finding the evidence that a lesson has been drawn demands excellent access to key informants in informal decision-making processes. Such access is not often possible.

From the perspective of practice, two main shortcomings are evident. The first is that the study would have benefited from a reflection of how traditional organizations can become learning organizations. Rose (2005, pp. 104–105) argues that the strategic direction of public organizations are path dependent and characterized by 'inheritance rather than choice' in the sense that 'past commitments limit current choices'. Hence a set of recommendations on how to break from the 'wicked context' problem would have been extremely useful (see Common 2004). Second, a more detailed identification of potential obstacles to successful lesson-drawing would have provided important insights for practitioners into how to develop: (1) the type of learning organization conducive to the facilitation of successful lesson-drawing and (2) how to develop a model of prospective evaluation to guide effective lesson-drawing.

Ideational approaches

There are three main accounts of policy development using ideational-based studies that are worthy of brief discussion here: the social learning approach, the epistemic community approach and discursive approaches. These approaches are united in arguing that it is systems of ideas which influence how politicians and policy-makers learn how to learn and they all address the problem of when and how politicians, other policy makers and societies learn how to learn.

Social learning approaches do not make explicit reference to the concept of policy transfer but rather seek to provide a general theory of policy change. The relationship between the two literatures, however, is self-evident as policy transfer is an intentional activity involving the movement of ideas between systems of governance in the aspiration of forging policy change. Peter Hall's (1993) social learning approach disaggregates the policy-making process into three dimensions: the overarching goals that guide policy in a particular field (third order change); the techniques or policy instruments used to attain these goals (second order change); and the precise settings of these instruments (first order change). Hall argues that in order to make sense of how policy learning takes place we need a theory of the policy process that takes into account the role of ideas. For Hall, public policy deliberation takes place within a broader system of ideas that is understood and accepted by the policy-making community. This system of ideas specifies not only the goals of policy and the instruments used to attain them, but also the very nature of the issues that are important and need to be addressed. Keynesianism or monetarism may be viewed as two illustrations of systems of ideas or what Hall also terms 'policy paradigms' emerging in periods of third order change.

Hall's work has proved particularly influential in the study of policy change but is yet to be applied directly to the study of policy transfer with the exception of the work of Ian Greener (2001) on macro-economic policy and the articles by Claire Dunlop and Sucheen Patel in this volume. Its potential utilization in this field, however, is rich with possibilities. For example, consider the 2008 financial crisis. Will it lead to a period of third order change and a new policy paradigm characterized by the demise of neo-liberalism and the revival of old forms of state intervention in the economy? What role will policy transfer play in this process of change? The British prime minister Gordon Brown is currently performing the part of an international agent of policy transfer and is, at least for the moment, being lauded as the saviour of global capitalism by finance ministers around the world and even the Nobel Prize-winning economist Paul Krugman. Brown's rescue plan has now been adopted by other governments in need of a quick fix to get them out of the financial crisis. The plan involved the British government taking a stake in three British banks (Royal Bank of Scotland, Lloyds and HBOS) and giving them £37bn finance to recapitalize to allow them to cope with current market volatility and the ongoing liquidity crisis. The package was received exceptionally well by the world's markets. In contrast, the US government's bailout package of US$700bn, which was originally intended just to buy off bad debts from failed banks, was badly received by the markets earlier in October 2008 and failed to stem the tide. In consequence, the US government has adopted the Brown plan and recapitalized nine banks (amongst them Goldmans and Morgan Stanley) at the cost of US$250bn. Gordon Brown's newly found role as the saviour of global capitalism is, of course, rich in irony. Brown did not anticipate the global credit crunch despite being in a uniquely privileged position in the capacity of Chairman of the International Monetary and Financial Committee since September 1999 (the IMF's most important advisory committee).

The study of epistemic communities as a method of understanding the movement of ideas in the international domain is a central preoccupation in the study of international relations (Haas 1980, 1989, Adler and Haas 1992, Haas 1997, Adler and Bernstein 2005). Diane Stone's influential research on think-tanks has been central in integrating the concerns of this literature with the study of policy transfer (see Evans and Davies 1999 for an alternative account). Stone (1996a,b, 1999, 2000a,b) identifies think-tanks as key agents of policy transfer within what are termed 'epistemic communities'. Epistemic communities are comprised of natural and social scientists or individuals from any discipline or profession with authoritative claims to policy relevant knowledge that reside in national, transnational and international organizations. The function of these communities is to facilitate the emergence of policy learning that may lead to policy convergence. Her research provides an understanding of the mechanisms by which think-tanks have been successful in influencing the formulation of public policies, specifically the spread of privatization ideas. The epistemic community literature has also been used to explain how international policy has converged in areas such as GATT, food aid, financial regulation and environmental protection. Stone's work is particularly useful in helping policy analysts to determine how policy-makers acquire and deploy knowledge. Moreover, it provides compelling evidence of the internationalization of policy paradigms (see also Dunleavy 1994, Hood 1995).

Stella Ladi's (2005) recent work on the role of think-tanks in mediating policy transfer in the EU emphasizes the influential role of the discourses of globalization and Europeanization in processes of policy transfer. Ladi argues that an understanding of the belief systems that agents of transfer hold with regard to globalization and Europeanization is crucial in order to evaluate the influence of the discourse within which a process of policy transfer takes place. She concludes that although the ideational sphere is important, it is interwoven with the material sphere and processes of policy transfer can only be successful if the material sphere is also satisfied. Ladi's work demonstrates the importance of taking structure and agency issues seriously in policy transfer analysis.

Comparative approaches

All studies of policy transfer should adopt a comparative methodology but few do. In most cases, thick qualitative description is provided to account for the indigenous policy environment and detail of the non-indigenous policy environment is largely ignored. Comprehensive qualitative policy transfer analysis requires thick description but this does make for tiresome narrative and few editors are likely to countenance it. However, the use of quantitative methods in policy transfer analysis can make for more accessible reading. Guy Peters (1997), for example, examines the diffusion of administrative reform policy transfers through the member countries of the Organization for Economic Co-operation and Development (OECD). He argues that policy learning in public management is a common activity for governments around the world, but that there are differences in the rates at which countries are able to learn and adapt. He attributes these differences to structural factors such as economic, ideological, cultural and institutional similarities. Those states that share common features are more likely to engage in policy transfer with one another. For example, the 'New Public Management paradigm' struck a chord with governments of the radical right such as the Thatcher (1979–1990) and Reagan (1980–1988) administrations in the UK and the USA who blamed 'Big Government' for global economic downturn and were seeking to roll back the frontiers of the state to redress market failures. Subsequently, New Zealand, Canada and Australia followed suit. Indeed, in relation to market reforms, the UK became a net exporter of administrative innovations first to the Commonwealth and later to developmental states (Common 2001).

Notably, the most popular administrative reforms within OECD countries have been participatory and quality related and apart from in Anglo-American countries there has been far less interest in market reform. The developmental states clearly buck this trend and follow the Anglo-American countries in this regard. He concludes that cultural variables play an extremely important role in the transfer of policy innovations among countries, particularly in relation to geographical proximity and political similarity. However, another set of policy ideas, those associated with political parties and ideologies, appear to have much less of a relationship with the spread of management reforms.

While Peters' work is scholarly and provocative, it does fall foul of the criticism that it is impossible to use this methodology to prove that policy transfer has taken place. Hence, his explanation of why the diffusion of administrative reform has occurred through the member countries of the OECD is at best impressionistic (see also Olsen and Peters 1996). Moreover, such research provides few, if any, insights into the process of transfer. This appears a classic case of where quantitative analysis proves useful in highlighting potential critical variables for qualitative analysis. Cross-national aggregate comparisons of this sort are best contained within a mixed methods approach (see Wolman 1992).

Multi-level approaches

Multi-level approaches to the study of policy transfer are characterized by a concern with understanding outcomes of policy transfer through combining macro and micro (Dolowitz and Marsh 1996, 2000), or, macro, meso and micro (Evans and Davies 1999, Common 2001, Evans 2004b) levels of enquiry. The most influential accounts using this approach have been developed by David Dolowitz and David Marsh (1996, 2000), Mark Evans and Jonathan Davies (1999) and Evans (2004a).

Dolowitz and Marsh (1996) have led efforts within British political science to develop a comprehensive theory of policy transfer. In essence, they have drawn together a general framework of heterogeneous concepts, including policy diffusion, policy convergence, policy learning and lesson-drawing, under the umbrella heading of policy transfer. Dolowitz and Marsh suggest that all these phenomena can be organized into one framework as 'dimensions of policy transfer'. Thus lesson-drawing is categorized under the sub-heading 'voluntary transfer' and structured change is categorized within 'voluntary', 'perceptual' and 'direct' or 'indirect' coercive policy transfer. Dolowitz and Marsh provide an extremely useful framework which invites others to criticize and develop it, a map of the process of policy transfer which can only ever be a representation of a reality which needs to be proved or disproved through empirical investigation: '[w]e have suggested a series of questions which can be used both to organize our current knowledge of the process and to guide future work'. The framework developed by Dolowitz and Marsh is clearly designed to incorporate a vast domain of policy-making activity by classifying all possible occurrences of transfer, voluntary and coercive, temporal and spatial.

Dolowitz and Marsh's approach is generally regarded to be more inclusive than previous studies for two main reasons. First, their definition of transfer is broad enough to encompass both voluntary and coercive processes and transferences within and between nations. Second, the concept of policy transfer is used as both a dependent and an independent variable. In other words, they seek to explain what causes and impacts on the process of transfer as well as how processes of policy transfer lead to particular policy outcomes. As Dolowitz's (1997) analysis of how the British government learned from American employment policy demonstrates, the framework is extremely useful for organizing research questions and classifying the process of transfer under scrutiny. Similarly, Dolowitz *et al.* (2000), provide a compelling account of policy transfer and British social policy development. However, Dolowitz and Marsh are also criticized for failing to provide either an explanation of policy change (James and Lodge 2003), or an appropriate methodology for studying processes of policy learning (Page 2000, Evans 2004b). We will consider the work of Evans and Davies as a way forward in this regard in the penultimate section of this article.

Why do public organizations engage in policy transfer?

It has been argued by certain critics that policy transfer analysts fail to advance an explanatory theory of policy development (James and Lodge 2003) or, as Ed Page (2000, p. 12) puts it, the researcher should not expect from the literature 'firm guidance about how to frame the research questions or how to pursue them empirically'. Although it is accurate to criticize policy transfer analysts for failing to clearly stipulate their critical variables, it is quite simply incorrect to argue that all policy transfer analysts do not advance explanations for policy change. Most approaches to policy transfer are unclear in their specification of independent and dependent variables and clumsy in their theorization of the relationship between variables and between levels of enquiry. This is largely because most explanations of policy transfer emerge from inductive reasoning rather than deductive formal modelling. This is an inevitable corollary of applying heuristic models of policy development.

What are the knowledge claims of policy transfer analysis? The claim that policy transfer activity is on the increase is normally attributed to one or more of the following sources of policy change: global, international and/or transnational forces; state-centred forces; the role of policy transfer networks in mediating policy change; and micro-level processes of policy-oriented learning. This claim is, of course, non-falsifiable in the sense that there exists no comprehensive base-line data against which to compare contemporary transfer activity.

Global, international and transnational sources of policy transfer

Global, international and transnational sources of policy change provide opportunity structures for policy transfer to occur. Of course, the terms transnational and international should not be used interchangeably. This article recognizes as international those structures and processes which inform state-to-state relations such as the United Nations (UN) and as transnational the increasing importance of non-state actors, such as multi-national corporations and knowledge institutions, in policy-making at all levels of governance (Risse-Kappen 1995, Stone 1996a,b, 2000a,b). The phenomenon globalization is clearly more problematic. The lack of an agreed understanding of the term is one of the most commonly asserted problems in contemporary political science, yet even the growing band of critics of globalization explicitly place the study of the term at the centre of their analyses (Hirst and Thompson 1996, Callinicos 2003).

Irrespective of one's position within the globalization debate no serious scholar would deny that patterns of increased internationalization have occurred and that these have posed significant constraints on the ability of most nation states to forward independent national economic strategies. In particular, there have been significant changes in the organization of production and patterns of economic power in which a closer integration of national economies has been brought about by the reduction of the costs of transportation and communication and the breaking down of barriers to the flow of goods, services, capital, and, fundamentally to this book, knowledge, across borders.

Knowledge of policy initiatives in a wide variety of policy arenas at different levels of governance in nation states throughout the world is more accessible than ever before. Policy tourism via the Internet is now in the easy reach of most policy-makers, as the majority of public organizations provide detailed information of their activities on their web sites. If we wish to explore the latest economic development initiatives in Atlanta, Leeds, Delhi or Shanghai, they are available to use through our desktop or laptop search engines. Just 10 years ago, with the possible exceptions of the United States and the Netherlands, it would have been impossible to access such information via the Internet.

The advent of the Internet has also provided a unique opportunity for policy entrepreneurs, knowledge institutions and think-tanks to sell their expertise to governmental organizations throughout the world. The Internet has exposed a hitherto private realm of policy-oriented learning: transnational networks of epistemic communities operating in a system of global governance. The concept of global governance proceeds from the assumption that certain public policy problems such as the regulation of world trade and financial markets, global warming and ozone depletion, drug trafficking and terrorism cannot be dealt with at the level of the nation state alone but require a global response. Global governance thus refers to the process of political interaction aimed at solving problems that affect more than one state or region when there is no authority structure than can enforce compliance (see Rosenau 2000, p. 172).

What is the relationship between the concept of Global Governance and the concept of globalization? If we adopt Anthony McGrew's (1992, p. 23) definition of globalization as the multiplicity of linkages and interconnections between the states and societies which make up the modern state system we can see that 'Globalization has two distinct dimensions: scope (or stretching) and intensity (or deepening)'. It 'defines a set of processes which embrace most of the globe' thus politics and other social activities are becoming stretched across the globe. However, it also implies 'intensification in the levels of interaction, interconnectedness or interdependence between the states and societies which constitute the world community'. Thus Global Governance is the manifestation of the increasing scope and intensity of formal and informal processes of global social and political interactions. Formal processes of Global Governance focus on the activities of predatory agents of policy transfer including multi-lateral organizations such as the World Trade Organization and the Bretton Woods institutions (the International Monetary Fund and the World Bank). The influence of these global economic institutions has been particularly pronounced in developing countries, transition states and states emerging from conflict, which all depend heavily on external aid, loans and investment. Moreover, established international organizations such as the OECD have become proactive in pushing neo-liberal policy agendas in the international domain particularly in the areas of economic and administrative reform. The OECD is an international organization consisting of 30 member countries that share a commitment to democratic government and the market economy. With active relationships with some 70 other countries, NGOs and civil society, it has a global network of members and associates. The OECD is a committed agent of policy transfer with the stated aim of assisting '... governments in building and strengthening effective, efficient and transparent government structures through its Public Management Programme' (see www.oecd.org).

In contrast, informal processes of global governance would refer to networks of actors that seek to promote dominant policy discourses such as NPM or 'Neo-liberalism' (Biersteker 1992). The Internet has established a rich source for non-governmental policy-oriented learning for individuals and groups wishing to question the views of government. *Government is no longer the expert.* Of course, such a development poses threats as well as opportunities. The Internet does not provide a free market of ideas. Ideas are in imperfect competition with one another. Indeed, the think-tanks with the highest profile on the Internet tend to be deeply ideological, cloaking dangerous policies in creative evidence-based practice. Hence, policy analysis needs to be more rigorous than ever in discerning appropriate policy transfers.

In sum, the existence of the following institutional and ideational structures and the processes that emanate from them provide increased opportunity structures for policy transfer to occur:

- ideational discourses such as globalization, Europeanization, and neo-liberalism (the Washington Consensus; Ladi 2005);
- the activities of global economic institutions such as the IMF, the World Trade Organisation and the World Bank (Stiglitz 2002);
- the activities of international financial markets (Cerny 1994, 1997);
- the activities of international inter-governmental organizations such as the OECD (OECD 1997, Kiddal 2003, Huerta-Melchor 2006);
- the institutions and processes of Europeanization (Buller *et al.* 2002);
- international treaties such as the General Agreement on Tariffs and Trade (GATT) and the North American Free Trade Area (NAFTA) allowing for the free movement of goods, investment and services between Canada, Mexico and the United States; and,
- transnational and non-state organizations promulgating particular international policy agendas in the international domain (see Stone 2000a,b).

As well as acting as potential opportunity, structures for policy transfer these institutional and ideational structures and the processes that emanate from them can also act as sites of struggle between competing conceptions of globalization. For example, unaccountable bureaucrats have designed the global economic architecture, such as the development of banking standards that govern economic globalization, and this has engendered significant resentment in the developing world. The securing of loans by developing countries from the IMF and elsewhere has become conditional on the introduction of SAPS that are predicated on a Western interpretation of 'Good Governance' that also give rise to significant resentment (Grindle 2004).

State-centred explanations of policy transfer

State-centred explanations of policy transfer tend to be rooted in transformational theories, i.e. theories that see policy transfer as a key strategy for transforming the state. Evans and Cerny's (2004) competition state theory, for example, proceeds from the grounded empirical observation that over the past three decades the British State has transformed from an industrial welfare state into a competition state. It is observed that successive governments, regardless of their traditional ideological complexion, have increasingly assumed the policies of an enterprise association. The core concern of government is therefore no longer seen purely in terms of traditional conceptions of social justice but in adjusting to, sustaining, promoting, and, expanding an open global economy in order to capture its perceived benefits. The shift from an industrial-welfare state to a competition state reflects political elite perceptions of global realities and informs state strategies for navigating and mediating processes of globalization. In modernization terms this has been articulated in: leadership rhetoric and discourse; the changing architecture of the state; the nature of political agency in which politicians and bureaucrats have become entrepreneurial agents of globalization promoting 'Great Britain Plc' in the global economy; the decline of ideological differences between political parties and the gravitation of party politics to the electoral centre ground; and the internationalization of the policy agenda through policy transfer.

Changes in government clearly provide a significant opportunity structure for policy transfer activity in what Hall (1993) refers to as periods of third order change that give rise to new policy paradigms. For example, the assent of the Blair government to power in the UK in July 1997 led to a proliferation of policy transfer activity between Britain and the United States and signalled the rise of some new policy paradigms although there was also a significant degree of continuity with Conservative government policy particularly in economic matters. The close relationship which developed between the Blair and Clinton administrations was reflected in a long list of common policy initiatives that included: education (reduction of class sizes), crime (zero-tolerance, anti-truancy drives) and welfare (welfare to work and creation of work incentives) reform. In addition, the UK's former Chancellor of the Exchequer, Gordon Brown, became convinced of the need for Bank of England independence after discussions with Alan Greenspan, chair of the independent US Federal Reserve Board (Central Bank), and Robert Rubin, Clinton's Treasury Secretary. Many of these items may be viewed as part of an international policy agenda for the centre-left which was forged by Blair, Clinton and their advisors. On 6 February 1998, Blair addressed the US State Department outlining what he termed the 'five clear principles of the centre-left' common to both New Labour and the New Democrats:

(1) stable management and economic prudence in order to cope with the global economy;
(2) a change in the emphasis of government intervention so that it dealt with education, training, and infrastructure and not things like industrial intervention or 'tax and spend';
(3) reform of the welfare state;
(4) reinventing government, decentralization, opening-up government; and
(5) internationalism in opposition to the right's isolationism.

It is within this international agenda for the centre-left that we are most likely to find examples of policy transfer between Britain and America. For example, in public management (Common 2001, James 2001), urban (Wolman 1992) or welfare (Dolowitz *et al.* 2000) policies.

Hence, the upsurge of policy transfer activity between the two countries may be attributed partly to the sharing of similar policy problems and partly because of ideological similarities between the New Democrats and New Labour. It was made possible, however, because elites in the two countries share a common ontology and language, together with the existence of longstanding historical legacies that are embedded economically, socially and culturally.

In Britain, for example, processes of 'hollowing-out' have also created new opportunity structures for policy transfer. The term 'hollowing-out' infers that the political powers of the central state are being eroded in particular ways. Rhodes (1994, pp. 138–139) has argued that there are four key interrelated trends which illustrate the reach of this process in the UK: privatization and limiting the scope and forms of public intervention; the loss of functions by central government departments to alternative service delivery systems (such as Next Steps Agencies) and through market testing; the loss of functions from the British government to EU institutions; and the emergence of limits to the discretion of public servants through a public management that emphasizes managerial accountability and clearer political control created by a sharp distinction between politics and administration. A further dimension can be added to these four: the global trend towards regionalization and devolution. The rise of this new form of governance has facilitated cross-sectoral opportunities for policy transfer. Hence, the private sector is increasingly used as a source of policy learning due to its expertise in particular areas (e.g. banks and credit card fraud detection, management, risk assessment or logistics). Indeed the opportunity structures for policy transfer tend to increase in an era of what Rhodes (1996, p. 652) has termed 'the New Governance: Governing without Government'. In this context, New Governance refers to the increasing pervasiveness of 'self-organizing, interorganizational networks' which Rhodes argues compliment markets and hierarchies as governing structures for authoritatively allocating resources and exercising control and co-ordination in public policy-making. In times of uncertainty, policy-makers at the heart of networks will look to the 'quick fix' solution to public policy problems that policy transfer can provide.

Organizational-centred explanations for policy change

The most common explanation for the occurrence of policy transfer is that micro-level dissatisfaction with existing policy systems identified through monitoring systems or broader policy evaluation frameworks provide opportunity structures for policy transfer to occur. However, public organizations in both developed and developing countries often do not have the expertise to tackle all the problems they confront and increasingly look outside their organizations for the answers to their problems (Stone 1999). This depicts policy-makers as wholly reactive beings. There is evidence, however, that some governments have started to emphasize the importance of governmental organizations being rational learning organizations engaged in an ongoing process of evidence-based learning (Common 2004).

There are, of course, other organizational-centred explanations for policy change that are highlighted in the literature. Changes in organizational leadership often provide an opportunity structure for policy change to occur (Furlong 2001). Moreover, policy transfer may be introduced for political reasons to legitimate conclusions already reached by the organization (Robertson 1991). It may also be observed that processes of policy transfer can precipitate further processes of policy transfer. For example, it can be observed in the UK context in the case of New Labour's New Deal for unemployed 18–24-year-olds, that new service delivery approaches have been adopted including one-stop-shops on the United States Iowa model and the introduction of a single gateway to the benefit system (see Dolowitz *et al.* 2000).

Policy-oriented learning as a mechanism of policy change

Policy transfer studies of processes of policy transfer have emphasized the role of policy transfer networks as key instruments of policy-oriented learning (Evans 2004b, Ladi 2005, Huerta-Melchor 2006). These are collaborative decision structures comprised of state and non-state actors that are set up with the deliberate intention of engineering policy change. It is argued that policy transfer networks matter because they shape the nature of policy outcomes emerging from the process of transfer. Moreover, the creation of a policy transfer network provides an opportunity structure for the creation of further policy transfer networks. In this sense, policy transfer activity can have a momentum of its own through a process of functional spillover.

Policy transfer networks can act as agents of globalization or counteragents to globalization, for agents of policy transfer are often carriers of particular policy belief systems (e.g. new public management, privatization, etc) and use their membership of formal and informal international policy networks to disseminate international policy agendas.

Indeed, the content of policy transfers is often informed by notions of 'best practice' disseminated by international organizations, KIs and think-tanks in the international domain, suggesting that ideological considerations play a key role in informing the content of policy transfers. These agents of transfer play a key role in facilitating policy-oriented learning through imparting technical advice, for the content of policy transfers normally reflect areas where indigenous state actors lack expertise. Agents of policy transfer that have the capacity to bridge the indigenous knowledge gap can become important players in policy transfer networks.

The case for multi-level 'action-based' policy transfer analysis

So what is the way forward for policy transfer analysis? A multi-level 'action based' approach to policy transfer analysis would ameliorate some of the problems identified with the aforementioned approaches. In an article published in 1999 in the journal *Public Administration,* Evans and Davies mapped out a multi-level, interdisciplinary approach for understanding policy transfer (Evans and Davies 1999). The main submission underpinning this article was that policy transfer analysis provides a context for integrating some key concerns of domestic, comparative and international political science. It was also observed that the increasing complexity and uncertainty that underpins modern governance has increased the tendency for policy-makers at all levels of governance to engage in policy transfer activity. The article therefore focused on the tactics of research in policy transfer analysis and concluded that the process of policy transfer should be examined through a structure and agency approach with three dimensions: global, international and transnational levels, the macro-level and the inter-organizational level. This three-dimensional model employs the notion of a policy transfer network as a middle-range level of analysis which links a particular form of collaborative governance (policy transfer), micro-decision-making in organizations, macro-systems and global, transnational and international systems (see Figure 2).

As Figure 2 illustrates, a series of empirically testable hypotheses can be deduced from the above characterization of the process of voluntary policy transfer. These may be organized into a set of independent and dependent variables in which structures should be viewed as independent variables and functions as dependent variables. Any variation in the dependent variable (function) may be the result of variation in either the structure (independent variable) or in the intervening variable (process or mechanism). For example, exogenous or network environment changes may lead to the creation of a policy transfer network leading to policy change. These may be economic/market, ideological, knowledge/technical or institutional effects. If economic factors constitute the catalyst for change, the form of the response may be influenced by, for example, the ideology of the competition state. It may also be deduced that policy changes, which emerge from a policy transfer network, can be the product of endogenous factors such as the influence of the agent of transfer. However, as the multi-level nature of this approach dictates, policy transfer networks are but one component of an explanation of policy change.

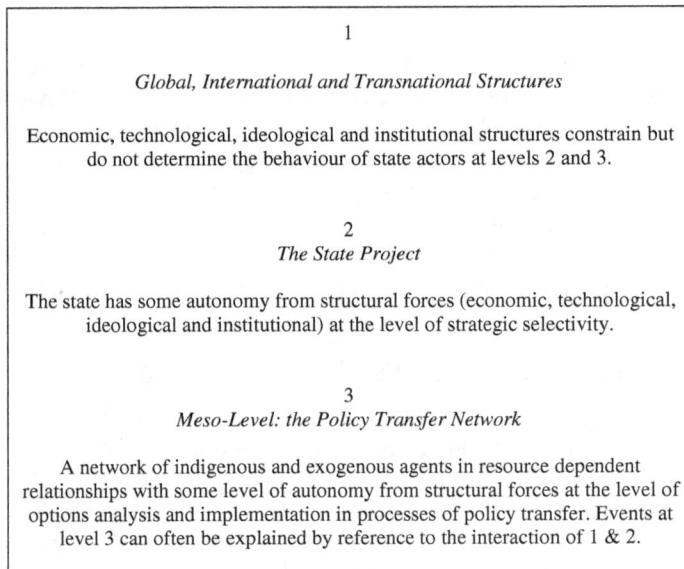

1

Global, International and Transnational Structures

Economic, technological, ideological and institutional structures constrain but do not determine the behaviour of state actors at levels 2 and 3.

2
The State Project

The state has some autonomy from structural forces (economic, technological, ideological and institutional) at the level of strategic selectivity.

3
Meso-Level: the Policy Transfer Network

A network of indigenous and exogenous agents in resource dependent relationships with some level of autonomy from structural forces at the level of options analysis and implementation in processes of policy transfer. Events at level 3 can often be explained by reference to the interaction of 1 & 2.

Figure 2.   Multi-level policy transfer analysis.
Source: developed from Evans and Davies (1999).

The development of the policy transfer network approach was primarily a response to the absence of an adequate methodology within the existing literature for investigating processes of policy transfer, the role of agent(s) of policy transfer within processes of policy transfer, and policy-oriented learning (Evans 2004b). The application of a version of policy network analysis, which incorporates the strengths of the epistemic community approach, was thus considered an essential research tactic because it allows policy transfer analysts to analyse the role of agents in the process of policy transfer. The notion of a policy transfer network can also help us to evaluate the cognitive dimension of decision-making, i.e. how decision-makers acquire knowledge. Thus through its emphasis on studying structural (organizational rules and imperatives) and interpersonal relationships (information and communication exchange) a method is provided for understanding forms of policy development within a multi-organizational setting.

Figure 3 illustrates how, *purely for analytical purposes*, the voluntary policy transfer process can be broken down into three broad stages involving various learning activities, pre-decision policy-oriented learning, decision processes and post-decision policy-oriented learning. The first stage involves the identification of a public policy problem, the search for ideas, the identification of agents of transfer and the establishment of a policy transfer network. The second stage involves processes of agenda-setting and decision-making and the third stage refers to post-decision processes of policy-oriented learning. The principle underpinning this scheme is the idea that policy is made and remade in the practice of implementation and is characterized by ongoing organizational learning in an evolutionary process. These putative activities within the process of voluntary policy transfer will be analysed in detail within the ensuing case study. *It must be noted that we are making no claims here about the rationality or otherwise of the policy transfer process.* The capacity for a policy to pass through these stages is contingent on environmental factors (e.g. prevailing economic conditions, changes in government) and the type of agent of transfer involved. Moreover, processes of policy transfer can break-off at any point past 'search' and still result in a form of transfer (e.g. the drawing of a lesson or the transfer of rhetoric).

The scheme that we present is thus wholly illustrative and provides a frame for organizing empirical research. However, in what sense is this approach action-based and relevant to practitioners? In order to ascertain the appropriateness of policy transfer research for public action the researcher should engage in the self-conscious integration of theory and practice. This works at two levels: practical application and communication for practice. The former involves identifying the elements of the research that are both relevant and irrelevant to practice and the elements that are missing from the research that would be relevant to practice. The latter focuses on developing a sense of audience. Getting research into practice is often a difficult process because policy-makers often describe research articles as being inaccessible (Shaxson 2005, Burton 2006).

These principles can be included within a logical framework matrix in order to aid the application of the principles to practical examples (see Gaspar 2000, Dale 2003). As Table 1 illustrates, the logical matrix summarizes the constituent elements of the research and links them to each other allowing for conclusions to be reached as to the utility of research for public action. Moreover, the logical framework also demonstrates the academic benefits of prescriptive analysis as it draws attention to

The pre-decision process of policy-oriented learning

Problem recognition	The search for ideas and contact	The emergence of an
economic crisis	**with potential agents**	**information feeder network**
globalization	**of transfer**	
modernization	*regime*	
policy failure	*international*	
electoral change	*transnational*	
conflict	*national*	
legitimation	*regional*	
	local	
	cross-sectoral	

Decision processes

Cognition	Elite and cognitive mobilization	Decision enters
and reception and the emergence	**and evaluation of options**	**formal policy**
of a policy transfer network	*(agenda-setting)*	**stream**

Post decision processes of policy-oriented learning

Implementation	Monitoring and evaluation	Ongoing processes of policy
(operational delivery)		**learning**

Process of policy evolution

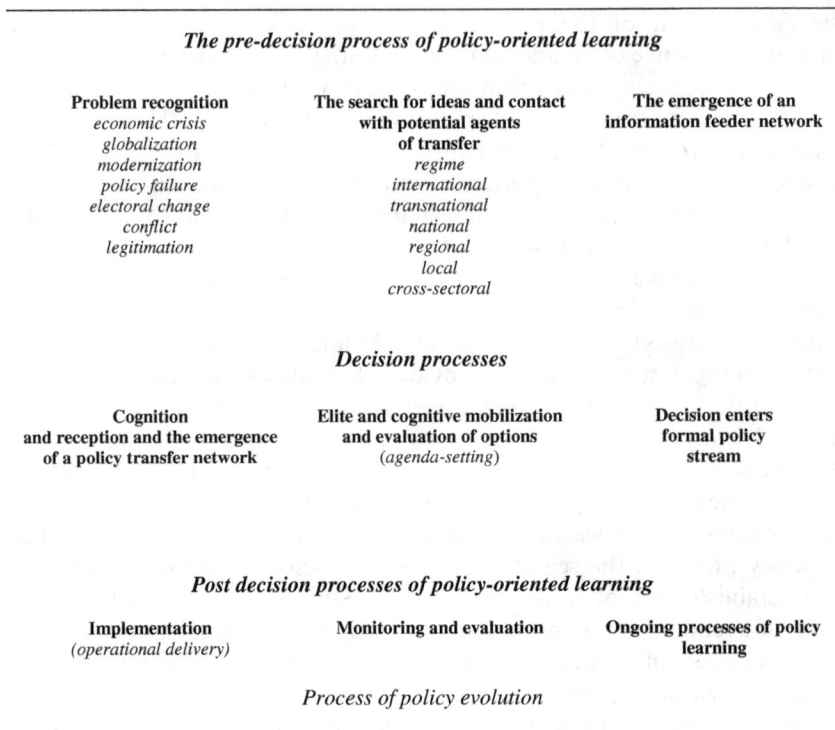

Figure 3.   The emergence and development of a voluntary policy transfer network.

putative problems in theorization, method, data analysis and synthesis. The matrix of the logical framework is organized around four columns: a narrative summary of the potential of the research for public action, verifiable indicators, means of verification and critical reflexivity.

Conclusions

This article's main concern has been with identifying the domestic and international circumstances likely to bring about policy transfer in Britain, the scope and dimensions of policy transfer and which aspects of the policy transfer framework should and should not be pursued in empirical work. It was hoped that this would allow for the development of a better understanding of the phenomenon of policy transfer and its relationship with global and domestic processes of economic, social and political change. It therefore remains to draw some general conclusions on the implications of our findings for the broader study of policy transfer in British public administration.

Policy transfer analysis can only be distinctive from the analysis of normal forms of policy-making if its focuses on the remarkable movement of ideas between systems of governance through policy transfer networks and the intermediation of agents of policy transfer. This should involve the study of different forms of voluntary and completed transfers, failed transfers and 'in process' transfers. Moreover, while policy transfer analysis remains weak as an explanatory theory of

Table 1. A logical framework for assessing the utility of policy transfer research for public action.

1. Narrative summary	2. Verifiable indicators of rigour	3. Means of verification	4. Critical reflexivity
Goal: the overall practical aim to which the research is expected to contribute	Identifying the measures that show the potential of the research for public action – theory, method, data, analysis	Identifying the sources of information and methods used to show achievement of the goal	Reflecting on the utility of the research for public action
Theoretical approach	Is the theory or approach verifiable? Can it be tested against the world of observation?	Is the theoretical approach tenable? If they exist, are the core propositions of the theory tenable?	Is there inherent bias in the theory? Does the theory need to be reconceptualized? What amendments to the theory need to be made to make for sounder knowledge claims?
Methodology	Does the methodology allow for the verification of the theory? Are these tried and trusted methods?	Have appropriate documentary, qualitative, quantitative or mixed methods been used?	Is there inherent bias in the method? Has the evidence been obtained properly?
Data analysis and synthesis	Is the evidence credible? Has enough evidence been generated?	Has the data been verified through triangulation and the use of counterfactuals?	Is the evidence reliable, and generalizable?
Self-conscious integration of theory and practice	What elements of the research are relevant to practice? What elements of the research are irrelevant to practice? What elements of the research could have been relevant to practice but are missing from the research agenda? Is the communication of the research accessible to practice?		

policy change if used in isolation from other theories of policy change, this article demonstrates that transfer analysts are busy developing a common idiom of theoretical and methodological discourse from which lessons can be drawn and hypotheses developed. Policy transfer analysis thus presents a valuable field of study for integrating common research concerns of scholars of domestic, comparative and international politics insofar as it provides a lens for observing both the changing nature of the nation state and the role of state actors and institutions in promoting new forms of complex globalization. Moreover, the most comprehensive explanations of policy change are yielded by multi-level models of policy transfer analysis that encompass global, international and/or transnational explanations of policy change, macro-level explanations of policy change, meso-level analysis of the role of policy transfer networks in mediating policy change, and micro-level analysis of the process of policy-oriented learning in and between policy transfer networks.

Notes

1. Note, however, that since the turn of the century the academic study of policy transfer from developed countries to the developing world and between developing countries has increased in scope and intensity (see Evans 2004b).
2. For examples of voluntary policy transfer see James's (2001) account of the transfer of 'business-like' central government agencies or Jones and Newburn's (2001) study of US influences on British crime control policy.
3. See Evans 2004a, chapters 6, 7 and 8.
4. See the Cabinet Office's overview of the *Professional skills for government* programme at: http://psg.civilservice.gov.uk/

References

Adler, E. and Bernstein, S., 2005. Knowledge in power: The epistemic construction of global governance. *In*: M. Barnett, *et al.*, eds. *Power in global governance*. Cambridge: Cambridge University Press.

Adler, E. and Haas, P., 1992. Conclusion: epistemic communities, word order, and the creation of a reflective research program. *International organisation*, 46, 367–390.

Bennett, C., 1991. Review article: what is policy convergence and what causes it? *British journal of political science*, 21, 215–233.

Biersteker, T., 1992. The 'triumph' of neoclassical economics in the developing world: policy convergence and the bases of governance in the international economic order. *In*: J. Rosenau and E. Otto Czempiel, eds. *Governance without government: order and change in world politics*. Cambridge: Cambridge University Press.

Buller, J., James, O. and Evans, M., eds., 2002. *Understanding the Europeanization of British public policy*. Cardiff: PPA/PAC.

Burton, P., 2001. Wading through the swampy lowlands: in search of firmer ground in understanding public policy-making. *Policy and politics*, 29 (2), 209–217.

Burton, P., 2006. Modernising the policy process: making policy research more significant. *Policy studies*, 27, 3.

Cabinet Office, 1999. *Modernising government*. London: HMSO.

Cabinet Office, 2001. *Better policy-making*. London: HMSO.

Cabinet Office, 2005. *Professional skills for government*. London: CMPS.

Callinicos, A., 2003. *The anti-capitalist manifesto*. Cambridge: Polity.

Cerny, P.G., 1994. The dynamics of financial globalization. *Policy sciences*, 27, 319–342.

Cerny, P.G., 1997. Paradoxes of the competition state: the dynamics of political globalisation. *Government and opposition*, 32, 251–274.

Common, R., 2001. *Public management and policy transfer in Southeast Asia*. Aldershot: Ashgate.

Common, R., 2004. Organisational learning in a political environment: improving policy-making in UK government. *Policy studies*, 25, 72–97.

Dale, R., 2003. The logical framework: an easy escape, a straitjacket, or a useful planning tool? *Development in practice*, 13 (1), 57–70.

Davies, H., Nutley, S. and Smith, P., eds., 2000. *What works? Evidence-based policy and practice in public service policy*. Bristol: Policy Press.

Dolowitz, D., 1997. British employment policy in the 1980s: learning from the American experience. *Governance*, 10, 23–42.

Dolowitz, D. and Marsh, D., 1996. Who learns what from whom: a review of the policy transfer literature. *Political studies*, 44, 343–357.

Dolowitz, D. and Marsh, D., 2000. Learning from abroad: the role of policy transfer in contemporary policy-making. *Governance*, 13, 5–24.

Dolowitz, D., *et al.*, 2000. *Policy transfer and british social policy*. Buckingham: Open University Press.

Dowding, K., 2001. There must be end to confusion: policy networks, intellectual fatigue and the need for political science methods courses in British universities. *Political studies*, 49, 89–105.

Dunleavy, P., 1994. The globalization of public services production: can government be 'best' in world? *Public policy and administration*, 9, 36–64.

Dunlop, C., 2009. Policy transfer as learning: capturing variation in what decision-makers learn from epistemic communities. *Policy studies*, 30(3), 291–313.

Evans, M., 2004a. Policy transfer in a competition state: Britain's new deal. *In*: M. Evans, ed. *Policy transfer in global perspective*. Aldershot: Ashgate, 64–78.

Evans, M., ed., 2004b. *Policy transfer in global perspective*. Aldershot: Ashgate.

Evans, M. and Cerny, P.G., 2004. Globalisation and public policy under New Labour. *Policy studies*, 25 (1), 84–107.

Evans, M. and Davies, J., 1999. Understanding policy transfer: a multi-level, multi-disciplinary perspective. *Public administration*, 77, 361–386.

Furlong, P., 2001. *Constitutional change as policy transfer; policy transfer as constitutional change. ESRC future governance programme*. Available from: http://www.hull.ac.uk/futgov/Papers/APSAFurlongPau.pdf

Gaspar, D., 2000. Evaluating the logical framework approach towards learning-oriented developmental evaluation. *Public administration and development*, 20(1), 17–28.

Greener, I., 2001. Social learning and macroeconomic policy in Britain. *Journal of public policy*, 21, 1–22.

Grindle, M., 2004. Good enough governance. *Governance*, 17 (4), 525–548.

Haas, E., 1980. Why collaborate? Issue-linkage and international regimes. *World politics*, 32, 357–405.

Haas, P.M., 1989. Do regimes matter? Epistemic communities and evolving policies to control Mediterranean pollution. *International organisation*, 43, 377–403.

Haas, P.M., 1997. *Knowledge, power and international policy coordination*. South Carolina: University of South Carolina Press.

Hall, P., 1993. Policy paradigms, social learning and the state: the case of economic policy-making in Britain. *Comparative politics*, 25, 275–296.

Hirst, P. and Thompson, G., 1996. *Globalisation in question*. Cambridge: Polity Press/Blackwell.

Hood, C., 1995. Contemporary public management: a new global paradigm. *Public policy and administration*, 10, 104–117.

Howlett, M., 2000. Beyond legalism? Policy ideas, implementation styles and emulation-based convergence in Canadian and US environmental policy. *Journal of public policy*, 20 (3), 305–329.

Huerta-Melchor, O., 2006. *Understanding international agents of policy transfer: the case of the OECD and Mexican administrative reform*. Thesis (PhD). University of York.

Ikenberry, J.G., 1990. The international spread of privatisation policies: inducements, learning and policy bandwaggoning. *In*: E. Suleiman and J. Waterbury, eds. *The political economy of public sector reform*. Boulder: Westview Press.

James, O., 2001. Business models and the transfer of business-like central government agencies. *Governance*, 14, 2.

James, O. and Lodge, M., 2003. The limitations of 'policy transfer' and 'lesson drawing' for public policy research. *Political studies review*, 2003, 179–193.

Jones, T. and Newburn, T., 2001. Learning from Uncle Sam? Exploring US influences on British crime control policy. *ESRC future governance programme*. Available from: http://www.hull.ac.uk/futgov/

Kiddal, N., 2003. *Perspectives on policy transfer: the case of the OECD*. Copenhagen: Rokkansenteret.

Ladi, S., 2005. *Globalisation, policy transfer and policy research institutes*. Cheltenham: Edward Elgar.

Majone, G., 1991. Cross-national sources of regulatory policy making in Europe and the United States. *Journal of public policy*, 11, 79–106.

May, P., 1992. Policy learning and failure. *Journal of public policy*, 12, 331–354.

McGrew, A.G., and Lewis, P.G., 1992. *Global politics*. Cambridge: Blackwell.

OECD, 1997. *Reviews of national policies for education*. Paris: OECD.

Olsen, J. and Peters, B.G., 1996. Learning from experience? *In*: J. Olsen and B.G. Peters, eds. *Lessons from experience: experiential learning in administrative reforms in eight democracies*. Oslo: Scandinavian University Press.

Padgett, S., 2003. Between synthesis and emulation: EU policy transfer in the power sector. *Journal of european public policy*, 10 (2), 227–245.

Page, E.C., 2000. *Future governance and the literature on policy transfer and lesson drawing*. ESRC future governance programme workshop on policy transfer, 28 January.

Patel, S., 2009. Accounting for policy change through multi-level analysis: the reform of the Bank of England in the post-war era. *Policy studies*, 30(3), 335–348.

Pedler, M., Burgoyne, J., and Boydell, T., 1991. *The learning company*. Maidenhead: McGraw-Hill.

Peters, B.G., 1997. Policy transfers between governments: the case of administrative reforms. *West European politics*, 20, 71–88.

Reschenthaler, G. and Thompson, F., 2001. Public administration in a period of change: moving to a learning organization perspective. *International public management network journal*, 1 (1), 1–59.

Rhodes, R.A.W., 1994. The hollowing-out of the state: the changing nature of the public service in Britain. *Political quarterly*, 65, 138–151.

Rhodes, R.A.W., 1996. The new governance: governing without government. *Political studies*, 44, 652–667.

Risse-Kappen, T., ed., 1995. *Bringing transnationals back in: non state actors, domestic structures and international institutions*. Cambridge: Cambridge University Press.

Robertson, D., 1991. Political conflict and lesson drawing. *Journal of public policy*, 11, 55–78.

Rose, R., 1993. *Lesson drawing in public policy: a guide to learning across time and space*. Chatham House: New Jersey.

Rose, R., 2005. *Learning from comparative public policy: a practical guide*. London and New York: Routledge.

Rosenau, J., 2000. Change, complexity and governance in a globalising space. *In*: J. Pierre and G. Peters, eds. *Debating governance: authority, steering and democracy*. Oxford: Oxford University Press, 167–200.

Sabatier, P., 1986. Top down and bottom up approaches to implementation research. *Journal of public policy*, 6, 21–48.

Shaxson, L., 2005. Is your evidence robust enough? Questions for policy makers and practitioners. *Evidence and policy*, 1 (1), 101–111.

Stiglitz, J., 2002. *Globalization and its discontents*. London: Penguin.

Stone, D., 1996a. *Non-governmental policy transfer: the strategies of independent policy institutes.* ESRC Research Seminar, Department of Politics and International Studies, University of Birmingham.

Stone, D., 1996b. *Capturing the political imagination: think tanks and the policy process.* London: Frank Cass.

Stone, D., 1999. Learning lessons and transferring policy across time, space and disciplines. *Politics,* 19, 51–59.

Stone, D., ed., 2000a. *Banking on knowledge: the genesis of the global development network.* London: Routledge.

Stone, D., 2000b. Non-governmental policy transfer: the strategies of independent policy institutes. *Governance,* 13, 45–62.

Tonry, M., 2004. *Punishment and politics: evidence and emulation in the making of English crime control policy.* Devon: Willan.

Tushman, M. and Nadler, D., 1996. Organizing for innovation. *In*: K. Starkey, ed. *How organizations learn.* London: International Thomson Business Press.

Walker, J.L., 1969. The diffusion of innovations among American states. *American political science review,* 63, 880–899.

Wincott, D., 1999. Globalization and European integration. *In*: C. Hay and D. Marsh, eds. *Demystifying globalization.* London: Macmillan, 168–190.

Wolman, H., 1992. Understanding cross national policy transfers: the case of Britain and the US. *Governance,* 5, 27–45.

Policy diffusion and policy transfer

David Marsh[a] and J.C. Sharman[b]

[a]Research School of Social Sciences, Australian National University, Australia; [b]Centre for Governance and Public Policy at Griffith University, Brisbane, Australia

This article argues that the literatures on policy transfer and policy diffusion are complimentary, but need to focus more clearly on five key issues drawing insights from both literatures. First, work in each area can benefit from a greater focus on the changing interactions between the various mechanisms involved in diffusion/transfer. Second, the diffusion literature privileges structure, while the transfer literature privileges agency, but we need an approach which recognizes the dialectical relationship between the two. Third, the diffusion literature concentrates on pattern-finding, while the transfer literature examines process-tracing, but any full explanation of transfer/diffusion needs to do both. Fourth, both literatures suffer from skewed case selection with, in particular, too little attention paid to developing countries. Finally, while both literatures need to be interested in whether diffusion/transfer is likely to be successful/unsuccessful, neither considers any criteria that might be used to establish policy success and failure.

Introduction

Scholars studying the spread of common policy trends across very different policy environments are faced with an embarrassment of riches when it comes to theories, concepts and mechanisms. Indeed, it is the terminological and conceptual diversity among scholars studying similar processes that strikes the casual observer. International relations, public policy, comparative politics, sociology and other fields have each been increasingly drawn to processes and outcomes variously labelled as policy transfer, policy diffusion, policy convergence, institutional isomorphism or any one of a number of other cognate terms. In this context, it is perhaps unsurprising that some authors have seen the lack of uniformity as a serious obstacle to extending our knowledge of diffusion and transfer, and in response have called for a process of standardization (James and Lodge 2003, p. 190, Holzinger and Knill 2005, pp. 775–776, Knill 2005, p. 764, Braun and Gilardi 2006, p. 298). However, in our view this will not be easy and, to date, there have been few, if any, attempts to combine the various literatures into an integrated approach (for partial exceptions, in the public policy literature see Evans and Davies 1999, Newmark 2002; in the international relations literature see Braun and Gilardi 2006). However, rather than seeking to effect any grand synthesis, our aim is to identify common challenges and potential cross-fertilizations. We explore the diffusion literature from international relations and the transfer literature from public policy in order to identify how the study of diffusion/transfer (which is clearly an important, and probably growing, phenomenon) might usefully be developed.

More specifically, we shall suggest:

- Following Meseguer and Gilardi (2006), that both literatures need to pay greater attention to the mechanisms involved in diffusion and transfer, the interactions between them and how they evolve over time, rather than simply treating them as either individually sufficient or jointly additive and as exerting a homogenous influence across time and space.
- Work on diffusion tends to emphasize structure while those writing on transfer tend to privilege agency. We need to recognize that the relationship between structure and agency is dialectical, that is interactive and iterative. Any explanation of transfer/diffusion needs to acknowledge this and examine how they interact to produce outcomes.
- In terms of method, the diffusion literature from international relations uses quantitative techniques to analyze a large number of cases to produce generalizations about the reasons for, and the results of, the process. In contrast, the public policy transfer literature uses qualitative analysis of a limited number of cases. As such, the literature raises the crucial question inevitable in any discussion of comparative methodologies or the relative advantages of quantitative and qualitative analysis. Large-N comparative studies allow generalizations, but many would argue that they don't permit sufficient consideration of the cultural differences, etc. among cases. In contrast, small-N studies allow a more nuanced analysis, but the results are not generalizable. We argue that there is potential for intellectual exchange between the work on diffusion and transfer to ameliorate, if not completely resolve, this tension.
- Both literatures, but especially that on policy transfer, should broaden the scope of their case selection. We need greater focus on both different regional patterns of diffusion and negative cases and, above all, a move away from an excessive preoccupation with Western countries. Only then can the extent of diffusion/transfer, and the dynamics underpinning it, be more fully explored.
- Greater attention needs to paid by both literatures to the question of the criteria used for establishing whether a policy is successful or not, given that a key question in both literatures, although particularly in the transfer literature, concerns the effectiveness (or otherwise) of the policy transferred/diffused.

Before examining each of these points in more detail, it is important to consider definitions of policy transfer and diffusion (and cognate concepts), and how they are related. The most quoted definition of policy transfer is by Dolowitz and Marsh (2000, p. 5) who see it as a process by which: 'knowledge about policies, administrative arrangements, institutions and ideas in one political setting (past or present) is used in development of policies, administrative arrangements, institutions and ideas in another political setting'. A common minimalist definition of diffusion views it as a process through which policy choices in one country affect those made in a second country (Simmons and Elkins 2004, p. 171, Braun and Gilardi 2006,

p. 299, Simmons *et al.* 2006, p. 781). Of course, under this definition, if a country sought to differentiate deliberately itself from its peers by adopting policies bearing as little resemblance as possible to those of any other country, this would involve diffusion, but it would bear little relationship to what those researching the topic clearly have in mind: a process of interdependent policy convergence.[1] Policy convergence itself involves a process in which policies in two or more countries becoming more alike over time (Knill 2005, p. 766). Of course, logically, this could be a product of entirely unrelated domestic factors, but, once again, the authors who employ the concept are typically interested in the process by which policies converge because of mechanisms operating at the international level. As far as the relationship between the concepts is concerned, some scholars argue that policy transfer is a type of diffusion (Newmark 2002), while others see diffusion as a type of policy transfer (Busch and Jorgens 2005) and Stone sees both as types of lesson-drawing (2001, p. 7 footnote 3). We are not over-concerned with classificatory schemes; rather our main point here is that it is clear that these literatures share an overlapping conceptual core and a complementary interest in a related class of empirical phenomena.

Mechanisms

As far as explaining diffusion/transfer is concerned, the two literatures, despite their different methodological approaches, generally identify four major mechanisms, learning, competition, coercion and mimicry, although these mechanisms receive differing degrees of attention in the diffusion and transfer literatures. For example, learning is the main mechanism identified in the transfer literature, while other mechanisms receive more attention in the diffusion literature.

Learning

In most transfer literature, learning implies a 'rational' decision by governments to emulate foreign institutions and practice to the extent that these measures produce more efficient and effective policy outcomes than the alternatives (Rose 1991). Learning can lead to complete or partial policy transfer and may take place on a strictly bilateral basis, or through transnational problem solving in international policy networks or epistemic communities. Of course, the assumption of rationality can be relaxed by employing a conception of bounded rationality. In this vein, Weyland in particular has emphasized the importance of bounded rationality and cognitive heuristics in learning (2004, 2005), which may lead to patterns of diffusion distinct from fully rational learning.

Competition

The idea of a 'race to the bottom' driven by international competition, whereby environmental, fiscal or labour standards convergence on a common low base, is a staple trope of much of the literature on globalization and policy diffusion (despite a conspicuous lack of supporting evidence, see Braithwaite and Drahos 2000, Drezner 2001). The argument is that the growing importance and mobility of capital explains why more and more countries have come to adopt broadly similar investor-friendly policies, including privatization, deregulation, balanced budgets, low inflation and strong property rights. In this view, differences between states disappear as footloose capital flows towards those states offering greatest returns and away from less favourable environments. In a related argument, it is suggested that governments need to ensure their exports remain competitive in the global market place by keeping pace with rivals' domestic economic policies.

Coercion

Most scholars are keen to allow some room for various forms of coercion as an explanation of growing similarities among different countries institutions and policies. Such coercion may come from powerful states, or from international organizations like the IMF and World Bank via the conditions attached to their lending. In practice, however, very few studies see coercion as a leading mechanism (for an important exception see Drezner 2001, 2005), although this may result from a pronounced case selection bias. Coercion is most likely to be important in explaining diffusion and transfer in the developing world, but a large majority of the empirical work in this field ignores counties outside the OECD, an issue examined in more detail below.

Mimicry

Mimicry, also known as emulation or socialization, explains the process of copying foreign models in terms of symbolic or normative factors, rather than a technical or rational concern with functional efficiency. States adopt the practices and institutional forms of social leaders (either states perceived to be more advanced or models provided by international organizations) and thereby are perceived by others and themselves as being advanced, progressive and morally praiseworthy. For the sociologists who introduced this concept, mimicry is driven by the deep, intertwined, structural forces of modernization and rationalization (DiMaggio and Powell 1991). Modernity is understood as: 'the organization of society and the nation-state around universalized notions of progress and justice, as built up of rationalized organizations and associations, and as composed of autonomous, rational and purposive individual citizens' (Strang and Meyer 1993, p. 501, see also Boli and Thomas 1999). Emulation in this way may be a deliberate ploy by governments to acquire legitimacy. As such, a government may know full well that the policy in question is technically ineffective but, nevertheless, place a greater value on the social pay-offs among domestic and foreign audiences. Another variant of this argument would see automatic, unreflective, copying as the result of deeply embedded shared conceptions of appropriate behaviour.

The interaction between mechanisms

Of course, although these mechanisms have been presented here as analytically separate and distinct from one another, this neat division is rather contrived. So we might ask: How bounded does rationality have to be before learning becomes unreflective mimicry? If poor countries find themselves under pressure to adopt costly and dysfunctional intellectual property rights laws to gain access to foreign markets, is this competition or coercion at work? Both conceptually and empirically, it is difficult to draw clear lines separating the operation of one mechanism from another, which can make empirical testing a difficult proposition.

Nevertheless, the key point is that it is often assumed that these mechanisms are individually sufficient or work in an additive way, despite much work in political science and sociology pointing out the limitations of such presumptions and emphasizing the importance of being aware of causal complexity (Ragin 1987, Elster 1999, Brady and Collier 2004). Different causal pathways may lead to the same result (multiple causation), small chance events may cause major changes (non-linear causation), and individual mechanisms may only produce changes when engaged in tandem with others (conjunctural causation). As an example, some countries may grant central banks independence to tame an inflationary crisis, while others may merely be following the dictate of the IMF.

In this vein, some authors speak of a 'tipping point' or 'threshold' (Finnemore and Sikkink 1998, Holzinger and Knill 2005, Braun and Gilardi 2006) when the decision of one or a few countries to join a group of policy pioneers precipitates a generalized rush to emulate. Perhaps the adoption of an epistemic community's favoured policy solution is more likely if there is a conspicuous policy failure or scandal in the adopting country. As such, 'Galton's Problem', which refers to the erroneous presumption that national policy choices are independent when they may be auto-correlated, always needs to be born in mind in the study of diffusion. Francis Galton criticized a late nineteenth-century study of the institution of marriage in 350 cultures which claimed that there were common patterns which showed that different cultures independently go through a common sequence of development. He pointed out that the similarities observed could have been the result of cross-cultural borrowing, rather than being independent developments (Jahn 2006, see also Most and Starr 1990).

Many of the large statistical investigations of diffusion cannot cope with these kinds of complications. One solution would be for diffusion scholars to undertake some detailed case studies, based on fieldwork and interviews, in order to tease out the relative impact of policy learning, norms, economic competition and so on. However, the need to combine what below we term process-tracing and pattern-finding research cuts both ways; public policy scholars could also begin to employ statistical techniques like event history, logit and probit tests to produce more generalizable conclusions about the relative importance of, and the interaction between, mechanisms.

A separate, but related, problem concerns the assumption that given mechanisms generate a uniform impact across different stages of the diffusion process, that is on initiators and on those joining the 'bandwagon' much later on, although some mechanisms are premised on the view that different motivations operate at successive stages of the diffusion process. As an example, in writing on the spread of female suffrage Finnemore and Sikkink (1998) hold that early adaptors give women the vote thanks largely to the efforts of domestic social movements and protest campaigns. However, by the time late adaptors legislated universal suffrage it had become an almost unquestioned norm, a taken-for-granted international standard (see also Collier and Messick 1975).

A more formal rendering of this kind of dynamic is provided by Granovetter's threshold model (1978), which some have sought to apply to diffusion processes (Braun and Gilardi 2006). Granovetter's idea, developed to explain patterns of collective action, is that different people have different thresholds that must be reached before they will engage in collective action. So, some people are happy to initiate a demonstration, others will join as long as someone else has made the first move, while some will hang back until almost everybody else is participating. According to this logic, depending on the distribution of these thresholds among individuals, tiny demonstrations may rapidly balloon into huge protests, as in East Germany in 1989 (Lohmann 1994). Moving to the idea of states emulating each other, some governments may wish to stake their claim as innovators, others may wait and see, while still some may only be reluctantly shifted from the status quo once all the other dominoes have fallen.

Not only do different individuals have different thresholds before emulating their peers, but these individuals may also be sensitive to the effects of different mechanisms simultaneously or sequentially at work (e.g. some to learning, some to mimicry). Of course, it is very difficult to present a detailed model able to cope with national variations which is consistent with the uneven progress of transfers and could establish the distribution of thresholds in a given population before a given bandwagon has run its course (Strang and Soule 1998). As such, this kind of cascade model may be useful for *post hoc* explanations, but also be hard to falsify for the same reason. While this approach can accommodate a wide variety of mechanisms and the interactions between them, the result will not appeal to those with a preference for parsimony.

Structure and agency

In our view, the diffusion literature tends to emphasize structural explanation, while, in contrast, the transfer literature places more emphasis on agency. Of course, many diffusion scholars reject the accusation made by Dolowitz and Marsh in their first article (1996, pp. 334–335) that diffusion is a process without agents. As just one example, Lee and Strang argue (2006, p. 888):

> Policy diffusion we should note, does not imply a world without agency. In both of the cases outlined above [public sector downsizing in Australia and Korea] key actors – most notably Australia's Prime Minister Bob Hawke and Korea's President Young-Sam Kim – allied themselves with foreign exemplars to achieve their policy goals.

Indeed, Newmark argues (2002, p. 164): 'Both literatures identify the importance of agents'. This seems to us to be a difficult position to defend. The only focus on the role of agents in the diffusion literature is in the limited process-tracing work and this is clear in Lee and Strang's article (2006). They have two pages on the role of agency in diffusion in which they review two case studies utilizing a process-tracing approach. However, this is little more than an aside in a piece which focuses on a statistical analysis of the role of structural factors like trade partnership, capital city proximity, geographical proximity, trade with the United States, previous economic outcomes, etc. Indeed, given the methodology adopted, it is difficult to provide any indicators of agency effect and impossible to take account of the meanings agents, whether leaders or electors, attach to these structural variables.

The transfer literature does acknowledge the importance of structures. So, for example, Dolowitz and Marsh (2000) highlight the role of structures of government, international economic and political pressures and the media, etc. Nevertheless, because their main focus, and indeed their entire empirical focus, is on voluntary transfer or learning, there is a clear privileging of agency, a focus upon who was involved in transfer, how and why. Thus, at best, they take an additive approach to the structure/agency problem, in which the outcome is influenced by both structure and agents, but the relationship between the two is not theorized.

The problem with both of these literatures is that they have an unsophisticated approach to the structure/agency problem. The one honourable exception is Evans and Davies (1999), who develop what they term a multi-level approach to policy transfer in which they adopt a dialectical approach, rooted in Giddens' structuration theory. Certainly, the best modern literature on structure and agency treats the relationship as dialectical; that is interactive and iterative. Structures provide the context within which agents act and they constrain or facilitate the agents' actions. However, agents interpret those structures and, in acting, change them. These new structures then provide the context within which agents act, and the process starts another cycle. This is not the place for a detailed consideration of the structure/agency literature (for good reviews see Hay 2001, McAnulla 2002). Inevitably, given its origins in Giddens' work, Evans and Davies' (1999) approach suffers from one of the problems that is regularly identified with structuration theory, that it doesn't allow one to study the interaction between structure and agency because, methodologically, either structure or agency, and usually the former, is held constant (see Hay 2001, McAnulla 2002). The key point here is that, when considering transfer, agents are faced with a structural context which may privilege certain decisions. However, they interpret that structural context and in acting change it. This has clear methodological significance: for example, one cannot study an iterative process without a temporal dimension, so any analysis should trace the evolution of policy over time. Given the limitations of structuration it seems to us that Archer's morphogenetic approach (see McAnulla 2002 for a clear exposition and defence of morphogenesis) is a more likely candidate if we want to examine the interaction between structure and agency over time (see Legrand 2007 which offers a way of approaching policy transfer from a morphogenetic perspective underpinned by critical realism).

Methodology and approach

Quantitative vs. qualitative methods?

There is a clear difference between most of the writers in the transfer and the diffusion literatures in terms of their methodologies and, consequently, ambitions (a similar point is developed by Newmark 2002). The transfer literature employs small-N qualitative case studies focusing on a detailed analysis of the transfer of a policy, or perhaps a series of related policies, between two, or sometimes more, countries. At the same time, its ambitions have been guarded. In contrast, the diffusion literature mainly uses large-N studies and aims to produce generalizable statements about both the causes and consequences of the diffusion process.

The thrust of the transfer literature is clear if we consider the two contributions by Dolowitz and Marsh (1996, 2000), and the heuristic framework that they developed, which is widely used in empirical studies of policy transfer. Initially, Dolowitz and Marsh (1996) suggested a series of questions that might be addressed when studying transfer: Who transfers policy? Why engage in policy transfer? What is transferred? Are there different degrees of transfer? From where are lessons drawn? What factors constrain policy transfer? In each case, they suggest a number of putative answers to the particular question. In their later article (Dolowitz and Marsh 2000), another question is added: How is the process of policy transfer related to policy 'success' or 'failure'? In addition, the questions are transposed into a conceptual framework, to produce a model (Dolowitz and Marsh 2000, p. 9, Table 1). The key point however, is that, even in this later formulation, Dolowitz and Marsh's claims for their model are modest. The model is presented as primarily: 'a heuristic devise that allows us to think more systematically about the processes involved' (Dolowitz and Marsh 2000, p. 14). In effect, it offers a series of questions that researchers can use to frame their empirical work; indeed, this is what has happened as there are a number of empirical studies which, sometimes critically, use all or elements of this model to organize the research (for example, Jacoby 2000, Jones and Newburn 2002, Lamour 2002).

This does not mean that Dolowitz and Marsh, or other researchers into policy transfer, are not interested in explanation (2000, p. 8). In fact, one of their main concerns in their second article is to examine the relationship between policy transfer and policy success/failure and they suggest that transfer is likely to be unsuccessful if it is uniformed, incomplete or inappropriate. The details need not concern us here, rather the key point is that Dolowitz and Marsh claim (2000, p. 21), with a number of subsequent caveats that: 'the research presented here supports the position that policy transfer is a useful explanatory variable'. There is an important issue here, because Dolowitz and Marsh, in common with all the transfer literature, consider a very limited number of cases (in this article the transfer of welfare to work policy and the Child Support Agency from the US to the UK). As a result, any claims they make about the general explanatory power of transfer need to be very circumspect.

In contrast, the diffusion literature is more ambitious. After briefly reviewing the diffusion literature, Lee and Strang (2006) introduce an interesting distinction between process-tracing and pattern-finding strategies. They argue (p. 886) that:

> Process tracing research follows the spread of a policy or practice from one location to another. The approach permits inspection of the role played by external models, and inquiry into why and how a concrete instance of learning or mimicry occurs. By contrast, pattern finding research tests a priori hypotheses about diffusion channels (. . .) this strategy asks whether structures of covariance and temporal ordering are generally consistent with a theoretically specified model of influence.

This distinction is useful, but seems difficult to apply to the diffusion literature, given that it is almost exclusively pattern finding. Weyland's (2005) effort to draw lessons for theorizing policy diffusion from an analysis of Latin American pension reform is a notable exception (see also the case studies reported in Lee and Strang 2006, pp. 886–889), but most diffusion research aims to 'find patterns' and establish generalizable statements about either what causes diffusion or what diffusion causes on the basis of aggregate data. This is clear if we briefly consider the contributions to a recent special issue of *International Organization* (*IO*) on diffusion.

Lee and Strang (2006) consider the diffusion of public sector downsizing. They use regression analysis to study the annual change in public sector employment between 1980 and 1997 in 26 OECD countries and conclude (Lee and Strang 2006, p. 903) that:

'the size of the public sector is linked not only to domestic economic and political conditions, but also to international policy diffusion'. More particularly, they contend (Lee and Strang 2006, p. 903) that: 'down-sizing appears to be contagious, while upsizing does not'. Gleditsch and Ward (2006) focus on the diffusion of democratization. They use a transition model to examine how international and regional factors influence the likelihood that there would be democratic transition between 1951 and 1997. They argue that there are clear diffusion effects. Thus, they conclude a higher proportion of democratic neighbours and a successful transition to democracy in a neighbouring country significantly decreases the likelihood that autocracies will endure (Gleditsch and Ward 2006, p. 925). Swank (2006) examines the spread of neo-liberal tax policy among 16 advanced nations between 1981–1998 using regression analysis. In contrast to the other studies in the *IO* volume, he finds: 'net of other factors in the model, national policymakers are not systematically influenced by the general course of recent policy change across the developed countries' (Swank 2006, p. 865). Elkins, Guzman and Simmons (2006) focus on the diffusion of bilateral investment treaties between 1960 and 2000 using an event history framework and regression analysis. Their analysis is different from that of the three other articles because diffusion is their dependent variable. As such, they argue that competition between countries (Elkins, Guzman and Simmons 2006, p. 836) and increased globalization, measured in terms of growing global foreign direct investment (p. 838) and coercion, measured in terms of the use of IMF credits (p. 840), help explain diffusion.

Our argument here is that the two literatures are complementary. The transfer literature produces much more nuanced understandings of the process involved in transfer and, as such, it fits well with the limited process-tracing approach in the diffusion literature. This approach can both suggest variables that might be included in pattern-finding studies and/or help interpret the results of pattern-finding research. The diffusion literature may produce generalizable conclusions using aggregate statistical data, but they are not always easy to interpret. To take one example, Gleditsch and Ward (2006) distinguish only two types of political system, democracies and autocracies, in terms of where they are located on a seven-point institutionalized democracy scale and then examine which factors are associated with a move from democracy to autocracy, or vice versa. The details need not concern us here, but we would suggest that the likelihood of a state moving towards the democratic end of the continuum will depend on both its leaders' and citizens' understanding of democracy and its leaders' and citizens' view of the democracy in the states from which the lesson is drawn. As such, an analysis which offers a more nuanced, process-tracing, approach to democratization has much to offer.

In other diffusion studies, the use of particular proxies for complex underlying concepts seems to verge on the heroic. Certainly, Lenschow *et al.*'s (2005) use of religion as a proxy for culture in order to compare the cultures of different countries seems a simplification too far. East Timor, Switzerland and Argentina are all predominantly Catholic countries, but 'explaining' any institutional similarities in their government bureaucracies by reference to their Catholicism is very little help. Similarly, the finding in another study that culture (indicated by religion) is one of the best predictors of economic liberalization seems to be a correlation in search of an explanation, rather than an explanation as such (Simmons and Elkins 2004). The tendency of decision-theoretic models to reduce symbolic and normative factors to nothing more than governments making deliberate means-ends calculations to maximize prestige or legitimacy, in the same way that individuals make investment decisions to maximize their wealth, is also problematic (March and Olsen 1989). The point here is not that a process-tracing approach is superior to a pattern-finding approach, rather that to explain and understand diffusion/transfer we need both approaches. We need to establish the patterns, but we also need to explain them.

Diffusion/transfer as an independent and dependent variable

As Dolowitz and Marsh (2000) point out, diffusion/transfer can be used as either a dependent or an independent variable. So, we can use diffusion/transfer as a variable to explain policy change/innovation or success or failure and/or we can try to explain under what circumstances diffusion/transfer is more likely to occur. Of course, these two approaches are not mutually exclusive, indeed a full explanation of a policy outcome surely has to cover both whether something has had an effect and how and why. As indicated, both sets of literature deal with both issues. Dolowitz and Marsh's framework focuses largely on the factors which make transfer more or less likely but, as we saw, in their second article they focus on the ways in which transfer might lead to outcomes which are successful or fail. Similarly, three of the articles in the *IO* special issue consider above use diffusion as an independent variable, while one uses it as a dependent variable.

If we use diffusion/transfer as an independent variable, then the null hypothesis is that particular national arrangements reflect particular national circumstances, or that even if pronounced similarities can be observed, these are independent reactions to common shocks or trends. In this case, there is no transfer or diffusion. As Holzinger and Knill put it, there is nothing too mysterious about a crowd of strangers all deciding to put up their umbrellas simultaneously as rain begins to fall (2005, p. 786). As such, most contemporary work on diffusion, and to a lesser extent transfer, springs from dissatisfaction with the previously conventional notion that states are self-contained, isolated units whose institutions and policies can only be explained by reference to domestic variables.

Outcomes of the process

One of the fundamental differences between the diffusion and the transfer literature lies in the focus the former has on policy convergence. As such, the international relations policy diffusion literature treats diffusion in particular countries as a dichotomous outcome. In contrast, public policy scholars are much more likely to see policy transfer as a matter of degree. In part, this difference may reflect the different methodologies, with the diffusion researchers having to simplify variables to enable statistical analysis. However, it is also interesting that even the limited international relations work that utilizes a qualitative, case study method tends to treat diffusion as a dichotomous variable (Finnemore and Sikkink 1998, Flockhart 2006).

Presenting diffusion as a dichotomous (adopt/don't adopt) variable may be a reasonably accurate rendering for some policies. However, in other cases such simplifications give grounds for concern. As Marcussen has noted, a seemingly simple dichotomous judgment, such as whether or not a central bank is independent, actually obscures a host of difficult decisions about classifications (2005, p. 907).

Indeed, McNamara has argued that findings about the effects of central bank independence on inflation and other macroeconomic variables may be artifacts of the way this notion has been shoehorned into a simple present/absent coding schema (McNamara 2002).

In contrast, in the public policy field researchers argue that policy transfer does not necessarily involve foreign institutions and practices being adopted *in toto*. Although such complete 'cut and paste' transfers are allowed for, they are seen as the exceptions, with hybridized combinations of outside and local knowledge much more common. As such, there is a much greater interest in the preconditions for transfer in the recipient state and how national differences may alter the speed, scope and extent to which outside examples are incorporated into the domestic policy-making process (Lenschow *et al.* 2005). These scholars are interested in what kind of actors are pushing the transfer process and what kind of actors are most receptive to these kind of epistemic imports at what stage of the policy cycle (Knill 2005). In addition, convergence may occur at different policy levels (Heichel *et al.* 2005). Of course, as we emphasized, the detail involved in such studies generally precludes the sort of large number-crunching studies common elsewhere in favour of comparisons of a few detailed case studies, generally drawn from amongst the rich industrialized countries.

The role of domestic factors

Although those studying diffusion may well resist replicating the fine-grained approach of policy transfer approach, it is clearly not acceptable to simply ignore domestic factors. While it is important to establish whether policies are growing more and more similar in their formal content, it is also crucial to recognize that they may be practiced and implemented in incredibly different ways in various national settings.

Crucially, a central premise of the diffusion literature in international relations, as well as institutional isomorphism in sociology, is that countries adopt similar policies almost regardless of domestic circumstances. Indeed, it is the incongruity of common policies across a wide variety of social and institutional environments (contrary to the prior conventional wisdom that policies reflect local circumstances) that put diffusion on the agenda in the first place. However, attention to exogenous factors should not mean an exclusive preoccupation with such factors. The public policy literature has retained a better sense of balance here, looking at how domestic circumstances affect whether, when and how governments accept transfers from abroad. Such domestic factors may include the structure of the bureaucracy, the number of veto players, stage in the electoral cycle, etc. (Lodge 2003, Lenschow *et al.* 2005). Those analyzing diffusion from an international relations background could profitably (re)incorporate these kind of domestic factors to help explain the uneven tempo and spread of given policies. This is especially the case if, as argued above, diffusion is coded in more than just a dichotomous fashion, as a matter of degree, depth and perhaps even effectiveness.

Is the world becoming more homogenized?

As a result of the difference between the synoptic, sparse, view presented by the policy diffusion literature and the more detailed public policy perspective, the two groups come to quite radically different conclusions about whether the world really has become more homogenized. For international relations scholars researching diffusion, countries become more alike as they democratize their political systems and liberalize their economies (Simmons *et al.* 2006). Sociologists in the world society tradition share such a conclusion for an even wider range of institutions and practices, from corporate governance to social movements (Strang and Soule 1998). On the other hand, for those looking at policy transfer, the fundamental trends may be very different. The logic of transfer does not necessarily entail convergence. Because transfer is seen as continuous variable, perhaps extending along several dimensions, and often a matter of combining foreign and local models, national distinctiveness remains alive and well. Radaelli (2005), for example, notes that although all European Union governments have committed to conducting Regulatory Impact Assessments, what this means in practice varies completely from state to state in line with diverse national priorities. Overall, some public policy scholars are fairly agnostic as to whether the world is becoming a more homogenous place (see especially Levi-Faur 2006), though others tend to share the views of their colleagues in international relations and sociology (Dolowitz and Marsh 2000).

Empirical scope and case selection

In terms of case selection, studies of diffusion and transfer tend either to deal with a subset of developed Western countries (particularly common in the public policy literature) or utilize large data sets with something approaching global coverage (more typical of diffusion in international relations). There are very few regional or small-*N* studies with a focus outside Europe, or at least the North Atlantic (some honourable and very enlightening exceptions are provided by Evans 2004, Weyland 2004, 2005). The states of Africa, the Middle East and most of Asia are either considered only in so far as they are present in global data sets, or ignored altogether. This failure is particularly damning as it relates to policy transfer scholars, whose case study approach could be productively applied even in environments where detailed quantitative data are absent. In part, this neglect reflects the fascination with the topics of Europeanization and globalization writ large in the 1990s. This pronounced selection bias is an important shortcoming for a number of reasons.

Many of the mechanisms that are said to drive transfer and diffusion could be expected to exert a stronger influence in the developing world than anywhere else. Most obviously, if the IMF and World Bank are powerful agents of homogenization through conditional lending, their influence will be felt in recipient countries, rather than donor countries. The same can be said of coercive transfer driven by core states (e.g. Drezner 2001, 2005). Because of their generally smaller domestic stocks of capital and higher risk premiums, developing countries are also more likely to fall prey to a 'race to the bottom' dynamic in attracting foreign investment, if such a dynamic exists. At the same time, developing states legitimize themselves by mimicking developed states, rather than vice versa. If sovereign states are converging on a progressive, enlightened, rational model, those in the developing world have the most distance to travel. If policies are adopted for symbolic reasons, rather than to meet functional needs, this disjuncture should be most apparent and consequential outside the West. As such, the developing world again provides a powerful testing ground for examining the relationship between policy transfer and effectiveness. For either confirming existing hypotheses or generating new ones, the answers lie disproportionately in the developing world.

When this neglect has been acknowledged (Drezner 2001, p. 65, Stone 2001, p. 1, Heichel *et al.* 2005, p. 819), it has been argued that the necessary data for developing countries are not available. However, this excuse seems thin. Developing countries are measured and surveyed more and more with each passing year, by outsiders and by their own statistical bodies. For the travel-shy or impecunious, the results are increasingly available on the web. For qualitative researchers, the previous reluctance of scholars to travel too far from their home base to examine the experiences of policy-makers on the receiving end of Western models should represent a tremendous opportunity for new detailed process-tracing studies and structured inter-regional and intra-regional small-N comparisons. The latter might extend to Africa, the Caribbean Basin, Southeast Asia, or a sample of developing countries might be selected on other grounds (former French colonies, or small island states).

Of course, uncritically amalgamating the experiences of developed and developing countries may serve to obscure important relationships. For example, although it is possible to observe a statistically significant relationship between central bank independence and low inflation in developed countries, this relationship disappears when extended to developing countries (which have nevertheless been no less reluctant to adopt this reform, see McNamara 2002). Harking back to the earlier discussion, different mechanisms or, more likely, different combinations of mechanisms may be at work in the periphery and in differing regions of the developing world. Finally, and foreshadowing the next point, some regions may be especially resistant to taking on outside policy innovations, prompting questions of why 'holdouts' may be geographically clustered.

Despite the explosion of literature on diffusion, transfer and cognate concepts, the idea of why countries reject outside models and stick with local solutions has received relatively little attention. For example, why has the South African government been so reluctant to accept the policy model advanced by core states, international organizations and the relevant epistemic community in its efforts to combat AIDS? Incorporating negative cases in line with the 'possibility principle' could be particularly valuable in qualitative comparisons. As Mahoney and Goertz argue (2004, p. 653), the principle in question: 'advises researchers to select only negative cases ... if one or only a small number of independent variables predict its occurrence'. For argument's sake, in relation to diffusion this might involve geographically proximate, culturally similar countries, at similarly low levels of economic development, which nevertheless maintain highly distinctive, or even steadily diverging, policies across time. To productively apply the possibility principle, the relevant theory must be refined enough to confidently specify a small number of independent variables. With reference to diffusion and transfer, some explicitly dispute this point. Nevertheless, this possibility principle approach would represent a new and relatively low-cost means by which to shed new light on existing problems.

Policy success and failure

The policy transfer literature is concerned with how transfer relates to policy outcomes. Transfer is seen generally as improving the effectiveness of government operations (Dolowitz and Marsh 2000, p. 6, Radaelli 2000, p. 38). This presumption is present even more strongly in related earlier work on lesson-drawing (see Rose 1991), perhaps because the word 'learning' itself inherently entails these positive, progressive connotations (Alderson 2001, p. 424). Here, the idea is that, just as individuals learn through observing the experiences of others and modify their own behaviour as a result, governments can similarly draw upon a stock of knowledge concerning how particular policy measures have fared in other contexts, rather than having to work from scratch every time.

In the international relations (and sociological) literature there is no such presumption of improving effectiveness or efficiency through importing foreign models. Scholars working from these perspectives have generally bracketed-off the question of effectiveness. However, as we emphasized, this literature pays less attention to learning as a mechanism of diffusion and suggests that importing models from outside as a result of competition, coercion or mimicry, will more often than not produce policy ineffectiveness and dysfunction. For example, the view that governments mimic others to conform with dominant templates of appropriate structure and behaviour is explicitly counterposed to the view that policy diffusion is a rational process involving replacing ignorance with knowledge to enhance functional outcomes. This argument has been bolstered by empirical work that shows that the policies countries objectively 'need' to solve a particular problem are not always the ones they actually adopt for reasons of prestige or legitimacy (e.g. Lee and Strang 2006). Similarly, if countries have been coerced into adopting particular policies by powerful external actors, the policies themselves may be inherently unsuited to local conditions, or sabotaged by embittered domestic actors during the implementation. Even if learning is said to play a role, actors may have only bounded rationality and thus may generalize inappropriately from a few proximate examples and hold on to initial conclusions even in the face of repeated subsequent disconfirmations (Weyland 2005).

Despite this, we would argue that scholars interested in transfer and diffusion should be interested in policy effectiveness. Indeed, existing explanations of diffusion/transfer nearly always make implicit claims about its effectiveness (or perceived effectiveness, which only pushes the problem one-step back). More specifically, if governments are to learn, then they must gather information and sort previous experiences into instances where the policies have had the desired effect and those where they have not, before emulating the former. In addition, as noted above, it is the very lack of effectiveness of many of the outside models adopted internationally that provides the most compelling evidence for other mechanisms of diffusion; if policy solutions were clearly functional and efficient under local conditions there would be little to explain concerning why they were adopted.

There are also persuasive, practical reasons why scholars working on diffusion and transfer should confront the issue of effectiveness more directly, despite the sobering challenges this poses. For example, many NGOs claim that the imposition of Western models of water privatization in the developing world are causing massive economic deprivation and death (e.g. Public Citizen 2003). The fact that thousands of lives may hang in the balance makes evaluating the effectiveness of common water policy models more than just an interesting intellectual exercise. The conspicuous reluctance of countries like South Africa to accept policy transfer from abroad when it comes to fighting the spread of AIDS noted earlier seems to be in a similar category. For scholars to say that data and conceptual problems make questions of evaluating the effectiveness of models transferred from outside too hard seems overly pusillanimous.

The big problem here is that there is no generally accepted framework for judging policy success and indeed the academic literature in this field is very poor.[2] A Google search entering 'policy success' produces over 200,000 hits of five broad types: media pieces assessing the success/consequences of policy; claims by government and government agency of policy successes either in the media or in official documents; interest group or voluntary organization's assessments/claims about policy successes; blogs on policy outcomes; and academic articles assessing policy success.

Obviously, the latter are most interesting here but, unfortunately, they are limited and most could be categorized broadly as policy evaluation studies, which are very narrow. Fortunately, there is an exception to the general poor quality of the literature. Bovens *et al.*'s (2001) aim is to assess policy success/failure in four areas where there are challenges to governance in six European countries (UK, Netherlands, France, Germany, Sweden and Spain): (1) management of decline (the steel industry); (2) management of institutional reform (health services); (3) management of innovation (financial sector); and (4) management of crisis (HIV AIDS). Of course, it is the criteria they establish against which success can be judged that is of relevance here. The key distinction they make is between programmatic and political success. Programmatic success is established in relation to the three criteria of effectiveness, efficiency and resilience. Political success is characterized as follows: 'the political dimension of assessment refers to the way in which policies and policy makers become represented and evaluated in the political arena' (Bovens *et al.* 2001, p. 20). More specifically, they assert: 'Indicators of political failure or success are political upheaval (press coverage, parliamentary investigations, political fatalities, litigation) or lack of it, and changes in generic patterns of political legitimacy (public satisfaction with policy or confidence in authorities and public institutions)' (Bovens *et al.* 2001, p. 21). However, they also acknowledge that the detailed measures of success will be policy dependent, so their collaborators in this edited volume were asked to develop specific criteria for their four cases (the particular programmatic and political assessment criteria are laid out in Bovens *et al.* 2001, p. 21, Table 2.2). They also acknowledge that these criteria might produce contradictory results. So, policies may be unsuccessful in programmatic terms, but spun to appear a political success, or successful in programmatic, but represented as a failure and so being politically negative for the government (Bovens *et al.* 2001, p. 20).

This seems to be an important attempt to establish criteria to judge policy success or failure and it is a useful starting point for the diffusion/transfer literature to address this crucial question. However, there is one significant weakness with the discussion of success in Bovens *et al.*, because they have no discussion of the process dimension of policy. Yet, in many cases, a government may regard a policy as successful, if it is passed, virtually unamended. Thus, a government faced with a urgent political dilemma or issue may propose a solution, perhaps transferred from abroad, which moves the issue off the political agenda. In common parlance this may be a 'quick fix', which in a longer timeframe results in programmatic failure, although in the short term in may be a political success as the government is viewed as decisive, perhaps in the run-up to an election.

Of course, even if we could agree that these three dimensions of success, process success, programmatic success and political success, are adequate ones (or even just more adequate than previous ones) and then agree measures for how these criteria could be assessed, we are still left with the question of the extent to which an objective assessment is possible. Here, epistemological issues cannot be avoided. This issue is raised by Bovens *et al.* (2006), who argue that 'policy evaluation is an inherently normative act' (p. 319) and 'It is only a slight exaggeration to say, paraphrasing Clausewitz, that policy evaluation is nothing but the continuation of politics by other means' (p. 321). Bovens *et al.* (2006) distinguish between what they call rationalistic and argumentative approaches to evaluation, so they are contrasting approaches rooted in positivist and interpretivist/constructivist epistemologies. Of course, positivists, would say objectivity is possible, although perhaps with some reservations emphasizing that different people have different perceptions of success, a point developed below. In contrast, most interpretivists and constructivists would say no, because all such criteria are merely social constructions and do not reflect an underlying reality (for a discussion of these issues see Marsh and Furlong 2002).

In response to this seeming impasse, Bovens *et al.* (2006) quote Majone (1989, p. 182) with approval (p. 329) and we would agree with this argument:

> It is not the task of analysts to resolve fundamental disagreements about evaluative criteria and standards of accountability; only the political process can do that. However, analysts can contribute to societal learning by refining the standards of appraisal and by encouraging a more sophisticated understanding of public policies than is possible from a single perspective.

There is a related, if more limited, but still very important, issue concerning 'success for whom'. The nature of politics, especially liberal democratic politics, means that 'success' will always be contested to some degree. So, we should not expect government, politicians, civil servants, interest groups, citizens, etc. to all agree on whether or not any aspect of a particular policy is successful. Of course, this raises crucial issues about power relations: do outcomes serve particular interests? More narrowly, Bovens *et al.* (2006) argue: '(Even in relatively) uncontroversial instances, policy evaluations are entwined with processes of accountability and lesson-drawing that may have winners and losers. However, technocratic and seemingly innocuous, every policy programme has multiple stakeholders who have an interest in the outcome of an evaluation: decision makers, executive agencies, clients, pressure groups' (Bovens *et al.* 2006, p. 322). They also emphasize that interested parties attempt to influence evaluations (Bovens *et al.* 2006, p. 324).

Obviously then, there are difficult questions here. However, it is both important and possible to judge the success or failure of transferred or diffused policies. We need to acknowledge the issues raised in the last two paragraphs, but not become obsessed by them. In essence, we rest on Majone's claim that (1989, p. 183): 'The need today is less to develop "objective" measures of outcomes – the traditional aim of evaluation research – than to facilitate a wide-ranging dialogue among advocates of different criteria'. A framework which allows us to identify different indicators of success, we suggest process, programmatic and political indicators, is crucial here. However, it is also important to acknowledge that judgements about success may reflect power relations and be different for different individuals/groups. Indeed, some would claim that policy success itself is nothing more than a social construct reflecting power relations.

Conclusions

This article has shown that the transfer and the diffusion literature share a great deal in common. They both suggest that diffusion/transfer is an important factor in policy change. In addition, they identify a similar range of mechanisms as driving transfer/diffusion. The next step for each is to look at how mechanisms interact, and to allow for the differential functioning of these mechanisms in different regions, and on leaders as opposed to laggards. Diffusion and transfer differ significantly in terms of the structural cast of the former versus the agent-centred approach of the latter. In our view, it would be productive for each to utilize a dialectical conception of structure and agency. At the same time, there are few process-tracing studies in the diffusion literature, yet little else in transfer literature, while the diffusion literature focuses upon pattern finding, which is absent in the transfer literature. We argue here that we need to integrate these approaches if we are to both establish patterns and explain how and why they came about. This might be achieved by transfer scholars increasing their sample sizes and those working on diffusion looking in more depth at the processes which explain the aggregate patterns they uncover.

Despite the recent flurry of publications, little attention has been paid to the experiences of developing countries or regions (Latin America excepted), or negative cases of where policy transfer/diffusion has not occurred. This bias may retard the development of the field overall, for example in understating the significance of coercive transfer/diffusion. Finally, there is a need to confront the issue of policy success and failure, for compelling conceptual and practical reasons. Such evaluations undoubtedly raise a host of complicated issues, but they cannot be avoided and we suggest a putative way forward here which distinguishes between the policy, programmatic and political dimensions of success.

Notes

1. Although this article follows the currently usual approach in both international relations and public policy by referring to transfer and diffusion across states, the same processes may well be occurring between other units as well. The diffusion literature initially focused on the spread of policies among the 50 states of the United States (see Walker 1969). Indeed, Newmark's (2002) article still focuses almost exclusively on this type of diffusion research. Similarly, sociologists analyze 'institutional isomorphism' (another cognate term) between firms, local governments and professional associations (Strang and Meyer 1993, Strang and Soule 1998). As such, a future avenue of research for diffusion/transfer researchers might be to examine the degree to which international organizations, governmental and non-governmental, come to resemble each other or adopt similar practices.
2. This discussion of policy success is based on Marsh and McConnell (2009), 'Towards a model of policy success'.

References

Alderson, K., 2001. Making sense of state socialisation. *Review of international studies,* 27 (July), 415–433.

Boli, J. and Thomas, G., eds., 1999. *Constructing world culture: international nongovernmental organizations since 1875.* Stanford: Stanford University Press.

Bovens, M., t'Hart, P., and Peters, B.G., 2001. *Success and failure in public governance: a comparative study.* Cheltenham: Elgar.

Bovens, M., t'Hart, P., and Kuipers, S., 2006. The politics of policy evaluation. *In*: M. Moran, M. Rein and R.E. Goodin, eds. *Oxford handbook of public policy.* Oxford: Oxford University Press.

Brady, H.E. and Collier, D., eds., 2004. *Rethinking social inquiry: diverse tools, shared standards.* Lanham, MD: Rowman and Littlefield.

Braithwaite, J. and Drahos, P., 2000. *Global business regulation.* Cambridge: Cambridge University Press.

Braun, D. and Gilardi, F., 2006. Taking 'Galton's problem' seriously: towards a theory of policy diffusion. *Journal of theoretical politics,* 18 (3), 298–322.

Busch, P.-O. and Jorgens, H., 2005. The international sources of policy convergence: explaining the spread of environmental policy innovations. *Journal of european public policy,* 12 (October), 860–884.

Collier, D. and Messick, R., 1975. Prerequisites versus diffusion: testing alternative explanations of social security adoption. *American political science review,* 69, 1299–1315.

DiMaggio, P.J. and Powell, W.W., eds., 1991. *The new institutionalism in organizational analysis.* Chicago: University of Chicago Press.

Dolowitz, D.P. and Marsh, D., 1996. Who learns what from whom: a review of the policy transfer literature. *Political studies,* 44 (2), 343–357.

Dolowitz, D.P. and Marsh, D., 2000. Learning from abroad: the role of policy transfer in contemporary policy-making. *Governance,* 13 (January), 5–24.

Drezner, D.W., 2001. Globalisation and policy convergence. *International studies review,* 3, 53–78.

Drezner, D.W., 2005. Globalisation, harmonisation, and competition: the different pathways to policy convergence. *Journal of european public policy,* 12 (October), 841–859.

Elkins, Z., Guzman, A., and Simmons, B., 2006. Competing for capital: the diffusion of bilateral investment treaties 1959–2000. *International organization,* 60(4), 811–846.

Elster, J., 1999. *Alchemies of the mind: rationality and the emotions.* Cambridge: Cambridge University Press.

Evans, M. and Davies, J., 1999. Understanding policy transfer: a multi-level, multi-disciplinary perspective. *Public administration,* 77 (2), 361–385.

Evans, M.G., 2004. *Policy transfer in global perspective.* Aldershot: Ashgate.

Finnemore, M. and Sikkink, K., 1998. International norms dynamics and political change. *International organization,* 52 (Autumn), 887–917.

Flockhart, T., 2006. Complex socialisation': a framework for the study of socialisation. *European journal of international relations,* 12 (1), 89–118.

Gleditsch, K.S. and Ward, M.D., 2006. Diffusion and the international context of democratization. *International organization,* 60 (Fall), 911–933.

Granovetter, M., 1978. Threshold models of collective behavior. *American journal of sociology,* 83 (May), 1420–1443.

Hay, C., 2001. *Political analysis.* Basingstoke: Palgrave.

Heichel, S., Pape, J. and Sommer, T., 2005. Is there convergence in convergence research? An overview of empirical studies on policy convergence. *Journal of european public policy,* 12 (October), 817–840.

Holzinger, K. and Knill, C., 2005. Causes and conditions of policy convergence. *Journal of european public policy,* 12 (October), 775–796.

Jacoby, W., 2000. *Imitation and politics: redesigning modern Germany.* New York: Cornell University Press.

Jahn, D., 2006. Globalisation as 'Galton's problem': the missing link in the analysis of diffusion patterns in welfare state development. *International organization,* 60 (Spring), 401–431.

James, O. and Lodge, M., 2003. The limitations of 'policy transfer' and 'lesson drawing' for public policy research. *Political studies review,* 1, 179–193.

Jones, T. and Newburn, T., 2002. Learning from Uncle Sam: exploring US influence on British crime control policy. *Governance,* 15 (1), 97–119.

Knill, C., 2005. Introduction: cross-national policy convergence: concepts, approaches and explanatory factors. *Journal of european public policy,* 12 (October), 764–774.

Lamour, P., 2002. Policy transfer and reversal: customary land registration from Africa to Melanesia. *Public administration and development,* 22, 151–161.

Lee, C.K. and Strang, D., 2006. The international diffusion of public sector downsizing: network emulation and theory-driven learning. *International organization,* 60 (Fall), 883–909.

Legrand, T., 2007. *Overseas and over here: the politics and pathways of policy transfer.* Thesis (PhD). University of Birmingham.

Lenschow, A., Liefferink, D. and Veenman, S., 2005. When the birds sing. A framework for analysing domestic factors behind policy convergence. *Journal of european public policy,* 12 (October), 797–816.

Levi-Faur, D., 2006. Regulatory capitalism: the dynamics of change beyond telecoms and electricity. *Governance,* 19 (July), 497–525.

Lodge, M., 2003. Institutional choice and policy transfer: reforming British and German railway regulation. *Governance,* 16(2), 78–159.

Lohmann, S., 1994. The dynamics of informational cascades: the Monday demonstrations in Leipzig, East Germany, 1989-91. *World politics,* 47 (October), 42–101.

Mahoney, J. and Goertz, G., 2004. The possibility principle: choosing negative cases in comparative research. *American political science review,* 98 (November), 653–669.

Majone, G., 1989. *Evidence, argument and persuasion in the policy process.* New Haven: Yale University Press.

March, J.G. and Olsen, J.P., 1989. *Rediscovering institutions: the organizational basis of politics.* New York: Free Press.

Marcussen, M., 2005. Central banks on the move. *Journal of european public policy,* 12 (October), 903–923.

Marsh, D. and McConnell, A., 2009. Towards a framework for establishing policy success. *Public administration,* (forthcoming).

Marsh, D. and Furlong, P., 2002. A skin not a sweater: ontology and epistemology in political science. *In*: D. Marsh and G. Stoker, eds. *Theory and methods in political science.* Basingstoke: Palgrave, 17–41.

McAnulla, S., 2002. Structure and agency. *In*: D. Marsh and G. Stoker, eds. *Theory and methods in political science.* Basingstoke: Palgrave, 271–291.

McNamara, K., 2002. Rational fictions: central bank independence and the social logic of delegation. *West european politics,* 25 (January), 47–76.

Meseguer, C. and Gilardi, F., 2006. What's new in the study of policy diffusion? A critical review. 2006 unpublished paper, previously presented at the International Studies Association 2005 Hawai'i.

Most, B. and Starr, H., 1990. Theoretical and logical issues in the study of international diffusion. *Journal of theoretical politics,* 2 (4), 391–412.

Newmark, A.J., 2002. An integrated approach to policy transfer and diffusion. *Review of policy research,* 19 (Summer), 152–178.

Public Citizen, 2003. *Water privatization fiascos: broken promises and social turmoil.* Available from: http://www.citizen.org/documents/privatizationfiascos.pdf

Radaelli, C.M., 2000. Policy transfer in the European union: institutional isomorphism as a source of legitimacy. *Governance,* 13 (January), 25–43.

Radaelli, C.M., 2005. Diffusion without convergence: how political context shapes the adoption of regulatory impact assessment. *Journal of european public policy,* 12 (October), 924–943.

Ragin, C.C., 1987. *The comparative method: moving beyond quantitative and qualitative strategies.* Berkeley: University of California Press.

Rose, R., 1991. What is lesson-drawing? *Journal of public policy,* 11 (1), 3–30.

Simmons, B.A. and Elkins, Z., 2004. The globalisation of liberalisation: policy diffusion in the international political economy. *American political science review,* 98 (February), 171–189.

Simmons, B.A., Dobbin, F. and Garrett, G., 2006. Introduction: the international diffusion of liberalism. *International organization,* 60 (Fall), 781–810.

Stone, D., 2001. *Learning lessons, policy transfer and the international diffusion of policy ideas.* Centre for the Study of Globalisation and Regionalisation Working Paper, No.69/01 University of Warwick.

Strang, D. and Meyer, J.W., 1993. Institutional conditions for diffusion. *Theory and society,* 22 (4), 487–511.

Strang, D. and Soule, S.A., 1998. Diffusion in organisations and social movements: from hybrid corn to poison pills. *American review of sociology,* 24 (1), 265–290.

Swank, D., 2006. Tax policy in an era of internationalization: explaining the spread of neoliberalism. *International organization,* 60 (Fall), 847–882.

Walker, J.L., 1969. The diffusion of innovation among American states. *The american political science review,* 33 (September), 880–899.

Weyland, K., ed., 2004. *Learning from foreign models in Latin American pension reform.* New York: Woodrow Wilson Center Press.

Weyland, K., 2005. Theories of policy diffusion: lessons from Latin American pension reform. *World politics,* 57 (January), 262–295.

Policy transfer as learning: capturing variation in what decision-makers learn from epistemic communities

Claire A. Dunlop

Department of Politics, University of Exeter, Exeter, UK

Almost two decades ago, Peter M. Haas formulated the epistemic community framework as a method for investigating the influence of knowledge-based experts in international policy transfer. Specifically, the approach was designed to address decision-making instances characterized by technical complexity and uncertainty. Control over the production of knowledge and information enables epistemic communities to articulate cause and effect relationships and so frame issues for collective debate and export their policy projects globally. Remarkably, however, we still know very little about the *variety of ways* in which decision-makers actually learn from epistemic communities. This article argues that variety is best captured by differentiating the control enjoyed by decision-makers and epistemic communities over the production of substantive knowledge (or means) that informs policy from the policy objectives (or ends) to which that knowledge is directed. The implications of this distinction for the types of epistemic community decision-maker learning exchanges that prevail are elaborated using a typology of adult learning from the education literature which delineates four possible learning situations. This typology is then applied to a comparative study of US and EU decision-makers' interaction with the epistemic community that formed around the regulation of the biotech milk yield enhancer bovine somatotrophin (rbST) to illustrate how the learning types identified in the model play out in practice.

Introduction

Though the epistemic community concept enjoys good currency across political science and nearly two decades after it was first unveiled (Haas 1990, 1992a), the epistemic communities' framework continues to buck the academic trend of conceptual revision through the application of empirical findings observed in similar approaches (notably, the study of policy communities and the advocacy coalition framework).[1] Despite the presence of a healthy empirical literature using the idea of an epistemic community in different ways and in conjunction with different approaches, only a handful of studies have related their findings back to the original framework itself (Radaelli 1995, Dunlop 2000a, Zito 2001). Significantly, none of these interventions address the central mechanism that underpins epistemic communities' influence: the ability to transfer policy by assuming control over knowledge production and in doing so guiding decision-maker learning.

It is evident that epistemic communities can stimulate policy transfer inducing changes in state interests (Bennett 1991, p. 224, Haas 1992b, Dolowitz and Marsh 2000, p. 10) and resulting in global forms of public policy (Stone 2000, 2008). Decision-makers are not always situated behind an all encompassing veil of ignorance, however (indeed arguably a more common problem is information overload), and policy issues with transboundary implications are often addressed through divergent approaches and rival policy standards (Vogel 1995, Drezner 2007). We should not assume that experts have no role in these instances of non-transfer of course. We know from the knowledge utilization literature for example that even when technical uncertainty associated with an issue is high, decision-makers may know their own policy preferences calling upon experts to offer advice on discrete aspects of an issue (Weiss 1979). Epistemic actors are also brought together by decision-makers to advise them in situations where their technical rationality is relatively unbounded. The experts role here is to legitimize and endorse learning that has already taken place rather than directly feed into decision-makers' thinking (Lipsky 1977).

By conflating decision-maker uncertainty with comprehensively bounded rationality, Haas's approach overstates the level of influence ascribed to epistemic communities and in particular their ability to shape decision-makers' intentions. The variety of roles and levels of influence epistemic communities have over decision-maker learning are not captured by the framework as it stands and, as a result, we have no systematic way of ordering analysis and comparing learning within and across cases. How can the variety of ways in which epistemic communities influence decision-makers' belief systems be captured by the framework? How can we conceptualize learning exchanges where epistemic communities advise decision-makers who possess their own knowledge and have other epistemic resources at their disposal? Specifically, how can we model the different levels of control over learning enjoyed by epistemic communities and decision-makers? This article suggests that variety is best captured by differentiating between the control enjoyed by decision-makers and epistemic communities over the production of substantive knowledge (or means) that informs policy on the one hand and the policy objectives (or ends) to which that knowledge is directed on the other. The implications for the types of epistemic community decision-maker learning exchanges that prevail are elaborated using a typology of adult learning from the education literature which delineates the four possible learning types that flow from this distinction. We should be clear; this article aims to contribute to the 'reflective research programme' that Haas and his colleagues originally hoped to precipitate (Adler and Haas 1992, Haas and Haas 2002). Rather than re-invent any wheels, the intent here is to make 'smart' revisions that expand the framework in a manner that is both compatible with the theoretical logic that underpins it and consistent with the findings of empirical studies of epistemic communities in action.

The article also has the wider aim of improving the explanatory power of policy transfer analysis which has been criticized for covering too many processes and as a consequence being inconcrete (see James and Lodge 2003 for a particularly trenchant critique). Decision-maker learning is one of the key aspects of policy transfer that needs to be made more specific. The 'renaissance' in academic interest in the role of ideas in the policy process (Radaelli 1995), of which epistemic communities and policy transfer were key features, involved a sustained revisitation of how, what, when and from whom decision-makers learn (Bennett and Howlett 1992, May 1992, Dolowitz and Marsh 1996, Dunlop and James 2007). This literature has struggled to move beyond the seminal contributions made over 30 years ago however (most notably, Braybrooke and Lindblom 1963, Heclo 1974). One of the main problems is that despite the potential synergies with literatures elsewhere (most obviously in psychology, management and education) the study of policy learning remains remarkably parochial. While aspects of the study of policy analysis are relevant (most notably the literature on knowledge utilization; Radaelli 1995) the lack of lesson-drawing from the arguably more authoritative literatures may explain why policy learning tends to be broadly conceived (see Laird 1999 for a notable exception). The result has been the absence of any detailed specification of different knowledge acquisition processes (Dowding 2003, p. 413, see James and Lodge 2003 for more detailed critique). Rather, the conceptualization of learning as control over knowledge production is explored using broad notions such as endogenous lesson-drawing (Rose 1991 for a rational account, Braybrooke and Lindblom 1963 for an incremental one) and exogenous policy transfer and coercion (Dolowitz and Marsh 1996, Heclo 1974, pp. 305–306). Though this distinction acknowledges that decision-makers can take control of their own learning as well as being more passive actors, it does not *differentiate* this control in terms of the different knowledge components which have different functions and so leaves the different learning types unexplored.

Opening up one aspect of the cognitive dimension of policy transfer makes two contributions to policy transfer analysis. At a basic level, by providing a way to order how decision-makers receive the new ideas that powerful groups of experts create and attempt to export, analysis can be made more concrete. Moreover, taking an intentional approach to decision-makers' learning, where individuals' preferences and values mediate what is learned and from whom, highlights the often localized and unsuccessful sides of policy transfer. As a result, this approach widens the empirical vista of transfer studies to cases of non-transfer, the partial or sub-optimal use of ideas and fluctuations in transfer across time.

The article is organized around two substantive sections and a set of conclusions. Section one examines how the epistemic community framework currently organizes and captures variation in decision-maker learning, outlines a possible learning typology and addresses the likely criticisms of this enterprise. The potential usefulness of this typology requires empirical investigation. Section two of the article uses a comparative study of United States (US) and European Union (EU) decision-makers' interaction with the epistemic community that formed around the regulation of the milk yield enhancer bovine somatotrophin (rbST) to explore how the learning types identified in the model play out in practice. The third and concluding section has two aims. First, it examines how well the learning types measure up against three of the main desiderata for assessing such schema: mutual exclusivity, joint exhaustiveness and theoretical coherence and fruitfulness (Hood 1996, p. 208). Following this, the implications of opening up one aspect of the cognitive dimension of policy transfer for policy transfer analysis is explored.

Variation in epistemic community decision-maker interactions

Epistemic communities are amalgams of professionals working across both the social and natural sciences that produce issue-relevant knowledge. They possess a specific blend of beliefs covering four elements:

> [1] a shared set of normative and principled beliefs, which provide a value-based rationale for the social action of community members; [2] shared causal beliefs, which are derived from their analysis of practices leading or contributing to a central set of problems in their domain and which then serve as the basis for elucidating the multiple linkages between possible policy actions and desired outcomes; [3] shared notions of validity—that is, intersubjective, internally defined criteria for weighing and validating knowledge in the domain of their expertise; and [4] a common policy enterprise—that is, a set of common practices associated with a set of problems to which their professional competence is directed, presumably out of the conviction that human welfare will be enhanced as a consequence (Haas 1992a, p. 3).

Emphasizing learning as a potentially central mechanism effecting policy development, change and transfer, the epistemic communities framework complements existing theories of international behaviour that focus upon calculations of costs and benefits (neorealism), control over economic resources (dependency theories) and the use of words and discourse (poststructuralism) (Haas 1992a, p. 6). This blend of beliefs and highly specialized expertise distinguish epistemic communities from interest groups and policy networks (Haas 1992a, p. 22) enabling them to make legitimate claims to being *the* main producers of knowledge in an issue area giving them the potential to occupy the elevated position of what might be called 'principal teachers' to decision-makers. While epistemic communities' central role in information production gives them the authoritative status to occupy this principal position, we cannot assume that they will be able to exert control over every aspect of what is known about an issue or that the control they do enjoy will be uniform across time and space. To understand the different roles epistemic communities occupy in the policy process we must have a clear, coherent and systematic way of describing variation in this explanandum. Thus, when we speak about ordering the analysis of epistemic community decision-maker interactions, the aim is to categorize the range and diversity of influence enjoyed by these expert enclaves by settling on a small number of relevant types of learning. Before constructing such a learning typology, we must first establish why this gap exists in epistemic community analysis. Specifically, how does the epistemic communities framework as it stands deal with decision-maker learning and in what ways is it incomplete?

The deficit model of learning in the epistemic community framework

In his exposition of the epistemic communities' framework, Haas provides a clear definition of learning. Learning is a process of informing decision-makers' beliefs about the four key components of complex technical issues embodied by epistemic communities with particular attention drawn to epistemic communities' influence on the 'substantive nature of ... policy arrangements' and their more overtly political role as the 'nonsystemic origins of state interests' (Haas 1992a, p. 4). Experts' potential to stimulate learning within and across states is assured by the control they enjoy over the production of knowledge relating to an issue (Haas 1992a, p. 2) and the influence they exert a function of decision-makers' uncertainty.

Despite this clarity and specificity, the framework fails to produce an internally coherent account of the possible forms of learning that arise between epistemic communities and decision-makers. Though Haas sees analysis as underpinned by a logic of 'limited constructivism' (1992a, p. 23, see Haas 2007 for a fuller account) where the learning that epistemic communities stimulate is mediated by structural realities and decision-makers' own intentions and political support (Stone 2000, p. 66, 2005, p. 94), the framework emphasizes a single form of learning that depicts control over knowledge as something which epistemic communities have and decision-makers, whose bounded rationality initiates their call for advice, do not have (Haas 1992a, pp. 14–16). The manner in which uncertainty is defined is the root of the problem here. Epistemic communities' entry into the policy arena is a function of decision-makers' technical uncertainty, however by conflating this uncertainty with comprehensively bounded rationality we are left with a single learning category where decision-makers experience extreme epistemic deficiencies which need to be filled. And so, despite disaggregating belief systems into individual components in the definition of what an epistemic community actually is and highlighting the difference between inputs that are substantive and political, the epistemic resources experts control and pass on to decision-makers are portrayed as a unified good.

This deficit model of learning, where epistemic communities are required to fill decision-makers knowledge gaps, reflects the case which informed the original development of the epistemic communities approach. Haas's major study *Saving the Mediterranean* (1990) from which the framework was developed illustrates the extreme level of influence that epistemic communities can have and policy transfer they can effect. In this case, the epistemic community had the power to make decision-makers cooperate and develop policies in ways they would not otherwise have. Such ideal typical cases yield important examples of what is possible, however they highlight extreme phenomena. If it is to explain the role of epistemic communities in 'who learns what, when, to whose benefit and why' (Adler and Haas 1992, p. 370) the analytical framework must be able to account for the variety of these actors' learning interactions. To do so we follow through on the 'limited constructivist' logic that Haas argues should underpin analysis and focus upon the ways in which decision-makers' intentions mediate the learning processes in which they engage. This is something that Haas himself acknowledges at points. Using a less restrictive definition of uncertainty for example, Haas describes a scenario where decision-makers rely on epistemic communities for only *certain aspects* of policy knowledge with an epistemic community providing substantive policy inputs associated with normative convictions [component 1], cause and effect beliefs [component 2] and shared notions of validity [component 3] that justify policy alternatives [component 4] that are the product of decision-makers' political preferences and do not necessarily reflect the epistemic community's preferred policy agenda (Haas 1992a, p. 15). Where intentions are unclear or controversial uncertainty is generated and gaps appear in which epistemic communities can insinuate themselves. Learning may also be differentiated across time and space as well as knowledge components; epistemic communities can be 'called in' to provide one type of input and find that the scope and intensity of their influence may increase, decrease or change in emphasis (Haas 1992a, p. 16). As yet, however, we have no systematic way of describing this variation within or between cases which compromises the internal coherence of the framework itself.

The external consistency of the framework also suffers as a result of the undifferentiated conceptualization of learning. In addition to ideal typical cases, where epistemic communities' influence *both* substantive policy detail and decision-makers' policy objectives, empirical studies themselves illustrate that more varied types of learning exchanges exist between these actors. One of the best examples can be found in the 1992 *International Organization* special edition edited by Haas. In Ikenberry's study of Anglo-American postwar economic settlement (1992), an epistemic community was assembled by decision-makers to provide technical and normative guidance to facilitate a move away from policies based on unregulated free trade. A similar instance of decision-makers delimiting the policy ends is provided by Verdun in her study of the Delors' Committee that was called upon to provide epistemic resources to decision-makers seeking to deliver and diffuse Economic and Monetary Union (EMU) (1999).

Rather than dismiss these as 'limiting' cases (Haas 1992a, p. 5), the line taken here is that these studies illustrate the importance of extending the framework to accommodate the variation in influence enjoyed by epistemic communities over decision-maker learning across time and space. Significantly, they resonate with the distinction between two types of knowledge inputs implied by Haas: where what decision-makers learn about the substantive detail of an issue is distinct from the policy objectives or ends to which this information is directed (1992a, p. 4). It is suggested here that these represent the two 'outstanding' (Weber 1904 cited in Watkins 1953, p. 724) dimensions along which interactions between epistemic communities and decision-makers vary and upon which a more nuanced categorization of learning types should be constructed. Identification of these dimensions is central to the construction of a typology of epistemic community decision-maker learning exchanges which is necessarily a selective and abstractive enterprise that highlights the most relevant dimensions of a framework and isolates extraneous 'disturbing factors' (Watkins 1953, pp. 724–725). Here uniformities are identified by isolating certain elements of data that are the most relevant to the problem at hand rather than through the consideration of the 'totality of knowledge' (McKinney 1966, pp. 2–3).

Constructing a typology of epistemic community decision-maker exchanges: learning from the adult education literature

With the main dimensions of variation in epistemic community decision-maker learning exchanges identified, attention must now turn to the question of *how* such a typology is to be constructed. The lifelong learning literature provides a way to elaborate this conceptualization and create a common language with which to describe and explain these exchanges. In their work on adult learning, Mocker and Spear (1982) argue that to understand the interactions between teachers and learners we need to view adult learners as intentional actors who choose to learn and aim to control the learning processes in which they become engaged. It is not assumed however that learners have it all their own way all of the time. Learning is heavily conditioned. While they are 'intendedly rational' (Simon 1947), learners' (and decision-makers') ability to control knowledge production and take ownership of their learning is mediated by variables which determine the extent to which their rationality is bounded, notably their pre-existing 'mental maps' (Denzau and North

1994), values and knowledge (Tolman 1948, Brown 1995) and perception of the socio-political and institutional 'lifespaces' they inhabit (Lewin 1951, Argyris and Schön 1978, Lave and Wenger 1991, John-Steiner 1997).

Empirical studies of learning confirm this tension between intention and limited cognition. Echoing the logic and findings of the epistemic communities approach, the education literature illustrates that the knowledge adult learners need is often both complex and important to them; factors that can make it difficult for them to take the lead in substantive terms or immediately identify *and* progress their objectives. Thus, to explain adult learning we must distinguish between the different levels of control enjoyed by learners over what is to be learned in terms of the form, mode of delivery and timing of a subject's substantive content ('learning means') and the objectives to which those means are directed ('learning ends') (Mocker and Spear 1982, p. 2).

The distinction between the control enjoyed by teachers and learners over what is learned and how this is applied results in a simple two-by-two matrix in which Mocker and Spear (1982) position four different types of learning: self-directed learning, informal learning, formal learning, and non-formal learning (Figure 1 provides a schematic illustration). Comprehensive typification is the aim here. Because their typology is constructed upon empirical reality as well as theoretical assumptions of intended rationality, the learning situations Mocker and Spear describe are well-grounded and involve a sufficiently low degree of abstraction that capture specific learning dynamics whose occurrence is 'objectively probable' as opposed to the 'objective possibility' associated with single ideal types (McKinney 1966, chapter 2 provides a comparison of ideal types and constructed typologies).

The theoretical focus on learners' intentions and differentiation between means and ends this typology shares with the rationale and empirical findings of Haas's framework are suggestive of its potential to elaborate decision-maker-epistemic communities learning exchanges. To operationalize it, the four components identified by Haas can be reclassified quite simply into the foci of means and ends with shared normative beliefs [component 1] cause and effect postulates [component 2] and intersubjective understandings of validity [component 3] making up the substantive

LEARNERS' CONTROL OVER LEARNING
OBJECTIVES / ENDS

	HIGH	LOW
HIGH 'LEARNERS' CONTROL OVER LEARNING CONTENT / MEANS	Self-Directed Learning	Informal Learning
LOW	Non-Formal Learning	Formal Learning

Figure 1.   Mocker and Spear's lifelong learning typology (1982, p. 4).

means produced around an issue and the most overtly political component of epistemic communities the common policy enterprise [component 4] equating to the end objectives. Along with its potential fit with the epistemic communities' framework, this distinction avoids the controversial assumption implicit in some of the policy transfer literature that a positive correlation exists between control over substantive knowledge and the identification of policy goals.[2]

The four components are outlined in further detail below where they are related to epistemic community decision-maker learning exchanges (see Figure 2 for an adapted illustration). It is worth repeating that this article's interest is in how well these exchanges can be classified within the typology and it does not engage in formal congruence testing. Therefore, the aim here is to describe what constitutes each of the four learning types not to build hypotheses. As well as describing the balance of power envisaged by each category for these actors, attention is also paid to how the phenomenon can be observed. Though tentative, suggesting evidential requirements for each learning type reduces the risk of reification and moves us closer to the wider ambition of establishing a systematic approach (see Bailey 1992, Elman 2005 for a wider discussion of reification). Achieving such clarity about the property space that constitutes decision-maker learning will also ensure a non-tautological operationalization of learning where decision-makers' ability to define the substantive means and policy alternatives are gauged without referencing the influence of epistemic communities we are seeking to explain. With learning defined as a knowledge acquisition process, we are interested in who takes the lead and assumes control over knowledge production over the course of policy making rather than the ultimate policy outcomes. After all, while policy change can be the result of

DECISION-MAKERS' CONTROL OVER
LEARNING OBJECTIVES / ENDS

		HIGH	LOW
DECISION-MAKERS' CONTROL OVER LEARNING CONTENT / MEANS	**HIGH**	**Self-Directed Learning** Epistemic communities' role is weak	**Informal Learning** Epistemic communities' role is moderate
	LOW	**Non-Formal Learning** Epistemic communities' role is moderate	**Formal Learning** Epistemic communities' role is strong (ideal type – Haas 1992a)

Figure 2. Visual representation of decision-makers' and epistemic communities' control over knowledge based on Mocker and Spear's lifelong learning typology (1982).

learning, learning can be present when outcomes appear to remain stable and not alter at all.

Self-directed learning is individualized and experiential. Here, learning is unstructured and driven by the learner. With their learning unrestricted by any disciplinary silos or paradigms and pre-determined goals, learners enjoy control over all aspects of learning seeking out knowledge from a variety of sources, constructing the problem and establishing their own solutions in their own time: 'learning what they want for as long as they want and stopping when they want' (Rogers 2004). In its most extreme form, self-directed learning can result in learners both adjudicating and creating evidence rejecting that possibility that any expertise is superior to their own (Rogers 2002, p. 275). More usually, knowledge creation here is not entirely autodidactic, notably learners in the self-directed mode may take advice from a range of teachers on the veracity of the information they find (Hiemstra 1994). They do not however identify with a single actor to inform the content and direction of policy. The avoidance of single paradigms or knowledge hierarchies to structure what they learn implies that where decision-makers direct their own learning, epistemic communities may simply represent one possible information source among many or may be shut out altogether.

Demonstrating self-directed learning requires evidence that teachers (epistemic communities for our purposes) play a weak role in setting both learning content and ends to which it is directed. This is only serves as a *prima facie* indicator however. Epistemic communities can be treated as one teacher among many, ignored or their evidence contested by decision-makers who are not engaged in self-directed learning. Following the experiential learning literature, true self-directed learning requires evidence that decision-makers have either learned from critical reflection of experience or are learning by doing (Kolb 1984, Boud 1985, Jarvis 1987) where evidence is sought out from a wide range of sources and pieced together in a way that creates something different and becomes what they know (for more on this 'epistemological bricolage' see Freeman 2007).

Informal learning treats learners as task-conscious where learning is not enlightenment for its own sake but rather revolves around assembling the means to dispatch a specific task which has been effectively set for them (Rogers 2003, pp. 18–21). While the learner directs the selection and production of substantive resources, the presence of externally determined objectives bound this scope for choice; the development of 'know-how' requires that learners are conscious of extrinsic evaluation where the substantive arguments they amass will be assessed in terms of goals that are determined by other actors.

In relation to decision-makers and epistemic communities, informal learning describes circumstances where experts have a moderate role in the policy process having set policy targets or standards for decision-makers to comply with in the policy that they themselves design. That decision-makers may be coerced to meet certain policy ends is well know (Dolowitz and Marsh 1996). Demonstrating informal learning within epistemic community decision-maker exchanges requires evidence that decision-makers recognize the goals anchoring their learning and are engaged in creating or gathering evidence of 'what works' in terms of delivering them.

Formal learning refers to externally imposed learning where the learner's control over both the substantive content of knowledge and ends to which it is applied is severely constrained (Coombs and Ahmed 1974). Learning here takes the form of guided episodes from teacher to learner where there is acceptance on both sides that learning *needs* to occur (Rogers 2002, p. 279). This captures the type of learning and locus of control between epistemic communities and decision-makers posited by the original framework where the epistemic community assumes the role of principal teacher able to influence decision-makers' thinking about both the substantive means and policy ends of an issue. At its most extreme, epistemic communities determine the length, pace and level of the learning process.

Epistemic communities' knowledge creation is insulated from the political world occupied by decision-makers and learning exchanges limited affairs where these experts' inputs are privileged above others. To demonstrate that formal learning has taken place, we would expect to see epistemic communities' belief systems show up in policy outputs through the supplementation or change of decision-makers' under-standings and policy preferences.

Non-formal learning refers to situations where information is moulded to learners' own circumstances and the teacher's role is that of facilitator. Here, learners' awareness of what they want to do with what they learn ensures that their engagement with codified knowledge is mediated by pre-existing expectations for determining the use or success of that knowledge (Tough 1971, Heimlich 1993). In relation to epistemic communities and decision-makers, an epistemic community may control key resources that determine what learning around an issue proceeds but lack influence over the ends to which those resources are directed. In this scenario, how decision-makers interpret the problem is central to the learning experience. The epistemic community's role is to provide the information required to manage complex issues framed by decision-makers.

For non-formal learning to be identified, evidence is required of decision-makers' dependence on epistemic communities for the delivery, legitimization or justification policy preferences that have been formed independently of their relationship with these experts. Most obviously, this would take the form of scenarios where experts have been commissioned to comment on a specific initiative. It should not be assumed however that learners will always receive the substantive resources they require to achieve their goals. In the education literature, non-formal learning exchanges are often failed cases of formal learning where the learner has not conformed to teachers' goals or goal-oriented structures have been absent or unclear (Pigozzi 1999). The result can be a mismatch between the knowledge that teachers are willing and able to impart and the information learners need in order to achieve their personal goals. So for example, decision-makers may commission a piece of research or consolidate an epistemic community within a bureaucracy but remain unable to exert influence over the nature and timing of the epistemic resources that are delivered. Thus, the fact that decision-makers' have autonomously determined the ends to which they want to put information is no guarantee that an epistemic community will provide suitable goods or relax the hierarchy of knowledge in which they believe.

The value-added of typologies

The usefulness of the typology requires empirical investigation. Before doing this, a likely criticism must be addressed. Critics are liable to ask: why categorize learning exchanges at all? In his discussion of the proliferation of typologies relating to policy networks, Judge warns against the academic tendency toward 'overly desiccated ... exchanges' (1993, p. 121). The policy transfer literature has been similarly criticized (Bennett 1997). Accordingly, we must be certain that such an enterprise is analytically useful and not merely an opportunity to revel in the esoteric. Two functions are addressed by adapting Mocker and Spear's (1982) typology.

First, typologies serve as parsimonious 'criterion points' (Bailey 1992, p. 2188) that, at their most basic level, help organize empirical material and allow for the systematic comparison of cases (Elman 2005, p. 294). That epistemic communities' role in helping decision-makers think about the ideational components of an issue goes through peaks and troughs is a discernable feature of many of the studies of policy diffusion however the absence of any basic categorization of learning types frustrates nuanced analysis, systematic comparison and identification of patterns of epistemic communities' influence both within and between cases. Delineating a relevant property space for epistemic community decision-maker learning exchanges provides a valuable steer to scholars who otherwise face choosing from a range of different and, in some instances, competing conceptualizations of learning from across disciplinary and theoretical traditions. The merit of this approach is particularly strong in relation to epistemic communities where analysis of learning exchanges is obscured by the 'thick description' (Geertz 1973, pp. 3–30) that epitomizes the research methodology. Single case study analyses of international policy controversies usually spanning decades are both a gift and burden. The analytical virtues of in-depth single case studies are well known; most notably they are renowned for their capacity to show us the 'moving picture' of politics in all its complicated glory as opposed to the often too simple and acontextual 'snapshot' (Pierson 1996). Without an agreed system to organize key aspects of analysis however, ordering and comparing phenomena in a meaningful way is difficult if not impossible.

Second, epistemic communities theoretical precision can be developed using this typology as a starting point. Though the ambitions of this article are to explore the suitability of an adult learning typology for capturing variation in epistemic community decision-maker learning exchanges this will provide a platform to further the more ambitious goal of building and testing hypotheses. More specifically, new institutional economics (NIE) variants of rational choice theory implicit in the framework that accepts 'limited constructivist' analysis with its incorporation of bounded rationality, cognitive constraints and uncertainty could be used to unpack variables associated with decision-makers' intentions. Such congruence testing will undoubtedly enhance the analytical purchase of the framework and advance the epistemic communities' research programme. First, however, we need to be sure that the typology itself is fit for purpose.

Applying the typology: learning in the USA and the EU in the regulation of bovine somatotrophin

The viability and usefulness of this learning model is explored through an empirical examination of the relationship between decision-makers in the USA and EU and the epistemic community promoting the milk yield enhancer bovine somatotrophin (rbST). In both cases decision-makers learned about rbST, however only in the US case was the epistemic community able to adopt a strong role in decision-makers' learning. Analysis follows a 'process tracing' approach (George 1997) with the account informed by actors' perceptions of the locus of control what is learned and how policy ends are conceived identified using interview data,[3] scientific reports and official documentation. The aim of analysis is to make a conceptual contribution to our limited knowledge of epistemic community-decision-maker interactions in general and how the learning exchanges between these actors evolve and differ across time and space in particular.

rbST is a genetically modified milk aid. In short, bovine somatotrophin is a naturally occurring substance that, with the advent of biotechnology in the 1970s in the USA, was synthetically produced for the mass market of dairy farmers. rbST was developed, tested and steered through the regulatory approval process by an epistemic community of agricultural economists, biotech scientists, veterinary experts, toxicologists and lawyers associated with pharmochemical manufacturer Monsanto and its university partners, notably Cornell University's Department of Animal Science. These actors were united by a normative belief that the product should go to market as it promised dairy farmers greater flexibility in how they managed their herds, a certainty that milk yields could be increased by rbST safely, shared values on the centrality of quantitative risk assessment methods in assessing and evaluating the product and finally a policy aim to get rbST to world market by the end of the 1980s at the latest.

This section outlines the regulatory review of rbST in the USA and EU that spanned nearly two decades. The story is structured by the four mechanisms identified through which epistemic communities are expected to engage decision-makers in learning and exert influence: policy innovation; policy diffusion; policy selection; policy persistence (Adler and Haas 1992). Approaching the narrative in this way helps to organize a large amount of information and locates any fluctuations in learning at different stages of the policy process. As this is a single case study no attempt can be made to discuss possible patterns across these stages, however following Adler and Haas's structure is consistent with the wider aim of systematizing epistemic community case studies to enable such comparative analysis in the future.

Policy innovation

Policy innovation captures the early stages of epistemic community decision-maker exchanges where the epistemic community aims to frame the range of political controversy, define state interests and set standards for how the evidence on an issue is to be evaluated (Adler and Haas 1992). Such formal learning did not prevail in the case of rbST however. Rather, the product's scientific development ran concurrent to the establishment of a regulatory framework on biotechnology in the USA. Convinced of the huge commercial potential of these innovations and the scientific safety of the technology, the Food and Drug Administration (FDA) took the lead role in establishing a cross-agency 'co-ordinated' regulatory framework. The policy goal here was clear, as a flagship biotech product the FDA was committed to getting rbST approved for market as quickly as possible providing that product safety and efficacy could be established by product developers (Miller 1988).

Accordingly, the early engagement between the rbST epistemic community and the FDA's Centre for Veterinary Medicine (CVM) bore the hallmarks of non-formal learning. In 1982, the first investigational application was submitted for rbST and the epistemic community began conducting field and clinical trials of the product (Miller 1988). The product review process followed the iterative norms of knowledge production institutionalized in the US regulatory framework, with the epistemic community engaged in ongoing discussion and providing additional data when the CVM requested (Juskevich and Guyer 1990). Indeed, the application alone amounted to over 55,000 pages of studies and analysis leading CVM director Gerald Guest to conclude that rbST would be the most extensively studied product the agency had ever handled (in Gibbons 1990, p. 852).

This is not the whole picture of learning however. While CVM decision-makers' learning about rbST was non-formal, at certain points it was tinged with self-direction (see Figure 3 for a visual representation of the case study). One particular episode is instructive in this regard. An increased incidence of the udder infection mastitis among dairy cows injected with rbST was detected in trial data. Mastitis is recognized universally amongst dairy farmers as one of the most financially costly diseases they face because of the intensive antibiotic treatment it requires and the corresponding possibility of lost revenue from spoilt milk (Bramley and Dodds 1984). Clearly, the threat of a positive correlation between the administration of an rbST product and an increased incidence of mastitis was potentially very damaging for the prospects of the product's uptake in the dairy industry. While some academic veterinarians both from within and beyond the epistemic community (Bauman 1990, Kronfeld 1987, respectively) agreed that multi-lactational studies were required into the link between rbST and mastitis, neither the epistemic community nor the CVM believed that the licensing process should be held up by such research (Deakin 1990). With both sets of actors aware of the potentially infinite costs of the product review

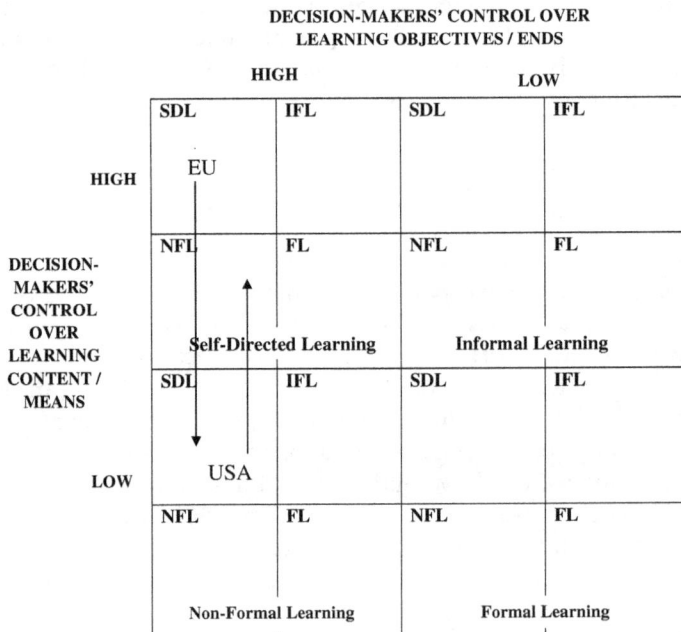

Figure 3.   Visual summary of EU and USA decision-makers' learning on rbST across time.

process and the target that had been established that the product would reach the market by 1990 (Deakin 1990), decision-makers at the CVM preferred to convene a subcommittee of the Research Committee of the National Mastitis Council to develop guidelines for the evaluation of mastitis levels in the trial studies to enable it to evaluate the findings before any additional studies were commissioned.

Policy diffusion

The framework suggests that epistemic communities' innovations are diffused through communication with scientific colleagues beyond the nation state through conferences and specialist literatures. The epistemic community's aim here is to engage with experts occupying similar positions to their own in ways that enable these new actors to cascade ideas down to and 'exert concurrent pressure' on decision-makers at their local level (Adler and Haas 1992, p. 379). This is, of course, an ideal typical account of knowledge transfer between elites and Adler and Haas readily acknowledge that in reality we should expect the process to be far messier and politically contingent than this stylized description suggests (1992, p. 379). Indeed, the rbST case confirms that epistemic communities that are successful teachers in one place may not be able to assume the same status in another.

The interpretative context surrounding rbST in the EU created the conditions for self-directed learning among decision-makers and effectively blocked the epistemic community from engaging decision-makers in any sustained learning exchanges. In 1987, when the first product applications were submitted in the EU, the policy debate about biotechnology was in its infancy and dominated by concerns from environmentalists that evidence of the scientific safety of rDNA technology were not robust and that, in normative terms, its applications posed unnecessary threats to the 'European way of life' (Bud 1993, p. 207). Such an environment would represent a tough challenge for any epistemic community aiming to help decision-makers learn about its biotech innovation, however, in this case the barriers were raised higher still. By boosting milk production, rbST would hit what was arguably the weakest link in the Community's enervated agricultural policy (Gardner 1996, p. 65). Indeed, in their first contact with Monsanto members of the epistemic community in 1984, European Commission officials from Directorate General (DG) Industry pointed out that the introduction of the milk quota system that year made a yield enhancer a very poor fit for the EU in policy terms (Cantley 1995, p. 635).

While the USA had worked through similar debates in the 1970s 'gene wars,' these had been succeeded by a regulatory infrastructure underpinned by a strong biotech lobby (Dunlop 2000b), supportive scientific community integrated into industry and quantitative risk assessment techniques all of which were fundamentally supportive of the pedagogic efforts of science-based epistemic communities such as that which existed around rbST. In the EU however, there was no established network of experts working on biotech able to act as idea conduits, nor was there a science-based regulatory framework. Rather, rbST was assessed on the basis of its' potential socio-economic and environmental impacts as well its safety, quality and efficacy in scientific terms (Commission 1989). While the rbST epistemic community engaged the independent scientists on the Committee on Veterinary Medicinal Products (CVMP) in a thorough and iterative process of formal learning, this committee's conclusions that rbST products were safe and should be licensed were not binding and rejected outright by decision-makers (Commission 1991, 1992 annexes 1 and 2).

Between 1988 and 1994, rbST was under kept review and the subject of successive moratoria prohibiting its use within the Community. Despite efforts to engage sceptical decision-makers (European Parliament 1988), the epistemic community failed to gain an audience with decision-makers during this 'review period'. The almost annual renewal of the moratorium was justified by the need to gather further evidence on the substance. Decision-makers in DG Industry (with the support of the European Parliament's Environment Committee) engaged in self-directed learning; collecting evidence focussed upon the risks associated with rbST's socio-economic impact and its implications for animal welfare and consumer confidence to construct an alternative paradigm. The result was a further moratorium set until 2000. While the development of this belief system by EU decision-makers has been documented in detail elsewhere (Dunlop 2007), what happened to the epistemic means proffered by the epistemic community again illustrates that one learning type can be tinged with aspects of another. DG Industry contested the epistemic community's interpretation of rbST as safe for animals citing the community's own data on mastitis (Commission 1992, 1993a,b). This use of outlier evidence from the rbST trials conducted by the epistemic community to bolster their own policy objective to prohibit use of the substance indefinitely suggests that while learning was self-directed it was tinged by non-formal logic and reliance on substantive knowledge created by the epistemic community, albeit not as that community intended. This deracination of epistemic community evidence also illustrates that intentional analysis highlights the little discussed phenomenon of sub-optimal knowledge transfer (Dowding 2003).

Policy selection

Adler and Haas (1992, p. 381) acknowledge that the influence of an epistemic community is often a function of the political 'fit' between that group's belief system and those of decision-makers. The expectation here is that where there is resistance, epistemic communities will aim to make their ideas more politically palatable by adapting their message to particular domestic circumstances. Despite the expectation within the CVM and epistemic community that rbST would reach the USA market by 1990, questions raised by individuals in the wider scientific community about trial evidence of deleterious impact of rbST for both animals and humans resulted in wider government attention and specifically two Congressionally mandated audits of the CVM's review of rbST (OTA 1992, GAO 1992). These challenges are notable not simply because they effectively delayed rbST reaching the market for a further 4 years but also because it was the CVM and not the epistemic community that sought to address them. Defending their policy decision to grant rbST a license, decision-makers at the CVM were transformed from learners to teachers explaining and defending the epistemic means that had been given to them by the epistemic community.

One episode exemplifies this transformation and move to an extreme form of self-directed learning. In the late 1980s, Samuel Epstein, a Professor of Occupational and Environmental Medicine at the University of Illinois and longstanding critic of the standards applied by regulatory agencies to the regulation of carcinogens, began warning of what he viewed were the potentially carcinogenic implications that rbST carried for humans (Epstein 1988). Epstein was the first scientist to suggest publicly that rbST could carry serious implications for human health. This concern centred upon the discovery of a noticeable increase in the trial milk of rbST treated cows of another hormone called 'insulin-like growth factor' (IGF-1) (Epstein 1988). IGF-1 has long been regarded by the mainstream scientific community as one of the most powerful growth hormones occurring in nature and is found in all milk, including human breast milk. It is therefore identical across the species and in small levels is benign. Epstein argued however that as a growth-promoting hormone, IGF-1 could have a mutagenic effect, inducing cell division and tumour growth if consumed at 'sustained incremental levels' (Epstein 1988, p. 193). This led him to extrapolate that if IGF-1 could exert a biological influence on the humans consuming milk where its levels were increased, in particular promoting premature growth in children (Epstein 1988) and breast cancer in women (Epstein 1990).

Despite the entirely hypothetical nature of these claims, in 1990 the CVM took the unprecedented step of publishing some of the Monsanto dose response data in international journal *Science*. The paper, written by CVM scientists and whose publication was advertised in the *Journal of the American Medical Association (JAMA)* and *Science News*, confirmed the FDA's agreement with the epistemic community that, while rbST-stimulated milk did contain higher levels of IGF-1, no further toxicological studies were necessary as the levels fell within the 'normal' range found in human breast milk and furthermore would be destroyed by pasteurization (Juskevich and Guyer 1990, p. 875).

This effectively closed down the IGF-1 controversy for US decision-makers. The CVM's paper was succeeded by a chain of endorsements from the US scientific establishment (notably the American Cancer Society and US National Institutes of Health). Of even greater significance was the international approval conferred upon rbST in June 1992 of the Joint FAO/WHO Expert Committee on Food Additives (JECFA 1993). This paved the way for the product finally being granted a license in November 1993.

Epistemic communities that focus their efforts on trying to convince others that their interests would be satisfied by switching to the epistemic community's way of thinking are less likely to succeed than those which focus on compromise (Adler and Haas 1992, p. 383). The pronounced mismatch between the policy goals of EU decision-makers and those of the epistemic community however made rbST a zero sum game. After a decade of review, in October 1999, the European Commission's DG for Health and Consumer Protection (DG Sanco) which had been newly empowered following the BSE crisis, announced its intention to propose a permanent ban on rbST. This proposal represented a significant departure from the past not simply because it bolted the already closed door on rbST but by virtue of the epistemic justification upon which it rested.

When DG Sanco assumed charge over the rbST issue the long anticipated trade dispute with the USA over rbST was looming. Decision-makers used their experience at the World Trade Organization (WTO) in a similar and ongoing dispute with the USA on hormone growth promoters (see Dunlop and James 2007) and post-BSE institutionalization of the precautionary principle to guide it in the types of evidence and standards that were scientifically justifiable in banning rbST. As a result, decision-makers replaced their self-directed learning with non-formal learning commissioning scientific reports from two DG Sanco committees on the 'adverse effects' of rbST for animals and consumers. The first report from the Scientific Committee on Animal Health and Welfare (SCAHAW) advised that the evidence on mastitis was now sufficient to sustain prohibition (Commission 1999a). The second scientific contribution, made by the Scientific Committee on Veterinary Measures Relating to Public Health (SCVPH), concerned IGF-1 and in particular reviewed studies that appeared to add weight to Epstein's cancer postulate arguing that more research was required before rbST milk could be assumed to be safe for human consumption (Commission 1999b).

We should be clear about the status of these committees and the non-formal learning exchanges in which they were engaged. This episode of non-formal learning was tinged with self-direction among EU decision-makers. While the experts were independent academic scientists, they had been vetted and appointed by decision-makers whose policy objectives were explicit. This made the possibility of adverse selection remote. Indeed, the post-BSE empowerment of DG Sanco and accompanying explication of a precautionary interpretation on all food related risks ensured that scientists opposed to this agenda would be unlikely to be interested in participating in any case. More specifically, the Commission's enduring interest in the scientific evidence that was available concerning rbST's risks had informed the research agendas of most of the committee members in throughout the 1990s.

Policy persistence

Policy persistence is underpinned by socialization processes where what has been learned is consolidated and sustained (Adler and Haas 1992, pp. 384–385). In both the US and EU cases, opposing belief systems that had either resulted from or been consolidated through non-formal learning have been internalized and defended by decision-makers. For Adler and Haas the longevity of these interpretations are expected to be affected by changes in the degree of consensus held by the epistemic community; where a community's authority is diminished so too is the basis for socialization. When we put decision-makers at the centre of analysis the picture is quite different however. Both cases illustrate that while a scientific consensus can be attacked, judgements about whether or not it has been undermined and the authority of an epistemic community/committee diminished are subjective. Throughout the rbST saga, contrary evidence was rejected by both sets of decision-makers and the experts from whom they have learned.

Perhaps the greater challenge for decision-makers would be how to change direction or 'unlearn' on rbST. This is not as far-fetched scenario as it may first appear. In the USA for example, the increasing salience of 'pure' and organic food movements has raised the profile of scientific studies associating IGF-1 with various human health disorders[4] and resulted in a growing number of EU dairy processors and retailers going 'rbST-free' (Pollack 2006, Fox 2008). Meanwhile in the EU, awareness of the significant changes in global dairy consumption and concerns that the dairy market is uncompetitive may yet put rbST back onto the agenda. The non-formal nature of how both sets of decision-makers have learned about rbST, and their delegation to epistemic communities/committees for the epistemic means that underpin policy, could complicate any plans for policy succession, termination or reversal.

Conclusions: assessing the usefulness of the lifelong learning typology for epistemic community and policy transfer analysis

What is the value-added of this typology to the analysis of epistemic communities' role in the policy process? Our concern with 'mutual exclusivity' centres upon the internal coherence of the four learning types. The empirical illustration of rbST provides grounds for optimism suggesting that each of the types are readily distinguishable from one another and provide a parsimonious account of learning exchanges and basis for ordering empirical findings across cases and comparison within them. Further empirical assurances are required that the typology does not contain self-contradictory ideas and in particular more needs to be known about the interaction effects between control over substantive means and ends.

Claims that the learning categories are 'jointly exhaustive' are a function of the extent to which the typology addresses what is intended. Though the study sheds light on only two of the four learning types, it does support the broad argument that no single one of the learning types can lay an overriding claim to being the 'natural' descriptor of epistemic community decision-maker learning exchanges. The empirical exploration again offers *prima facie* evidence that the adapted adult learning typology is a lens which enables us to zoom-in on variation in epistemic community decision-maker interactions. The contrast between the EU and US in the rbST case illustrates that the typology increases awareness of the simultaneous presence of alternative states of learning across space. Such dynamism is also temporal. Even where the overall policy outcome was not in doubt, the learning process and the balance of power between decision-makers in both the USA and EU and the rbST epistemic community were not static. The EU example illustrates the dynamism of learning exchanges where institutional changes enabled decision-makers to alter their learning strategy switching from self-directed to the non-formal mode where two new epistemic groups were consolidated within the bureaucracy as rivals the rbST epistemic community and US decision-makers. Clearly, congruence testing of the four learning categories is required that goes beyond this case; this could easily start with the examination of the sizeable bank of epistemic communities case studies that already exists.

The empirical illustration here suggests that the typology also has the virtue of 'stretchability' (Hood 1996) meaning it can be drilled into further to offer a fine-grained analysis of a range of learning types that exist *within* each of the four categories. To avoid a danger common to typologies where each cell becomes a 'sponge type' that absorbs an ever increasing variety of scenarios (McKinney 1966, p. 27), and to improve the level of abstraction associated with the typology, additional learning sub-types were created by applying the two-by-two matrix to each quadrant where learning types found in the corners represent ideal or 'polar types' (see Mars 1982, p. 38 cited Hood 1996 for discussions of this in relation to Mary Douglas's grid group analysis). Thus, while the CVM decision-makers were still engaged in non-formal learning over mastitis, and as such were heavily reliant on epistemic agents for substantive inputs, the manner in which they set the boundaries of the empirical work to be done had much in common with self-directed learning.

It is hoped that the adult learning typology will form the basis for a more purposive theoretical research agenda on epistemic communities and the role of experts and decision-maker learning in policy transfer. The intentional approach pursued here matches Haas's own ambition that the approach be used and developed in concert with macro-level theories and fits the 'limited constructivism' that underpins the framework as it stands. It also addresses anomalies found in empirical studies where epistemic communities' influence is more limited than the original framework's focus on international policy coordination suggests without denying the possibility that they can be 'principal teachers' to decision-makers. By putting decision-makers at the heart of analysis we have a clear analytical way forward where hypotheses can be constructed to explain epistemic communities' influence in terms that are independent of the communities themselves.

Going beyond the epistemic communities framework, what contribution does this expanded approach to epistemic community-decision-maker exchanges make to the explanatory power of policy transfer analysis? The policy transfer literature has been criticized as strong on concepts but weak on systematic empirical analysis (Bennett 1997, p. 214). The expansion of epistemic communities outlined here will no doubt have added to this conceptual noise however the enterprise will facilitate empirical ambitions. At its most basic level, the typology provides a way of tracking decision-maker learning and ordering analysis of cross-national, cross-temporal policy transfer cases in ways that will isolate learning as a mechanism of policy choice. Narrowing our focus to explore this cognitive dimension of policy transfer, and specifically the use of intentional analysis where individuals' preferences and values mediate what is learned and from whom, underlines policy transfer processes as variously strategic, unpredictable, highly specified and difficult to steer, even for experts who initiate the process. The main consequence of such intentional analysis, something with which the literature is not traditionally associated, is to widen the empirical field of vision. Three particular areas for empirical development stand out.

First, lifting the analytical veil in this way reminds us that policy learning is not synonymous with policy adoption; decision-makers can learn 'negative lessons' where learning from the ideas that are diffused help crystallize what ideas and policy paths they *do not* wish to follow (see Stone 1999, p. 52 who suggests the UK's handling of BSE as a possible example of this). Furthermore, as the rbST case illustrates, where those attempting to export an idea have epistemic authority and political backing, this process of non-policy transfer requires significant resources and commitment. The EU could not casually reject rbST but rather resisted by assuming complete control over the policy end to be achieved and guided knowledge acquisition both directly, using the epistemic community's outlier data on mastitis to undermine the case for transfer, and indirectly, commissioning research from experts on other aspects of rbST's potential impact. In short, decision-makers worked hard to block transfer over a protracted period learning different lessons to those being given by the epistemic community and USA. Second, differentiating the ways in which individual decision-makers learn across knowledge components brings into relief cases where what has been learned has been partial or sub-optimal. As the EU's appropriation of outlier evidence illustrates, what decision-makers learn from epistemic communities cannot always be controlled by the experts. Finally, focussing on individuals' engagement with epistemic communities and raises questions about what happens over time as individuals' understandings mature or circumstances change and also when there are personnel changes in key decision-making positions. This latter point links to the questions raised by the rbST case concerning the extent to which decision-makers can become socialized into a learning type selected by their predecessors which erodes incumbents' abilities to terminate a policy which has been transferred or to revisit those rejected. For example, while policy persistence cannot necessarily be assumed, the political ratification of an epistemic paradigm that non-formal learning entails may raise considerable barriers to change locking decision-makers in to certain ways of thinking. In such situations it may make more sense to think in terms of the institutionalization of learning types than policy itself. Addressing individuals' thought processes over time and what happens when new decision-makers appear carries specific evidential and methodological requirements. To gain a window on decision-makers' minds, in-depth interviews are essential. So too is taking the long view – raising the spectre of historical case studies where analysis spans decades.

Acknowledgements

This article is based on doctoral research funded by Economic and Social Research Council (ESRC) studentship R00429834387. Previous versions were presented at the ECPR joint sessions in Rennes on 11–16 April 2008 and British International Studies Association (BISA) annual conference at the University of Exeter on 15–17 December 2008. The author is grateful to the participants of workshop 23 (on 'The Politics of Evidence-based Policy-making') and panel 3.5 (Epistemic Communities, International Experiences and Policy Transfer) respectively for their constructive comments and feedback. Particular thanks are extended to Peter Haas, Hanne Foss Hansen, Atsushi Ishii, Oliver James, Sara Kutchesfahani, Simone Ledermann, Mark Monaghan, Claudio Radaelli, Fritz Sager and John Turnpenny for their helpful suggestions.

Notes

1. In the five citation indexes in the *Web of Science*, Peter M. Haas's introductory article in the 1992 *International Organization* special edition edited by him has been cited 537 times (accessed 6/2/2009).
2. Notably, James and Lodge criticize the policy transfer model presented by Dolowitz and Marsh (2000) for collapsing these two analytical dimensions onto a single continuum (2003, pp. 184–185).
3. The author conducted 38 semi-structured interviews with active and retired scientists, civil servants, industry representatives, politicians and interest group actors.
4. Two particularly high profile studies have associated IGF-1 with a higher risk of diabetes (Baur *et al.* 2006) and identified milk produced by rbST administered cows as one of three major contributors to increased human twinning (Steinman 2006).

References

Adler, E. and Haas, P.M., 1992. Conclusion: epistemic communities, world order and the creation of a reflective research program. *International organization*, 46 (1), 367–390.
Argyris, C. and Schön, D., 1978. *Organizational learning: a theory of action perspective.* Reading, MA: Addison-Wesley.
Bailey, K.D., 1992. Typologies. *In*: E.F. Borgatta and M.L. Borgatta, eds. *Encyclopedia of sociology volume 4.* New York: Macmillan.
Bauman, D.E., 1990. *Bovine somatotrophin: review of an emerging animal technology.* US Office of Technology Assessment Washington, DC: Congress of the US.

Baur, J.A., *et al.*, 2006. Resveratrol improves health and survival of mice on a high-calorie diet. *Nature*, 444, 337–342.

Bennett, C., 1991. What is policy convergence and what causes it? *British journal of political science*, 21 (2), 215–233.

Bennett, C.J., 1997. Understanding ripple effects: the cross-national adoption of policy instruments for bureaucratic accountability. *Governance*, 10 (3), 213–233.

Bennett, C.J. and Howlett, M., 1992. The lessons of learning. *Policy sciences*, 25 (3), 275–294.

Boud, D.J., 1985. Problem-based learning in perspective. *In*: D.J. Boud, ed. *Problem-based learning in education for the professions*. Sydney: Higher Education Research and Development Society of Australasia.

Bramley, A.J. and Dodds, F.H., 1984. Reviews of the progress of dairy science: mastitis control – progress and prospects. *Journal of dairy science*, 51 (3), 481–512.

Braybrooke, D. and Lindblom, C., 1963. *A strategy of decision*. New York: Free Press.

Brown, G., 1995. What is involved in learning? *In*: C. Desforges, ed. *An introduction to teaching: psychological perspectives*. Oxford: Blackwell.

Bud, R., 1993. *The uses of life*. Cambridge: Cambridge University Press.

Cantley, M.F., 1995. The regulation of modern biotechnology: a historical and European perspective. *In*: D. Brauer, ed. *Biotechnology: volume 12 legal, economic and ethical dimensions*. Weinheim: VCH.

Commission of the European Communities, 1989. *Proposal for a Council decision concerning the administration of bovine somatotrophin (bST)*. COM (89) 379, September, Brussels.

Commission of the European Communities, 1991. *Promoting the competitive environment for the industrial activities based on biotechnology within the Community*. SEC (91) 629, April, Brussels.

Commission of the European Communities, 1992. *Second report from the Commission to the Council and to the Parliament concerning bST*. SEC (91) 2521, January, Brussels.

Commission of the European Communities, 1993a. *Veterinary medicinal products containing bovine somatotrophin: final scientific reports of the committee for veterinary medicinal products on two applications for marketing authorization submitted in accordance with directive. 87/22/eec*. CEC DGIII/C/3, Summary Document, 1 February, Brussels.

Commission of the European Communities, 1993b. *Opinion of the group of advisors on the ethical implications of biotechnology to the European Commission: the ethical implications of performance enhancers in agriculture and fisheries*. SEC (93) 8286, 12 March.

Commission of the European Communities, 1999a. *Report on animal welfare aspects of the use of bovine somatotrophin*. March, Brussels.

Commission of the European Communities, 1999b. *Report on the public health aspects of the use of bovine somatotrophin*. March, Brussels.

Coombs, P.H. and Ahmed, M., 1974. *Attacking rural poverty*. Baltimore, MD: John Hopkins University Press.

Deakin, R., 1990. BST: The first commercial product for agriculture from biotechnology. *In*: P. Wheale and R. McNally, eds. *The bio-revolution: cornucopia or Pandora's box?*. London: Pluto Press.

Denzau, A.D. and North, D.C., 1994. Shared mental models: ideologies and institutions. *Kyklos*, 47 (1), 3–31.

Dolowitz, D. and Marsh, D., 1996. Who learns what from whom: a review of the policy transfer literature. *Political studies*, 44 (2), 343–357.

Dolowitz, D. and Marsh, D., 2000. Learning from abroad: the role of policy transfer in contemporary policy-making. *Governance: an international journal of policy and administration*, 13 (1), 5–24.

Dowding, K., 2003. Policy transfer. *In*: I. McLean and A. McMillan, eds. *Concise dictionary of politics*. 2nd ed. Oxford: Oxford University Press.

Drezner, D.W., 2007. *All politics is global*. New Jersey: Princeton University Press.

Dunlop, C.A., 2000a. Epistemic communities: a reply to Toke. *Politics*, 20 (3), 137–144.

Dunlop, C.A., 2000b. GMOs and regulatory styles. *Environmental politics*, 9 (2), 149–155.

Dunlop, C.A., 2007. Up and down the pecking order, what matters and when in issue definition: the case of rbST in the EU. *Journal of European public policy*, 14 (1), 39–58.

Dunlop, C.A. and James, O., 2007. Principal-agent modelling and learning: the European Commission, experts and agricultural hormone growth promoters. *Public policy and administration*, 22 (4), 403–422.

Elman, C., 2005. Explanatory typologies in qualitative studies of international politics. *International organization*, 59 (2), 293–326.

Epstein, S.S., 1988. BST: the public health hazards. *The ecologist*, 19 (4), 128–129.

Epstein, S.S., 1990. Potential public health hazards of biosynthetic milk hormones. *International journal of health sciences*, 20 (1), 73–84.

European Parliament, 1988. *Hormones and the bST hormone in the dairy and meat industry.* A2-30/88/PE 115.204/fin, March, Brussels.

Fox, C., 2008. Got rbST-free milk? Available from: www.greenrightnow.com [Accessed 28 February 2008].

Freeman, R., 2007. Epistemological bricolage. *Administration and society*, 39, 476–496.

Gardner, B., 1996. *European agriculture: policies, production and trade.* London: Routledge.

Geertz, C., 1973. *The interpretation of cultures.* New York: Basic Books.

George, A.L., 1997. From groupthink to contextual process analysis. *In*: P. d'Hart, E. Stern and B. Sundelius, eds. , *Beyond groupthink.* Ann Arbor, MI: University of Michigan Press.

General Accounting Office (GAO), 1992. FDA's review of recombinant bovine growth hormone. GAO/PEMD-92-26, 6 August, Washington, DC: GAO.

Gibbons, A., 1990. FDA publishes bovine growth hormone data. *Science*, 249, 852–853.

Haas, P.M., 1990. *Saving the Mediterranean: the politics of international environmental co-operation.* New York: Columbia University Press.

Haas, P.M., 1992a. Introduction: epistemic communities and international policy coordination. *International organization*, 46 (1), 1–36.

Haas, P.M., 1992b. Banning chloroflurorcarbons: epistemic community efforts to protect stratospheric ozone. *International organization*, 46 (1), 187–224.

Haas, P.M., 2007. Epistemic communities. *In*: D. Bodansky, J. Brunnée and E. Hey, eds. *The oxford handbook of international environmental law.* Oxford: Oxford University Press.

Haas, P.M. and Haas, E.B., 2002. Pragmatic constructivism and the study of international institutions. *Millennium*, 31 (3), 573–601.

Heclo, H., 1974. *Modern social politics in Britain and Sweden.* New Haven, CT: Yale University Press.

Heimlich, J., ed., , 1993. *Nonformal environmental education: toward a working definition.* Information Bulletin 502E, Columbus, OH: ERIC.

Hiemstra, R., 1994. Self-directed learning. *In*: T. Husen and T. N. Postlethwaite, eds. *The international encyclopedia of education.* Oxford: Pergamon Press.

Hood, C., 1996. Control over bureaucracy: cultural theory and institutional variety. *Journal of public policy*, 15 (3), 207–230.

Ikenberry, G.J., 1992. A world economy restored. *International organization*, 46 (1), 289–321.

James, O. and Lodge, M., 2003. The limitations of 'policy transfer' and 'lesson drawing' for public policy research. *Political studies review*, 1 (2), 179–193.

Jarvis, P., 1987. *Adult learning in the social context.* London: Routledge.

JECFA, 1993. *Evaluation of certain veterinary drug residues in food. WHO Technical Report Series 832.* Geneva: WHO.

John-Steiner, V., 1997. *Notebooks of the mind: explorations of thinking.* New York: Oxford University Press.

Judge, D., 1993. *The parliamentary state.* Oxford: Sage.

Juskevich, J.C. and Guyer, G.C., 1990. Bovine growth hormone: human food safety evaluation. *Science*, 249, 875–884.

Kolb, D.A., 1984. *Experiential learning.* Englewood Cliffs, NJ: Prentice Hall.

Kronfeld, D.S., 1987. The challenge of BST. *Large animal veterinarian,* December, 14–17.

Laird, F., 1999. Rethinking learning. *Policy currents,* November, 3–6.

Lave, J. and Wenger, E., 1991. *Situated learning.* Cambridge: University of Cambridge Press.

Lewin, K., 1951. *Field theory in social science.* New York: Harper and Row.

Lipsky, M., 1977. *Commission politics.* Brunswick, NJ: Transaction Publishing.

Mars, G., 1982. *Cheats at work: an anthropology of workplace crime.* London: Allen and Unwin.

May, P.J., 1992. Policy learning and failure. *Journal of public policy*, 12 (4), 331–354.

McKinney, J.C., 1966. *Constructive typology and social theory.* New York: Meredith.

Miller, H.I., 1988. FDA regulation of products of the new biotechnology. *American biotechnology laboratory*, 6, 38–43.

Mocker, D.W. and Spear, G.E., 1982. *Lifelong learning: formal, nonformal, informal, and self-directed. Information Series No. 241.* Columbus, OH: ERIC.

Office of Technology Assessment (OTA), 1992. *US industry at a crossroad: biotech and policy (part 1 of 5).* Washington, DC: Congress of the United States, OTA.

Pierson, P., 1996. The path to European integration: a historical institutionalist analysis. *Comparative political analysis*, 29 (2), 123–163.

Pigozzi, M., 1999. *Education in emergencies and for reconstruction.* New York: UNICEF.

Pollack, A., 2006. Which cows do you trust? *The New York Times*, 7 October, p. C1.

Radaelli, C.M., 1995. The role of knowledge in the policy process. *Journal of european public policy*, 2 (2), 159–183.

Rogers, A., 2002. *Teaching adults.* 3rd ed. Maidenhead: Open University Press.

Rogers, A., 2003. *What is the difference?* Leicester: NIACE.

Rogers, A., 2004. *Non-formal education: flexible schooling or participatory education?.* Dortrecht: Kluwer.

Rose, R., 1991. What is lesson-drawing? *Journal of public policy*, 11 (1), 3–30.

Simon, H., 1947. *Administrative behaviour: a study of decision-making processes in administrative organization.* New York: The Free Press.

Steinman, G., 2006. Mechanisms of twinning: VII. Effect of diet and heredity on the human twinning rate. *The journal of reproductive medicine*, 51 (5), 405–410.

Stone, D., 1999. Learning lessons and transferring policy. *Politics*, 19 (1), 51–59.

Stone, D., 2000. Non-governmental policy transfer: the strategies of independent policy institutes. *Governance*, 13 (1), 45–62.

Stone, D., 2005. Knowledge networks and global policy. *In*: D. Stone and S. Maxwell, eds. *Global knowledge networks and international development.* London: Routledge.

Stone, D., 2008. Global public policy, transnational policy communities and their networks. *The policy studies journal*, 36 (1), 19–38.

Tolman, E., 1948. Cognitive maps in rats and men. *Psychological review*, 55, 189–208.

Tough, A., 1971. *The adult's learning projects.* Toronto: Ontario Institute for Studies in Education.

Verdun, A., 1999. The role of the Delors Committee and EMU. *Journal of european public policy*, 6 (2), 308–329.

Vogel, D., 1995. *Trading up.* Cambridge, MA: Harvard University Press.

Watkins, J.W.N., 1953. Ideal types and historical explanation. *In*: H. Feigal and M. Brodbeck, eds. *Readings in the philosophy of science.* New York: Apple-Century-Crofts.

Weiss, C., 1979. The many meanings of research utilization. *Public administration*, 39, 426–431.

Zito, A.R., 2001. Epistemic communities, European Union governance and the public voice. *Science and public policy*, 28 (6), 465–476.

Exporting public–private partnerships in healthcare: export strategy and policy transfer

Chris Holden

Centre on Global Change and Health, London School of Hygiene and Tropical Medicine, Keppel Street, London WC1E 7HT, UK

The literature on policy transfer has paid insufficient attention to the role of commercial interests in the transfer of policy. The British government has developed a healthcare industrial strategy that includes an attempt to export Public Private Partnership (PPP) services. This article analyses the application of the strategy to export PPP services in healthcare to developing and eastern European countries through a review of 'scoping reports'. The analysis reveals that the strategy involves an attempt to utilize the UK Department for International Development, international financial institutions such as the World Bank, and private sector consultancies to influence developing country governments towards adopting the British Private Finance Initiative (PFI) model, in order to lay the basis for the winning of consultancy, construction and other contracts by British firms. The debate concerning the suitability of PPP/PFI arrangements for the financing of healthcare facilities in Britain is considered in terms of its implications for the adoption of such arrangements by developing and eastern European countries. The purported efficiency gains of PPP/PFI in the UK are unproven, yet the drawbacks of the model may be even more problematic for public health service organizations in developing and eastern European countries, where the expertise to negotiate, monitor and enforce robust contracts with the private sector may be more limited. The article concludes that the attempt to export PPP services entails a strategy of trying to 'export' the policy itself, despite the fact that the public sector technical capacity needed to make the policy effective may be lacking in the target countries.

Introduction

The introduction of market mechanisms and greater involvement of for-profit companies into the British National Health Service (NHS) and other public services has attracted widespread commentary and debate. One particularly controversial means of involving the private sector has been through Public–Private Partnerships (PPPs), particularly through the Private Finance Initiative (PFI). However, another aspect of market-oriented policy is less well-known, that is, the utilization of the NHS to enhance the British healthcare industry and boost its exports. Such exports currently take the form primarily of healthcare devices and equipment, but also include health consultancy services and services related to the development of PPPs for the financing, building and maintenance of hospitals and other healthcare facilities. The Department of Health's international department, DH International (DHI), plays a key role in liaising with other government departments and with industry interests to facilitate the export strategy, including conducting scoping reports in order to identify priority markets to be targeted in both developed and developing countries.

This article analyses the nature of the export strategy as it applies to PPP services, and considers the suitability of the British PPP/PFI model as a means of financing healthcare facilities in developing and eastern European countries. Whilst that aspect of the industrial policy related to healthcare goods (as opposed to services) may also influence the nature of health services ultimately provided to patients, the article focuses specifically on attempts to export the British model of PPP, a policy that has provoked widespread controversy in the UK. It also focuses specifically on developing countries and eastern European countries as those countries where the activities of external actors, including donor governments, international institutions and private sector consultancies, may have most influence over system reform, and yet where PPP-type policies are potentially least appropriate.

The article first reviews the literature on policy transfer, elucidating its relevance for the present study. It then outlines the rationale and basis for the British healthcare industrial strategy, followed by an elaboration of its export-oriented components. Following this, it provides an outline of debates relating to the implementation of PPP policies in Britain, in order to explicate the rationale for their adoption domestically and the main points of contention. The article then presents a systematic analysis of country scoping reports relating to the export of PPP services to developing and eastern European countries in order to identify UK government and industry strategy in this area. The implications of the attempt to export PPP arrangements to these countries are then considered. It is concluded that the attempt to export PPP services entails a strategy of trying to 'export' the policy itself by utilizing various means of influencing government policy in target countries, despite the fact that the public sector technical capacity needed to make the policy effective may be lacking in those countries.

Policy transfer, lesson-drawing and coercion

According to Dolowitz and Marsh (1996, p. 344), 'Policy transfer, emulation and lesson-drawing all refer to a process in which knowledge about policies, administrative arrangements, institutions, etc. in one time and/or place is used in the development of policies, administrative arrangements and institutions in another time and place'. Many of the earliest discussions of policy transfer focused upon policy *learning* or 'lesson-drawing' (Rose 1991), suggesting a rational process whereby the transfer of policy is based upon a careful appraisal of the evidence. As Rose (1991, p. 7) puts it, a lesson utilizes 'available experience elsewhere to devise a programme that is new to the agency adopting it and attractive because of the evidence that it has been effective elsewhere'.

As Dolowitz and Marsh (1996, p. 344) point out, however, the idea of policy *transfer* incorporates but is broader than that of lesson-drawing, since it can take either voluntary or coercive forms. They distinguish between 'direct coercive transfer' and 'indirect coercive transfer'. In the case of the former, one government may force another to adopt a policy, an international institution may ensure a government adopts a certain policy by, for example, attaching conditions to a loan, or a transnational corporation (TNC) may influence policy adoption by threatening to take investment elsewhere. In the case of indirect coercive transfer, externalities, functional interdependence, economic constraints, competition between countries and the emergence of international consensus may all influence policy adoption. In a study of the international spread of earlier forms of privatization, Ikenberry (1990, p. 99) observed how one state or its agents could provide 'incentives or inducements that lead other states to adopt the preferred policy', noting the role of the American State Department and Agency for International Development (AID) in working in accord with the reform programmes of the major multilateral financial institutions to encourage liberalization.

If we are to be concerned with the possibility of coercive transfer as well as of voluntary transfer, an identification of the possible agents of transfer is crucial. Dolowitz and Marsh (1996, p. 345) identify six main categories of actors involved in policy transfer: elected officials, political parties, bureaucrats/civil servants, pressure groups, policy entrepreneurs/experts and supranational institutions. Other literature places particular importance upon 'epistemic communities' (Adler and Haas 1992, Haas 1992) or various forms of policy networks (Evans and Davies 1999, Stone 2004). Despite this focus on the actors that may be important to policy transfer, and Dolowitz and Marsh's passing reference to TNCs (1996), there has been little explicit examination of the role of material interests in motivating actors, or of the role of private actors in such processes. Whilst international institutions such as the World Bank or the International Monetary Fund (IMF) are often identified as agents of coercive transfer, and it is well known that such institutions operate upon the basis of a specific set of pro-market ideological values and knowledge claims, the potential or actual beneficiaries of such coercive transfer are not often identified.

Evans and Davies (1999) make the most useful contribution here by explicitly incorporating questions of structure and agency into their model. Thus whilst policy transfer is defined by Evans and Davies 'in Rose's terms as an action-oriented intentional activity' (1999, p. 36), it is seen as crucial to 'place social and political action within the structured context in which it takes place' (1999, p. 370). Thus, exogenous economic, technological, ideological and institutional structures can constrain and/or facilitate endogenous structures such as the 'competition state' (discussed in the next section), which in turn may constrain or facilitate the micro-politics of agency. At the level of agency, Evans and Davies (1999) see the concept of 'policy transfer networks' as a means for 'evaluating the complex interaction of state and international policy agendas forged through the interaction of state, non-state, transnational and international actors'. Whilst the role of international institutions is particularly important in the transfer of pro-private sector policies, Ikenberry (1990) demonstrates that a coalition of groups, including sections of the national bureaucracy and the private sector, sometimes emerges around a strategy that includes privatization and collaborates with external agencies. These external actors can thus help to 'bolster national coalitions that favour privatization and public sector reform' (Ikenberry 1990, p. 100).

The role of non-state actors in policy transfer clearly requires greater attention. Stone (2004) demonstrates that non-state actors can be as important as state and international agencies in the transfer of policy. Of particular importance to the present study is the role of private consulting firms, which played a key role in the global spread of 'new public management' ideas and policies (Saint-Martin 2000, Stone 2004). Wedel (2001) and de la Porte and Deacon (2002) have demonstrated the significant role that consultancies have played in policy transfer to eastern European countries during the transition to capitalism. The UK Department for International Development (DFID) has regularly funded private sector consultancies to advise on privatization in developing countries. Rather than being disinterested, such advice may be aimed at winning further business, regardless of potential conflicts of interest (Hilary 2004, WDM 2005).

In the context of the possibility of coercive transfer, the focus of the present article on strategies to export health-related PPP services to developing and eastern European countries is important for a number of reasons. First, in order to sell PPP-related services, PPP policies must already be present. There is therefore an instrumental and self-interested reason to encourage the adoption of those policies, which may override the evidence about the efficacy of the particular policy in any particular setting. In other words, there is an incentive for what started as an export strategy to become a form of coercive transfer or 'inducement' (Ikenberry 1990). Second, because export strategies have economic goals, whereas health policy has primarily social and equity-oriented goals, the potential for conflicts of interest and the downgrading or subsumption of health policy's social and development goals is significant. Third, the evidence concerning the benefits or otherwise of PPP policies in the UK is mixed at best, as discussed in a later section of this article. It therefore makes a dubious candidate for positive lesson-drawing. Fourth, policy transfer from developed to developing countries may be particularly difficult, involving '[p]roblems of adaptation to different economic, social, political, legal and administrative cultures' (Minogue 2004, p. 178). As Hulme and Hulme (2008) point out, nearly all the literature points to the importance of local context and mediation in what policies are adopted and how they are implemented. Furthermore, as Rose (1991, p. 21) indicates, an important consideration is whether the resources required to make a policy work in one place can be matched in another. Such questions must be given particular consideration when transfer from developed to developing countries is proposed. The implications for the policy transfer literature of the present study will be returned to at the end of this article. Meanwhile, in the next section, the rationale behind the British healthcare industrial strategy is outlined.

A healthcare industrial strategy

Figures on British companies' share of the global healthcare market are scarce and often inconsistent, yet it is clear that the market is a substantial one. According to the Association of British Healthcare Industries (ABHI 2005, p. 8), the British healthcare sector as a whole exports £16 billion of products and services, with medical technology companies generating over £3 billion of this. Aside from pharmaceuticals, the medical devices industry is the largest component of health-related trade, and is at the centre of the current British healthcare export strategy. The world market for healthcare devices is close to $200 billion (US$), which is about half the size of the global pharmaceuticals market, and is growing at 7% per annum. Department for Trade and Industry figures put the UK medical devices market at between \$5.5 billion and \$6.3 billion (US \$), or 3–3.6% of the total world market. Despite the dominance of healthcare goods, services are also an important component of British healthcare trade, and there are 500 British healthcare consultancies active in countries throughout the world (ABHI 2005, p. 8), which earn around £25 million abroad annually (DHI 2004a). According to DH International, the UK's 40 building contractors currently earn a further £25 million a year from overseas healthcare projects, increasingly involving project management (DHI 2004a), whilst British Healthcare (2006) claims that, in 2001, these 40 companies earned £5 billion overseas, of which 10% was healthcare related.

The current policy focus for developing the British healthcare industry results from the Health Industry Task Force (HITF), which was set up in October 2003 and co-chaired by Lord Norman Warner, Minister for Health, and Sir Christopher O'Donnell, chief executive of the health technology multinational Smith & Nephew. The HITF's goal was to find synergies between NHS provision to meet the health needs of British citizens and the potential economic benefits that a thriving healthcare industry may generate. The NHS procures supplies of goods and services from a huge range of firms, and its sheer size means that it is able to create and sustain huge demand for these supplies. The HITF was a collaboration between government and industry, with key input being provided by organizations such as the Association of British Healthcare Industries (ABHI), the leading UK trade association for the healthcare industry. ABHI includes among its key aims to influence legislation, government policy, regulation and standards (ABHI 2009), and launched its own 'Healthcare Industries Manifesto' for the 2005 general election (ABHI 2005).

The HITF was organized around four key areas for investigation (HITF 2004, p. 5): market access ('how to increase and speed up NHS adoption of useful new products and procedures'); research and development (R&D) and the industrial base ('how to improve support for innovation in the home market and enhance the UK's reputation as an attractive location for healthcare manufacturers'); regulatory issues ('building on the existing working relationship between the UK regulator and industry, and maximizing the UK's influence in regulatory matters in the EU and overseas'); and international trade ('working together to improve opportunities in overseas markets for UK-based companies'). Each of these areas had its own working group which produced specific proposals.

The HITF's key document, *Better health through partnership: a programme for action* (HITF 2004), identifies the NHS as playing a major role in developing the healthcare industry as a key sector of a future globally competitive British economy:

> The explosion of healthcare technologies is a global phenomenon and the UK is in a position to benefit from the changes ahead. Innovation, entrepreneurship and evaluation are key elements in driving forward improvements in health and social care, and are essential ingredients in a thriving economy ... Our largest asset is the NHS itself, which needs to drive change and innovation in healthcare delivery more strongly. No other country has a single system with the NHS's resources and links to academia. An NHS that looks to innovate can capture the benefits of the emerging technologies and, in so doing, provide an engine for industrial development based on the knowledge economy. Viewed holistically, the healthcare 'supply chain' ... is already one of the largest activities in the UK economy. It could, however, become its major long-term growth engine (HITF 2004, pp. 32–33).

This is in line with wider contemporary thinking on economic and social policy, in which competitiveness in the global economy is seen as being based on innovation, skills and knowledge. In this view, synergies should be found between economic and social policy so that they work together rather than against each other, and where necessary social policy is subordinated to economic policy in the attempt to enhance competitiveness. Such policies represent a shift towards what Cerny (1990) calls the 'competition state', and whilst this shift is widespread, it is typified by New Labour in Britain (Cerny and Evans 2004). Education, labour market and social security policy, for example, have been aligned so as to enhance the competitiveness and flexibility of the labour market (Holden 1999, 2003). Similarly, the strategy for the healthcare sector relies on utilizing the NHS to more explicitly support and nurture the healthcare industry, thereby creating a dynamic, state of the art industry which is in a world leading position to export health-related goods and services abroad. High value-added industries are seen as key by many commentators if advanced economies are to remain competitive in a period of globalization (see, for example, Reich 1991), and the healthcare industry meets these criteria (Loeppky 2004).

A question arises then as to whether these two goals (meeting health needs on the one hand, and promoting a dynamic healthcare industry on the other) are always mutually compatible. Where tension arises, will health policy goals be (consciously or otherwise) subordinated to industrial policy goals? Examples from the pharmaceutical industry already demonstrate the tensions that can exist between the meeting of health policy goals and industrial policy, where an industry does become one that is large and important to an economy (Holden 2009).

Similar contradictions between health policy and industrial policy may be explored in relation to health devices in terms of whether health expenditure is targeted in the most effective way. For example, in managing the transition of their health services from Communist-type systems to a western European model, some eastern European countries upgraded their health technology, such as high-end imaging equipment, to a point where per capita ratios for some equipment exceeded those in many western European countries (Ho and Ali-Zade 2001, pp. 12–13). One factor in this process was the easy availability of suppliers' credits, sometimes backed by government guarantees from either a seller's or a buyer's country. The consequence has often been that, in conditions of severe budget constraints, these technologies have been unsustainable in the end, with hospitals unable to pay for operating supplies or repairs and the equipment rarely used to its full capacity.

However, the British healthcare export strategy is not only focused upon goods and technology, but also on consultancy and on the export of services related to PPPs. The Private Finance Initiative (PFI) and other variants of PPP have been highly controversial in the UK, but have been adopted as the principal mechanism for funding large healthcare facilities and other public infrastructure. It is therefore important to assess whether the export of PPP-related services are the best means of enhancing developing country health systems. The adoption of PPPs by other countries is of particular strategic importance to British firms, since these are already the market leaders in PPP due to its extensive use in the NHS.

A healthcare export strategy

The outcome of working group 4 of the HITF on international trade was a strategy document which forms the basis for export policy (DHI 2004a). The principal stakeholders involved in the strategy are identified as UK Trade and Investment (UKTI), which is the lead government trade promotion and development organization, bringing together all the overseas trade work of the Department for Trade and Industry (DTI), the Foreign and Commonwealth Office and regional trade bodies; the Department of Health (DH), for whom DH International (DHI) leads on international issues; and British Healthcare, the industry-driven focus for healthcare exports, which brings together trade associations and other intermediaries with government representatives. Whilst UKTI will ensure that 'healthcare will remain a priority area for development' of trade (HITF 2004, p. 42), DHI takes the lead in coordinating the strategy.

Among the specialist areas identified as providing opportunities for increasing exports are consultancy and project management. The expertise of consultancies includes design, commissioning and operation of hospitals, strategic planning, healthcare master plans and the provision of advice on the reform of health insurance. The strategy identifies how 'risk sharing and other financial engineering skills' can be built into project management packages, reflecting contractors' experience of the UK's lead in healthcare PFI schemes (DHI 2004a). The strategy involves identifying a number of priority markets where there are opportunities to increase UK healthcare exports. For each priority market it is intended that detailed action plans will be developed based upon in-country research carried out by government and its partners in industry. These action plans, 'will be both bespoke and long term. Market priorities will be reviewed regularly to deliver dynamic support to the industry where appropriate' (DHI 2004a). The performance target was to deliver 25 new exporters and introduce 75 existing exporters to new markets by March 2006 (DHI 2004a), although at the time of writing it was not clear whether this target had been met.

'Other supporting initiatives' are identified in the strategy document as including UK Department for International Development (DFID) programmes, multilateral aid agencies, 'special projects' (including Iraq reconstruction), United Nations (UN) programmes and World Health Organization (WHO) assemblies and meetings. In addition to the HITF proposals, UKTI had commissioned a review of trade support by all Whitehall departments. For health, this recommended that, because of the key role of the NHS, DH should retain the 'sector champion' role, 'but with safeguards to ensure that it [trade] is not marginalized as it has been in the past by the domestic policy agenda' (DHI 2003a, p. 8). It also recommended that other DH/NHS agencies such as the Medical Devices Agency and the National Institute for Health and Clinical Excellence should 'play an active role in trade development', particularly by promoting UK standards and 'highlighting excellence amongst British suppliers' (DHI 2003a, p. 8). Furthermore, it argued that DFID should establish a dialogue with DH, UKTI and British Healthcare about 'forthcoming opportunities and how UK firms can position themselves to tender for them'. This attempt to tie other agencies into trade promotion clearly raises the potential for contradictions to arise between trade promotion and the other policy goals which are and should be the priority for these other agencies.

The centrepiece of the export strategy are the action plans for priority markets, which are to follow from a number of scoping missions to identify opportunities in particular countries. Most of the 'top-priority markets' are developed countries, in particular the USA, Germany, France and Japan, as these are the countries with the most highly developed health systems and markets. The two developing countries included in the top category are China and India. Whilst India is identified as requiring a 'watching brief' (DHI 2005), China is clearly identified as 'likely to become the leading market in the world' (HITF WG4 2004). 'Priority markets' identified in the 2004 document are Brazil, Canada, Hong Kong, Israel, Malaysia, Mexico, Saudi Arabia, Singapore, South Africa, Taiwan and UAE (DHI 2004a). Markets identified as 'requiring further investigation/niche opportunities' are Chile, Colombia, Hungary, Poland, Romania, Italy, Greece and Portugal. Consultancy and/or PPP/PFI are identified as key opportunities in a number of these countries. The next section of this article outlines the key debates relating to the effectiveness of the PPP/PFI policy as it has been implemented in Britain. The following section then analyses the scoping mission reports that have been completed for developing and eastern European countries that include aspects relating to PPP/PFI, whilst the final section discusses the implications of this attempt to export PPP/PFI arrangements to such countries.

Public–private partnerships as British policy

The term 'public–private partnership' may be used in a number of different ways to describe some kind of collaboration between the public and private sectors. This article focuses primarily on a particular type of PPP developed in the UK, the Private Finance Initiative (PFI), a scheme set up by the Thatcher governments for funding the construction and maintenance of public infrastructure which has been greatly expanded under New Labour governments. This model entails a private sector consortium, usually a 'special purposes vehicle', raising the funds to finance the construction of a facility such as a hospital, building the facility and then maintaining and operating it for the life of the contract. The facility is leased to the public sector under a contract typically lasting 25–30 years, so that the consortium is guaranteed an income stream paid for by the public sector service provider. Safeguards are built into the contract which stipulate service levels and quality, with penalties if these are not achieved. At the end of the contracted period, the asset reverts to the public sector, or a further contract for refurbishment and/or maintenance may be negotiated. A variant of this idea, used more often in continental European countries, involves concessions or franchises, whereby the private sector partner builds, maintains or enhances the asset and then collects payment for the contracted period of time by way of user charges (such as in the case of a toll road).

The UK has been the leader in such innovations, and a number of British firms have benefited considerably from public sector revenue streams in this way. As the Chief Secretary to the Treasury, Andrew Smith, was already able to note by 2000, PPPs have provided 'a major boost to the construction industry' (HM Treasury 2000, p. 4). The export potential of the British PPP model being adopted elsewhere was also realized at this time: 'It is an area of public policy where the UK leads the world … PPPs … offer British companies the opportunity to use the skills and expertise they have developed in providing services within the UK to enter new export markets' (HM Treasury 2000, p. 7).

It has been claimed that PFI allows more public facilities to be built in a shorter amount of time, since the funds are raised by the private sector and not borrowed by the government. Investment in public infrastructure can therefore take place without any apparent impact on public sector debt. This is a weak argument, however, since if PFI is properly accounted for as an alternative form of government borrowing it is likely to be more expensive than traditional forms of borrowing, since the government can borrow more cheaply than the private sector. Furthermore, the fiscal rules adopted by the UK Treasury under Gordon Brown's Chancellorship allow for borrowing across economic cycles if necessary to fund public investment. The argument against these more traditional forms of borrowing for public infrastructure projects is then that projects financed in this way usually experience significant over-runs and unexpected cost increases. Therefore, because a PFI contract, and the costs to the public sector involved, can be negotiated at the beginning of the process, risk is born by the private sector partner, which must absorb any unforeseen costs. The private sector partner is also contracted to deliver services to a specified level and quality, and may suffer penalties if they do not. The claim that PPP/PFI transfers risk to the private sector has become the principal rationale for the British model, as reflected in this definition of PPP by the UK government: 'The Private Finance Initiative (PFI) and other arrangements where the public sector contracts to purchase quality services on a long-term basis so as to take advantage of private sector management skills incentivised by having private finance at risk' (HM Treasury 2000, p. 8).

However, these claims of risk transfer have been questioned by a number of writers, who have argued that the way risk has been valued is unrealistic and is done in a manner so as to ensure that the PFI project appears to be more cost-effective than the traditional route. The government's claims of cost-effectiveness are based upon a formula which inflates the cost estimates for buildings procured under the traditional route (the 'public sector comparator') by 2–24% of the original estimates, in order to take account of initial under-estimating, or the so-called 'optimism bias'. The application of this formula often leads to procurement taking place under PFI arrangements, and is the justification for the government's PPP policy both at home and abroad. Pollock *et al.* (2005) undertook a rigorous examination of the evidence base for this policy and found that, 'There is no evidence to support the Treasury's chief justification for the policy, namely, that PFI generates value for money savings by improving the efficiency of construction procurement' (Pollock *et al.* 2005, p. 3). Even the Institute for Public Policy Research, a think-tank sympathetic to New Labour, concluded that: 'In the case of most NHS hospital schemes the small projected savings could easily disappear if some assumptions relating to risk, or the discount rate, were altered' (IPPR 2001, p. 91). Value for money comparisons with traditional public procurement methods are made more difficult because of the lack of transparency that surrounds PFI projects, which are deemed to be commercially confidential (McKee *et al.* 2006, p. 892).

However, there are clear drawbacks for the public provider leasing the facility under PPP/PFI arrangements. Contracts are inflexible for the public sector partner, locking them into long-term arrangements and regular fixed payments. Since the 'availability charge' NHS organizations pay for the use of PFI buildings is greater than the capital charge they pay to the Treasury under traditional arrangements, an 'affordability gap' is created that must be met from revenue budgets, thus diverting money from clinical services (Hellowell and Pollock 2006). This has resulted in PFI hospitals being built with lower capacity than those they replace in order to try to contain costs at an early stage (Dunnigan and Pollock 2003). Despite this, PFI payments have an ongoing impact on NHS service providers, with a higher incidence of deficits in NHS organizations in England that have PFI projects than those that do not (Hellowell and Pollock 2006, p. 5). It has also been argued that PPP/PFI has led to a deterioration in employment practices, including changes to the terms and conditions of work and reductions in the numbers of maintenance and ancillary staff employed (Hebson *et al.* 2003, Farnsworth 2006, p. 833). Furthermore, there is evidence that the contractual and profit-based nature of PPPs undermines the public sector ethos (Hebson *et al.* 2003). The government itself has acknowledged that the performance of 'soft services' such as catering, cleaning and portering within PFI contracts has not reached hoped-for standards (HM Treasury 2006).

A further issue is the technical and management capacity that is needed to run PPP/PFI projects. In England, the Audit Commission has identified large-scale capital projects such as PFI as imposing a substantial management burden on NHS organizations, and as a contributory factor in financial failure. It found that organizations with such projects often gave 'priority to capital projects over and above the day-to-day running of the NHS trusts and the issues they were facing' (Audit Commission 2006, p. 27). Planning, designing and funding processes can take an extended period of time, and 'the attraction of the big building project ... makes it difficult to withdraw from negotiations or reshape the vision once strategic approval has been gained and detailed discussions are underway'. It concludes that: 'Management capacity and how the risks to effective management of the whole organization will be addressed should form a key criterion for judging whether intended schemes should proceed' (Audit Commission 2006, p. 28).

UK government documents acknowledge that in the early days of implementation in the UK, the expected benefits of PFI projects were not fully realized, partly because there were, 'inadequate project management skills for such a complex procurement process in the public sector', and because, 'public sector clients had insufficient commercial knowledge and experience, in many instances even to select suitably qualified advisors' (HM Treasury 2000, p. 27). As Hebson *et al.* (2003), p. 492) put it: 'Under the new contractual approach ... the quality of public services is not only as good as the quality of the contract but is also defined by the relative balance of legal expertise between partners ...' These issues are likely to be of even greater importance in developing countries, many of which 'suffer from very low administrative capacity' (Polidano and Hulme 1999). As Batley and Larbi (2004) demonstrate, the kind of indirect management necessary for the successful realization of public–private partnerships is likely to be *more*, rather than less, demanding on government capacity than familiar direct forms of state management. The design, management and monitoring of the kind of long-term and complex contracts required by PFI-type arrangements are likely to present particular problems for developing countries (Batley and Larbi 2004). PPP/PFI therefore clearly remains a contentious domestic policy, and one that may be particularly unsuited to developing countries. In the next section, those parts of the British healthcare export strategy relating to PPP/PFI in developing and eastern European countries will be outlined via an analysis of available scoping reports and associated documents.

A strategy for exporting PPPs

The lead role in the healthcare export strategy is played by DHI, which accepts the industry view that government involvement in export promotion is essential and that the Department of Health should act as the 'official sponsor' of the industry (DH 2005). One of the key roles of DHI is to organize programmes for visiting health ministers and other 'inward missions' to see the NHS approach to PPP/PFI and other issues. In 2002–2003, of a total of 32 visits by delegations from 16 different countries, 24 visits involving delegations from 13 countries included PPP/PFI issues as part of the visit (DHI 2003a). Country delegations including PPP/PFI in their itinerary were primarily from the developing world or eastern Europe, and included Mexico, China, Chile, Brazil, South Africa, Colombia, Botswana, Hungary, Estonia, Finland, Portugal, France and Canada. Similarly, in 2004–2005, of a total of 54 visits by delegations from 21 countries, 21 visits involving delegations from 11 countries included PPP/PFI issues as part of the visit (DHI 2005). Again, these countries were primarily developing or east European countries, and included Malaysia, Kuwait, China, Singapore, Turkey, Slovakia, Hungary, Spain, France, Japan and Canada. Of 15 visits made that year by delegations from China or its provinces, seven included PPP/PFI in their itinerary. These figures demonstrate the importance of PPP/PFI to the overall export strategy. DHI also has a key role along with UKTI in organizing the scoping missions for priority markets to identify export opportunities. The rest of this section consists of a detailed analysis of available reports relating to these that have been completed for developing and eastern European countries.

China is the key target of the UK healthcare export strategy in the developing world. China is seen as the key future market by all types of transnational healthcare corporations (Holden 2005a). According to DHI (2005, p. 8), the Chinese authorities are particularly interested in the NHS' 'modernization' reforms, including PFI, to the extent that they now regard the UK as 'partner of choice'. The scoping mission to China which took place in 2003 concluded that the country 'offers rich and fertile ground for mounting trade initiatives' and that there was significant interest by the Chinese authorities in 'exploring further the UK models of healthcare including PFI/PPP' (DHI 2004b, pp. 1–2). A PFI conference was scheduled for the autumn that would include healthcare as a major component. PFI was reportedly 'of significant interest to local healthcare leaders as a route to developing a major hospital rebuilding programme'. The sheer size of the country, and the relative autonomy of city authorities, led DHI and UKTI to adopt a regional strategy centred on those areas experiencing greatest economic growth, namely Guangdong/Shenzhen, Hong Kong, Shanghai and Beijing. China was 'best seen as a collection of relatively small markets, each based around a wealthy eastern city, rather than a single large market' (DHI 2004b, p. 16). A range of 'lobbying and promotional activities' were to be launched, including inward and outward missions, sponsored visits to the UK for influential Chinese decision-makers, and awareness raising seminars for relevant UK organizations on the healthcare opportunities in China (DHI 2004b, p. 28).

Whilst Chinese officials were seen as recognizing the advantages of PPP/PFI, they still had 'much to learn'. Although it was 'not fully understood', the PFI concept of using private funds to build public hospitals and then manage them with some degree of autonomy was 'very popular' in Guangdong and Shenzhen, and particularly in Shanghai (DHI 2004b, p. 3). UK firms involved in consultancy, project management and finance were seen to be in a position to exploit opportunities in PPP/PFI. In 2004, the UK signed two memoranda of understanding with Chinese authorities, one with the Ministry of Health in Beijing and the other with the Shanghai People's Government. These cover 'a range of partnership initiatives ... and business support' including a pilot PFI hospital in Shanghai. The need for China to update its infrastructure in Beijing, including hospitals and other healthcare facilities, in preparation for the 2008 Olympics was seen as a particular opportunity for British firms (UKTI 2006a, p. 9). DH and UKTI together now lead a 'China Delivery Group' to oversee healthcare business opportunities in China, and DH feeds into the 'Whitehall China Task Force' chaired by the Deputy Prime Minister which seeks to promote partnerships with China across all Whitehall departments.

India is also seen as a growth market. The Indian healthcare market is dominated by the private sector, so that most opportunities relating to the design and building of hospitals will come from the expansion plans of corporate chains. However, the government elected in 2004 committed itself to raising the historically low level of public expenditure on health from 0.9% of gross domestic product in 1999 to at least 2–3% over a 5-year period (UKTI 2006b, pp. 3, 9), potentially creating opportunities for PPP/PFI deals. A UKTI 'PPP Export Advisory Group' involving the British Consultants and Construction Bureau (an export promotion association for consultancy companies, now called British Expertise) and International Financial Services London (a similar export promotion and lobby organization for UK-based financial services firms and consultancies) undertook a PPP scoping mission to India in March 2005. This found that there was a lack of understanding of PPP in India, with the term 'being applied to describe almost any commercial investment where the state has any interest' (UKTI 2005a). However, if the British model of PPP was clearly explained, 'given India's legal, governmental and business legacy from the UK the application of a UK-based PPP model should be easier to integrate than in some other countries in Asia' (UKTI 2005a, p. 5).

Although the Indian government appeared to be committed to implementing PPP on a large scale quickly, lack of expertise, fragmented responsibility between government departments and widespread antipathy to private sector involvement in public infrastructure were obstacles. The Indian Ministry of Finance had commissioned a report on PPP implementation from the Public Private Infrastructure Advisory Facility (PPIAF), 'a multi-donor technical assistance facility aimed at helping developing countries improve the quality of their infrastructure through private sector involvement', developed by the UK's DFID and Japan and involving the World Bank (UKTI 2005a, p. 8). The scoping mission reported that, 'The Indian government made a specific point of asking that the mission took back a request that some form of "ODA" [Official Development Assistance] assistance from the UK would greatly help them in contracting the right sort of UK professional skills and expertise' (UKTI 2005a, p. 9). The report recommended that: 'DFID being a joint sponsor of PPIAF, providing around 50% of it's funding, should have a major role in directing its activities'. It should therefore be assessed whether, 'PPP related consultancy work could be met from DFID funding for technical assistance, given that PPP has aspects of improved governance. Normally DFID would not relate any assistance specifically to the UK, although the UK would be the most likely source of expertise in this case' (UKTI 2005a, p. 15).

However, there was a relative lack of interest in PPP for social goals such as healthcare, partly because of a lack of information needed to produce meaningful private sector comparators and partly because of the widespread acceptance of private healthcare provision (UKTI 2005a, p. 4). Opportunities for PPP were therefore limited at the present time and, 'A great deal of educational work with government officials [would] be needed to breed understanding in the partnership aspects of PPP' (UKTI 2005a, p. 14). Assistance should be given to the central government to establish a PPP taskforce, and similar help should be given to any state governments that were interested. 'An on-going programme aimed at senior Indian politicians in the use of PPP and of the benefits of external advisors may improve the UK advisors' chances of work in this market' (UKTI 2005a, p. 14).

In Chile, a UKTI/DHI scoping mission in August 2003 was followed by a visit to the UK by a Chilean ministerial team in February 2004. This was followed by a 'joint healthcare reform and modernization seminar' in Santiago in July 2004 which ultimately led to a request from the Chilean Ministry of Health for 'structured input' from the UK in support of a programme of four PPP hospital developments (DHI 2005, pp. 10–11). The resulting programme involves Barts and the London NHS Trust as the lead in helping the Chilean hospital management teams to learn how to manage the PPP process effectively. The UK visit to Chile included a director of PPP Solutions Ltd, a company which has extensive experience of providing PPP services to public and private sector clients in the UK as well as some other countries.

The scoping mission to Malaysia in 2003 resulted in the country being classed as a high priority market for healthcare exports (DHI 2003b). The country's 8th Malaysia Plan prioritized healthcare, with significant public funding for the construction, expansion and refurbishment of hospitals and health clinics, including the construction of 31 new hospitals. There were thus potential opportunities under some kind of PPP/PFI arrangement as well as opportunities for healthcare consultancies in designing and implementing a new healthcare financing mechanism.

The scoping mission to the Czech Republic in 2005 indicated that the government was considering greater private sector involvement in its mainly public healthcare sector, including PPPs and outsourcing of various services. The paediatric wing of the largest teaching hospital, Motol, was in need of serious replacement or refurbishment and was therefore identified as a potential candidate for PPP (UKTI 2005b, p. 7). The central government at the time was characterized as unlikely to make any bold changes to the health system but the regional governments, which ran most of the hospitals, were 'much more radical in their thinking' and therefore perhaps 'more open to new ideas of clinical management, investment (PPPs) or contract management by international companies' (UKTI 2005b, p. 15). A change of central government in an election could bring more market reforms. It was seen as likely that the country would in time go down the British route of using PPP to fund most capital projects, and even the current government was evaluating several possible pilot projects. Since, like many other eastern European countries, there was a relative over-supply of hospital (as opposed to primary care) provision, refurbishment of hospitals was seen as more likely than new-build at this time. At the time of writing, PPP Centrum, the Czech Ministry of

Finance's centre for PPP implementation, had information on three substantial healthcare PPPs alongside a range of other PPP infrastructure projects (PPP Centrum 2006a,b,c). One of these was the construction and maintenance under a 15–20 year contract of a green-field seven-floor wing of the Na Homolce Hospital in Prague, an acute hospital owned by the central Ministry of Health (MoH). The Ministry of Health envisaged the project as 'a pilot project to introduce PPP into [the] Czech health sector and from Czech MoH perspective it shall prove PPP projects can be successfully delivered' (PPP Centrum 2006b). The consultancy firm PricewaterhouseCoopers won the bid to be the principal advisor on this project.

The scoping mission to Romania included, among others, a representative of the International Hospitals Group, an international hospital construction, equipping, management, commissioning and consulting company based in the UK, and the healthcare consultancy HLSP, a member of the consulting group Mott MacDonald which provides technical assistance on PFI projects in the UK and globally. The report notes the shift, which Romania shares in common with a number of other eastern European countries (Holden 2005b), from a state owned and financed system to a social health insurance model, which allows for greater decentralization and some private sector participation, such as the plans for polyclinics to introduce 'choice and contestability' (UKTI 2005c, p. 8). The Romanian government had recently negotiated a World Bank loan of $168 million (US$) based on an agreed 8-year strategy that would include increasing the role of the private sector. This strategy would be binding on the current and any successor government, and would provide opportunities for foreign healthcare firms, including building and managing facilities. 'The parallel nature of healthcare reform' in the UK and Romania was seen by the scoping mission as one positive feature creating opportunities for British businesses (UKTI 2005c, p. 10).

The government planned to introduce 'aspects of privatization' such as PPPs for hospitals, although 'several interpretations had been drawn about how the concept might be implemented' (UKTI 2005c, p. 10). At the time, none of the major international healthcare corporations had been attracted to Romania, but this may have been about to change with the tendering for the management of the 1200 bed Fundeni Tertiary Hospital in Bucharest. This was to be a test case, so that if successful the government would seek to contract PPPs with other international hospital operators to manage hospitals. These PPP reforms were aimed at introducing professional management into hospitals, transferring the responsibility for capital expenditure to private partners, and allowing hospitals to treat private as well as public patients. Hospitals would therefore be run by private operators as concessions under long-term contracts, with the assets reverting to the government at the end of the concession period (UKTI 2005c, pp. 13–14). Operators would have an incentive to provide services for private as well as public patients, as a new law was to introduce private health insurance, with an expected uptake of 10–15% of the population.

Hungary was identified as a country where British healthcare companies already enjoy success, with future opportunities seen as lying in consultancy, investment projects, and healthcare and hospital management services, as well as medical equipment and consumables sales (UKTI 2006c). In Poland, the Public Private Partnership Act (2005) provided for a major expansion of PPP projects, including in healthcare. Poland was the biggest recipient of European Union funds, and the implementation of the new law would facilitate 'the absorption' of these funds (UKTI 2006d, p. 3). The UK, the report on Poland claims, 'is seen in Poland as the most experienced and competent administration in PPP matters, with an enviable practice of transparency, still lacking in Poland'. Therefore, 'In order to reduce resistance and encourage the process in Poland, some good first examples of successful PPP projects are required' (UKTI 2006d, p. 4).

Export strategy as policy transfer

The reports discussed above indicate that there are a number of potential opportunities for British firms in providing PPP/PFI services to developing and east European country governments. The reports claim that there is a widespread acceptance of PPP/PFI among many of these governments, although means of influencing them in this direction are also elaborated. As discussed above, however, the PPP/PFI policy has been extremely controversial in the UK and its benefits and drawbacks have been vigorously debated. It is possible that the drawbacks of PPP/PFI may be accentuated for developing countries as a result of severe resource constraints, locking them into long-term arrangements which may divert resources from elsewhere. PPP/PFI appears to release more resources in the short-term, but entails expensive commitments in the long-term, and cannot be renegotiated by the public sector without huge penalties. The apparent transfer of risk to the private sector may be even more illusory in developing countries than in developed countries, where technical know-how and the administrative capacity to enforce rigorous contracts with private sector providers may be lacking. The number of private sector firms willing to take on work in such countries may be fewer, and the firms themselves may consider developing countries to be more risky, and may therefore demand more guarantees and loopholes when taking on projects.

PPP/PFI needs to be evaluated in terms of whether it advances health policy goals in developing and eastern European countries. Health policy in any country may in fact pursue a number of different, sometimes competing goals. Given the resource constraints in developing countries, even more so than in other countries, efficiency and equity goals are paramount. This means that policy should attempt to bring about the greatest possible health gain with the resources available, but do so as far as is possible in an equitable manner. Ensuring access to suitable services for the poor becomes a particular challenge in such countries. It is doubtful that PPP/PFI provides the most effective means of meeting these goals, given its unproven efficiency and its long-term inflexibility. Furthermore, as the UK government acknowledges, all evaluations of PPP/PFI are constrained by the fact that most operational projects are still within the first five years of what could be 25-year contract periods (HM Treasury 2006, p. 46). The International Monetary Fund (IMF) similarly acknowledges that in relation to PPPs, 'there are as yet few general lessons that can be drawn, especially from the experiences of emerging market economies and developing countries' (IMF 2004, p. 6).

The management and technical capacity issues discussed above were seldom mentioned in any of the scoping reports, except to claim that PPP/PFI 'has aspects of improved governance' (UKTI 2005a, p. 15). This claim was used to argue that UK DFID should fund PPP-related consultancy work in India through the PPIAF facility. The UK government has tried to address problems of management and technical expertise at home by employing or contracting with private sector advisors, and introducing various means of expanding the capacity of the public sector to evaluate the quality of advice given to it and to negotiate and manage PFI contracts (HM Treasury 2003, 2006). Advice to developing and eastern European countries on these matters may come from donor countries and international institutions, often through facilities such as PPIAF or through private consultancies funded by these, as well as from Partnerships UK, the UK Treasury's own PPP whose mission is entirely to support public authorities in the implementation of PPPs. DFID (2002), the IMF (2004) and the World Bank all acknowledge the importance of 'the institutional capacity and expertise required to capture benefits while mitigating the associated risks', as Nikolic and Maikisch (2006, p. 6) put it, yet they all tend to argue that where services can be contracted out to the private sector they should be (see IMF 2004, p. 11). International institutions, donor governments and private consultancies, therefore, all act as conduits for policy transfer rather than simply as neutral advisors (Wedel 2001, Hilary 2004).

Greenaway *et al.* (2004) argue that PFI was ideologically-driven from the beginning, and characterize it as a 'meta-policy' developed outside of the health sector and imposed upon it. PFI has necessitated the inclusion of private sector policy networks in its implementation in the UK, whilst medical and other networks that have been critical of it have been excluded from the policy process (Greenaway *et al.* 2004, p. 521). Similarly, the very nature of the healthcare industrial strategy is such that private sector interests have been integrally involved in the development and implementation of it from the beginning. In seeking to export PPP/PFI services abroad, what started out as an export strategy necessarily ends up looking like part of a conscious process of policy transfer in order to create the environment for more business. A recurring theme in the scoping reports discussed above was the view that host country officials did not fully understand the concept of PPP/PFI and that they had to 'learn' this. This kind of argument was sometimes advanced alongside statements that the host country government was already keen on the policy. It was then concluded that various strategies should be put in place to either inform the host country of how PPP/PFI worked, or to convince them that it was the answer to their problems. These included utilizing existing mechanisms put in place by DFID and the international institutions.

The Romanian case detailed above is a good example of this, where the UK scoping report made it clear that opportunities had arisen from the strategy agreed by the Romanian government with the World Bank, which would be binding on the country for a period of 8 years, regardless of any change of government. European Union funds were seen as an important source of financing in Poland, which could be 'absorbed' by PPP projects. Similarly, bilateral aid between governments may have conditions attached, and the UK healthcare export strategy makes a point of involving DFID within it. In relation to the Indian example, it is suggested that PPP related consultancy work could be met from DFID funding for technical assistance even though, 'Normally DFID would not relate any assistance specifically to the UK' (UKTI 2005a, p. 15). For their part, developing country governments may request some form of aid as the price for adopting the model being sold to them, as in the case of the Indian government. The promotion of private sector solutions is in fact entirely consistent with DFID's approach, which is situated alongside the pro-private sector approach of the World Bank and other international institutions (DFID 2004).

The key role of consultancies in PPP/PFI advice and implementation, both domestically and abroad, potentially creates a self-reinforcing process in which greater private sector involvement is always seen as beneficial. The involvement of consultancies in health sector reform may therefore facilitate greater opportunities for foreign (particularly British) companies in PPPs and other services. As the UK was the originator of PPP/PFI reforms, UK companies have greater experience than those of other developed countries and are best placed to take advantage of the spread of such reforms internationally. The provision of genuinely impartial advice and the building of independent core public sector capacity in developing and eastern European countries in relation to these matters would seem to be crucial if they are to make informed and beneficial decisions that are consistent with their health policy goals. These goals need to be clearly identified and given priority before any consideration of whether PPP/PFI is an appropriate model for adoption by such countries.

Conclusions: policy transfer as export strategy

The drive to export PPP/PFI services is rooted in the wider British health industry export strategy, and is therefore informed not by health policy and its goals, nor by development policy as such, but by industrial and trade policy. It leads to an attempt to influence developing country governments towards adopting the British PPP/PFI model in order to lay the basis for the winning of consultancy, construction and other contracts by British firms. If successful, this strategy will itself become a mechanism of policy transfer, but one based primarily on what is good for British firms rather than what is good for the health of developing country citizens. This has important implications for the policy transfer literature since, as noted towards the beginning of this article, that literature has tended to neglect the role of material interests and private actors in policy transfer processes.

The analysis here suggests that reference to knowledge communities, or even ideology, is not sufficient to explain the form of attempted policy transfer described, whilst 'lesson drawing' is of little relevance. Consultancies and their knowledge claims are undoubtedly an important component of the process, yet the strategy is not driven primarily by these knowledge claims or even by the wider ideology within which these are situated. Direct material interests are evidently the key explanatory factor. At the level of 'endogenous structures' (Evans and Davies 1999), the strategy is clearly informed by the industrial and export needs of the British 'competition state'. At the level of agency, the strategy is an instrumental attempt at exporting particular services, to meet the needs of specific interests, regardless of the suitability to the local context of the policy that it requires to be adopted. The purported efficiency gains of PPP/PFI in the UK are unproven, yet the drawbacks of the model may be even more problematic for public health service organizations in developing and eastern European countries, where the expertise to negotiate, monitor and enforce robust contracts may be more limited. There is therefore no attempt at 'lesson-drawing', just an attempt to 'sell' the policy itself in order to literally sell specific services. The strategy is thus intentional and rational, but in the service of particular commercial interests rather than in the pursuit of better policy. The analysis thus illustrates an important form of attempted coercive transfer, and alerts us to a gap in the literature and its associated typologies in terms of the importance of material interests and commercial actors in policy transfer.

Acknowledgements
The author would like to thank Rob Hulme, Mark Evans and anonymous referees for their comments regarding the policy transfer aspects of this article.

References

ABHI, 2005. *The future of Britain's health: healthcare industries manifesto.* London: Association of British Healthcare Industries.

ABHI, 2009. http://www.abhi.org.uk/about/ABHIactivities.aspx [Accessed 24 April 2009].

Adler, E. and Haas, P.M., 1992. Conclusion: epistemic communities, world order, and the creation of a reflective research program. *International organization,* 46 (1), 367–390.

Audit Commission., 2006. Learning the lessons from financial failure in the NHS. London: Audit Commission.

Batley, R. and Larbi, G., 2004. *The changing role of government: the reform of public services in developing countries.* Basingstoke: Palgrave Macmillan.

British Healthcare., 2006. *A good prognosis.* www.britishhealthcare.org.uk [Accessed 28 September 2006].

Cerny, P., 1990. *The changing architecture of politics.* London: Sage.

Cerny, P. and Evans, M., 2004. Globalisation and public policy under new labour. *Policy studies,* 25 (1), 51–65.

de la Porte, C. and Deacon, B., 2002. *Contracting companies and consultants: the EU and the social policy of accession countries. GASPP Occasional Paper No 9/2002.* Helsinki: STAKES.

DFID, 2002. *Making connections: infrastructure for poverty reduction.* London: Department for International Development.

DFID, 2004. *Public private partnerships in infrastructure: a brief overview of DFID programmes of support.* London: Department for International Development.

DH, 2005. *DH international: overview.* http://www.dh.gov.uk/PolicyAndGuidance/Interna tionalTrade [Accessed 19 October 2005].

DHI, 2003a. *A year of progress.* London: Department of Health.

DHI, 2003b. *Malaysia: healthcare fact finding mission January 2003.* London: Department of Health.

DHI, 2004a. *Improving healthcare around the world: an export strategy.* London: Department of Health.

DHI, 2004b. *China: healthcare scoping mission, 10–20 March 2003.* London: Department of Health.

DHI, 2005. *International partnerships: annual report 2004/5.* London: Department of Health.

Dolowitz, D. and Marsh, D., 1996. Who learns what from whom: a review of the policy transfer literature. *Political studies,* 44 (2), 343–357.

Dunnigan, M.G. and Pollock, A.M., 2003. Downsizing of acute inpatient beds associated with private finance initiative: Scotland's case study. *British medical journal,* 326, 1–6.

Evans, M. and Davies, J., 1999. Understanding policy transfer: a multi-level, multi-disciplinary perspective. *Public administration,* 77 (2), 361–385.

Farnsworth, K., 2006. Capital to the rescue? New Labour's business solutions to old welfare problems. *Critical social policy,* 26 (4), 817–842.

Greenaway, J., Salter, B., and Hart, S., 2004. The evolution of a 'meta-policy': the case of the private finance initiative and the health sector. *British journal of politics & international relations*, 6 (4), 507–526.

Haas, P.M., 1992. Introduction: epistemic communities and international policy coordination. *International organization*, 46 (1), 1–35.

Hebson, G., Grimshaw, D., and Marchington, M., 2003. PPPs and the changing public sector ethos: case-study evidence from the health and local authority sectors. *Work, employment and society*, 17 (3), 481–501.

Hellowell, M. and Pollock, A.M., 2006. *The impact of PFI on Scotland's NHS: a briefing.* Edinburgh: Centre for International Public Health Policy.

Hilary, J., 2004. *Profiting from poverty: privatisation consultants, DfID and public services.* London: War on Want.

HITF, 2004. *Better health through partnership: a programme for action.* London: Healthcare Industries Task Force/Department of Health.

HITF WG4, 2004. *Progress summary/overarching assumptions.* Healthcare Industries Task Force Working Group 4. Available from: http://www.advisorybodies.doh.gov.uk/hitf/wg4summjan04.htm [Accessed 2 October 2006].

HM Treasury, 2000. *Public private partnerships: the government's approach.* London: The Stationery Office.

HM Treasury, 2003. *PFI: meeting the investment challenge.* London: The Stationery Office.

HM Treasury, 2006. *PFI: strengthening long-term partnerships.* London: The Stationery Office.

Ho, T. and Ali-Zade, N., 2001. Eastern European hospitals in transition. *EuroHealth*, 7 (3), 8–14.

Holden, C., 1999. Globalization, social exclusion and labour's new work ethic. *Critical social policy*, 19 (4), 529–538.

Holden, C., 2003. Decommodification and the workfare state. *Political studies review*, 1 (3), 303–316.

Holden, C., 2005a. The internationalization of corporate healthcare: extent and emerging trends. *Competition & change*, 9 (2), 185–203.

Holden, C., 2005b. Privatization and trade in health services: a review of the evidence. *International journal of health services*, 35 (4), 675–689.

Holden, C., 2009. Regulation, accountability and trade in health services. *In*: E. Mordini, ed. *Ethics and health in the global village: bioethics, globalization and human rights.* Rome: CIC Edizioni Internazionali.

Hulme, R. and Hulme, M., 2008. The global transfer of social policy. *In*: N. Yeates, ed. *Understanding global social policy.* Bristol: Policy Press.

Ikenberry, G.J., 1990. The international spread of privatization policies: inducements, learning, and 'policy bandwagoning'. *In*: E.Z. Suleiman and J. Waterbury, eds. *The political economy of public sector reform and privatization.* Boulder: Westview Press.

IMF, 2004. *Public–private partnerships.* Washington, DC: International Monetary Fund Fiscal Affairs Department.

IPPR, 2001. *Building better partnerships. Commission on public–private partnerships.* London: Institute for Public Policy Research.

Loeppky, R., 2004. International restructuring, health and the advanced industrial state. *New political economy*, 9 (4), 493–513.

McKee, M., Edwards, N., and Atun, R., 2006. Public–private partnerships for hospitals. *Bulletin of the world health organization*, 84, 890–896.

Minogue, M., 2004. Public management and regulatory governance: problems of policy transfer to developing countries. *In*: P. Cook, *et al.*, eds. *Leading issues in competition, regulation and development.* Cheltenham: Edward Elgar.

Nikolic, I.A. and Maikisch, H., 2006. *Public–private partnerships and collaboration in the health sector: an overview with case studies from recent European experience.* Washington: The World Bank.

Polidano, C. and Hulme, D., 1999. Public management reform in developing countries: issues and outcomes. *Public management*, 1 (1), 121–132.

Pollock, A.M., Price, D., and Player, S., 2005. *The private finance initiative: a policy built on sand. An examination of the treasury's evidence base for cost and time overrun data in value for money policy and appraisal.* London: Unison.

PPP Centrum, 2006a. *Information on PPP project: hotel-type lodging house and parking site in the central military hospital in Prague.* Available from: http://www.pppcentrum.cz/res/data/003/000509.pdf [Accessed 30 November 2006].

PPP Centrum, 2006b. *Information on PPP Project: Na Homolce Hospital, Prague.* Available from: http://www.pppcentrum.cz/res/data/003/000517.pdf [Accessed 30 November 2006].

PPP Centrum, 2006c. *Information on PPP Project: Pardubice Regional Hospital.* Available from: http://www.pppcentrum.cz/res/data/003/000501.pdf [Accessed 30 November 2006].

Reich, R., 1991. *The work of nations.* London: Simon and Schuster.

Rose, R., 1991. What is lesson-drawing? *Journal of public policy*, 11 (1), 3–30.

Saint-Martin, D., 2000. The formation of the new entrepreneurial state and the growth of modern management consultancy. *In*: D. Braun and A. Busch, eds. *Public policy and political ideas.* Cheltenham: Edward Elgar.

Stone, D., 2004. Transfer agents and global networks in the 'transnationalization' of policy. *Journal of european public policy*, 11 (3), 545–566.

UKTI, 2005a. *Public private partnerships scoping mission to India March 2005.* London: UK Trade & Investment.

UKTI, 2005b. *The Czech Healthcare sector: fact finding mission to the Czech Republic 6–8 June 2005.* London: UK Trade & Investment.

UKTI, 2005c. *British healthcare fact finding mission to Romania 4–6 October 2004.* London: UK Trade & Investment.

UKTI, 2006a. *Sector report: healthcare industry China.* London: UK Trade & Investment.

UKTI, 2006b. *Sector report: healthcare and medical India.* London: UK Trade & Investment.

UKTI, 2006c. *Sector report: healthcare sector Hungary.* London: UK Trade & Investment.

UKTI, 2006d. *Public private partnerships in Poland.* London: UK Trade & Investment.

WDM, 2005. *Dirty aid, dirty water: the UK Government's push to privatise water and sanitation in poor countries.* London: World Development Movement.

Wedel, J.R., 2001. *Collision and collusion: the strange case of Western aid to Eastern Europe.* New York: Palgrave.

Accounting for policy change through multi-level analysis: the reform of the Bank of England in the post-war era

Sucheen Patel

Department of Politics, Queen Mary College, University of London, Mile End, London E1 4NS, UK

This article examines the post-war institutional reform of the Bank of England. In 1946, the Attlee government nationalised the Bank of England as the first of a series of measures for public ownership. In 1997, some five decades on, the Blair government reversed this arrangement as its' first task in office, granting the Bank of England operational independence. Drawing on models of policy change an inductive analysis is undertaken of the factors that brought about these policies to shed light on their analogous nature. This involves the development of a multi-level explanation of policy change which integrates policy transfer analysis with incrementalism and the policy streams approaches. The empirical investigation explores the marginal changes to monetary policy leading to the decisions, the exogenous basis underlying the reforms and issues of economic control and credibility for the Labour Party. It observes that a combination of these dynamics was critical to the ensuing institutional adjustments in the status of the central bank.

Introduction

The institutional arrangements of the Bank of England (BoE) have been the subject of two fundamental developments since the Second World War: nationalisation in 1946 and independence in 1997. Both reforms have generally been considered as part of a slue of policy measures. The nationalisation of the BoE transpired in March 1946 after Clement Attlee's Labour Party was elected in July 1945, replacing the wartime coalition administration with a considerable mandate. Passage of the 1946 BoE Act was the first measure undertaken by the Labour government. In the inter-war period, proposals for central bank nationalisation (CBN) intensified as the merits of state intervention in society were reviewed in the political arena. At this juncture the central ideology of the rising political left was socialism, which supported the concept of nationalising public institutions. The origins of the reform can hence be traced to the collective ideals of the Labour Party and its perception of the way the economy should operate (see Labour Party 1926, 1928a,b, 1932, 1934, 1937).

Economic upheavals also had a part in stimulating proposals for CBN. The economic downturn of the late 1920s and the subsequent departure of sterling from the gold standard in 1931 certainly placed CBN on the political agenda. The idea was initially combined with a commitment to nationalise the BoE together with the joint stock banks (a synonym for the commercial banks of the time). The scope of the proposal adjusted with the passage of time and was refined to reflect Labour's judgement on the level of economic control required to govern effectively. The party's stance on the BoE solidified with the onset and conclusion of the Second World War. While the reform made little operational difference to the BoE (Dell 1997, pp. 76–77), it enabled the party to implement its political manifesto upon entering office.

An institutional shift in the status of the BoE emerged half a century after its nationalisation. The policy for BoE independence was implemented 5 days after Tony Blair's Labour Party entered office in May 1997. Underpinning this decision was the political benefits of the reform in terms of financial credibility. In this setting, a similar mindset to that of the 1945 period transposed the 1997 decision for independence amongst political actors, except this time the policy was turned on its head. The origins of BoE independence can be traced to a transformation in economic thought, which impacted upon political events beginning in the mid-1970s. An ideological shift from Keynesianism to monetarism validated arguments for depoliticising public institutions.

Specifically, political acceptance of the monetarist vertical Phillips curve (which refuted the perceived trade-off between inflation and unemployment) (Brown 2000), the push for and adoption of inflation targets from 1992 (HM Treasury 1992b,c), and the increased credibility of central bank independence (CBI) from theory to practice (Wood *et al.* 1993, pp. 11–12), are all central explanatory factors in the emergence of an independent BoE. A persistent push for CBI in the political process was also evident (HM Treasury 1988, 1991, 1992a, 1993). Labour's need to establish competence in managing economic policy via an autonomous BoE developed against this backcloth. By granting the central bank its independence, the government acquired the credibility to pursue economic growth. Fundamentally, policy-makers wanted to achieve the same objectives by using diametrically opposite measures: whereas in 1945 they thought monetary control was the appropriate measure, in 1997 this view was supplanted by a belief in monetary autonomy.

There has been no specific attempt to account for these reforms in a comparative context, an omission which this work sets out to repair. The contention of this article is that the fundamental driving forces behind the two monetary decisions are analogous and can be elucidated using models of policy change. This study is divided into two parts. Part one delineates the respective monetary reforms. It outlines the historical aspects underpinning BoE nationalisation and BoE independence and provides the setting for theoretical analysis. Part two discusses the models of policy change germane to the cases, namely: (1) incrementalism, to explain the long-term background to the reforms, (2) policy transfer, to account for the external influences, and (3) policy streams, to consider issues of monetary control and credibility that predisposed the Labour Party to adjust the institutional status of the BoE, thus reversing earlier policy from within the same party. It employs these models to demonstrate an association between the factors that brought about the policy for BoE nationalisation and a similar set of factors that set in motion the policy to grant independence to it.

Towards a nationalised Bank of England

The move to nationalise the BoE was situated against the need for greater government authority over finance and industry. The experience of deflation and unemployment in the 1920s induced plans for monetary control but lacked co-ordination and detail. An early attempt for CBN came in February 1926 when the left wing of the Labour Party presented a Private Member's Bill to legislate for government control of the BoE. Significantly, the Bill failed to set in motion and a Second Reading was not taken (see Hennessy 1992). The first key party statement that adopted the scheme came in 1928. *Labour and the nation* considered BoE nationalisation in a representative form. It did not advocate sweeping changes to the operation of monetary policy and signified a relatively moderate political stance. With its associated memorandum, *Banking and currency policy*, the party promoted the BoE as a public corporation. Hereafter the idea became more widely attached to the control of the joint stock banks.

Monetary control was deficient in the 1930s largely because the BoE was in private hands. Financial interests were served before the interests of the electorate, a situation galvanised by the exit from the gold standard in 1931, in which a Bankers' ramp brought down the Labour government. The role of the BoE in this debacle caught the attention of the political left hereon in. Mistrust of the financial sector advanced calls for sweeping nationalisation. Nationalisation of the BoE was seen as the natural remedy for preventing future economic crises. In response to this, the party developed extended plans for public control. Its General Election manifesto (Labour Party 1931) pledged to nationalise the banking and credit system. Hence, a key purpose of the proposal 'was as a reassuring therapy for Labour members, a symbol that the Bank could no longer sabotage a Labour Government ...' (Morgan 1984, p. 100). Tomlinson (2004, p. 175) writes:

> ... central to Labour's approach, if diffuse in its consequences, was the belief that the (unelected) City was too powerful in its ability to shape economic policy, compared with elected (Labour) governments. Labour believed the City had to be persuaded or coerced into supporting government aims. Such a view was built upon Labour's interpretation of the events of 1931, when the City was seen as having imposed its priorities on enough of the credulous Labour Cabinet to have caused the collapse of the government.

This event underpinned Labour's economic approach and provided the political context to its future monetary plans. For Chester (1975, p. 879), Labour had two purposes in mind: 'The first was to exercise some general control over the policies pursued by the Bank of England and the second was to control the general credit policy of the commercial banks.' Specifically, Singleton (1995, p. 18) adds: 'Public ownership of the Bank of England would assist the government to channel more funds into industrial investment.' While its 1932 policy document, *Currency, banking and finance*, advocated public control of the BoE alone, the party resolved to also nationalise the joint stock banks. The 1934 policy statement *For socialism and peace* reaffirmed this commitment. However, this branching out of policy to encompass the joint stock banks culminated in a departure back to the previous, more pragmatic policy and the idea that the BoE alone should be nationalised. The modification of its monetary strategy was embodied in *Labour's immediate programme* (1937). The BoE would be nationalised alone. This was a critical step, and one, which despite a transitory move for the control of the joint stock banks in 1944, was not significantly altered in regard to the eventual policy in 1946.

A growth of CBN overseas was also evident during this time. Other countries took ownership of their central banks in order to gain greater control of the levers of economic change. Indeed, prior to the BoE's nationalisation a number of Commonwealth and European countries had nationalised their central banks to guard their currencies from both endogenous and exogenous pressures and as a channel for managing the post-war reconstruction of their economies (see Table 1). By formulating a policy for public ownership of the BoE, Labour decision-makers realised that this would generate a framework to reconstruct the British economy. They subsequently identified the institutional position of a number of central banks to make the case for nationalisation of the BoE. In his memoirs, Chancellor Hugh Dalton (1962, p. 43) observed: 'Nowhere else in the Commonwealth was there a central bank of this kind. Everywhere there was either complete or substantial State ownership and State control.' Measures were subsequently set in motion to legislate for nationalisation. A Labour document addressed the issue of timing:

> The Tories talked stupidly about the Act's 'wasting our time' and distracting our attention from important things like getting industry and trade moving. This is nonsense—it's as if we began to build a house without clearing the ground for it, or without making certain that the foundations are sound and will endure. Building Britain's industry and trade is the biggest job we have to do and a healthy and sound financial system is an indispensable foundation (Labour Party 1946, pp. 16–17).

Towards an independent Bank of England

The economic context to CBI was situated by the need for greater government credibility over the financial markets after the failure to meet monetary and exchange rate targets in the 1980s. A depoliticised economic environment was cultivated in which rules replaced discretion. This helped to underline the benefits of an independent BoE as a compelling remedy to previous economic crises. Fundamentally, BoE independence is linked to the policy changes since 1992 and the recognition of long-run vertical Phillips curve inferences. A process of building on earlier monetary strategies was evident as decision-makers explored variables at

Table 1.   Nationalised central banks since the First World War.

Year	Central bank
1936	Denmark: Danmarks National Bank New Zealand: Reserve Bank of New Zealand
1938	Canada: Bank of Canada
1945	France: Banque de France
1946	United Kingdom: Bank of England
1948	Netherlands: Nederlandsche Bank Belgium: Banque Nationale de Belgique
1949	Norway: Norges Bank India: Reserve Bank of India

Source: Cappie *et al.* 1994.

the margin. These were predicated on the perceived best way to anchor monetary policy. The ERM crisis in 1992 redefined the problem of monetary policy, which was unsuitably fixed and thought to be opaque and unaccountable. The post-ERM framework led to a more open system of setting interest rates.

The policy preceding independence made technical modifications that were essential to its implementation in Britain. The objective of securing monetary credibility was a powerful one and the solutions included inflation targeting and CBI. Despite efforts by the Treasury in the late 1980s and early 1990s, and the BoE's yearning for independence, this was a conception whose time had not yet come (see Table 2). Instead, decision-makers settled for the former of the two policy options. Rather than using the money supply or exchange rate to modify interest rates to target inflation, by 1992 policy-makers resolved to use interest rates to target inflation directly. The establishment of inflation targets nevertheless helped to fashion proposals for CBI in the political field. Indeed, they were a key component for BoE independence.

The monetary policy community comprised academics and central bankers, who interacted with political actors. The consensus in the 1990s was that CBI would lower inflation expectations and, *ergo*, lower inflation in the long term. Former Conservative Chancellors, Lawson and Lamont, accepted the case for delegation. However, they considered it for different reasons, believing it to be the most appropriate solution to their respective political problems (see Patel 2008). From September 1993, it was decided that the Treasury would no longer scrutinise the BoE's *Inflation Report* in advance of publication. From November 1993, the BoE was given some discretion over the execution of monetary decisions. From April 1994, the minutes of the monthly monetary meetings between the Chancellor and the Governor were promulgated with a 6-week delay.

Acceptance of the implications of the vertical Phillips curve was significant, for it made CBI politically advantageous. For Goodhart (2003, p. 65), it was 'the most crucial change that has occurred in our way of thinking about the working of the macroeconomic system'. It was significant because with no trade-off this meant no political judgment had to be made:

Table 2.   Proposals for an independent Bank of England.

Date	Actor	Interest
September 1988	Nigel Lawson	Conservative Government
March 1991	Norman Lamont	Conservative Government
June 1992	Norman Lamont	Conservative Government
December 1992	Edward Balls	Fabian Society
January 1993	Norman Lamont	Conservative Government
November 1993	Eric Roll	Centre for Economic Policy Research
December 1993	Giles Radice	Treasury Select Committee
January 1994	Nicholas Budgen	Private Member's Bill
May 1997	Gordon Brown	Labour Government

> The period from 1992–97 set up a position in which independence was the next logical step. It was the last step to achieve a disproportionate amount of credit (Treasury official, personal interview, 27 September 2004).

In this vein, CBI was reconsidered in the early 1990s by Blair's Labour Party, which had faced a profound economic credibility deficit. Being seen as poor money managers and the party of inflation saw the appraisal of a new monetary strategy centring on institutional reform of the BoE.

The level of accountability required to make CBI an acceptable proposition was an important consideration for Labour. Previously this was unsatisfactory. However, from 1992, accountability became an issue that equated directly with monetary policy. The post-ERM measures implemented to fortify the transparency and accountability of the policy process also addressed, by default, many of the concerns of CBI. As such, these policies were crucial in paving the way for independence. Furthermore, in 1993 the Treasury Select Committee and the Roll Committee came to favour an independent and accountable BoE. As an all-party committee, the former softened the parliamentary process and tempered Labour's opposition to the reform, while the latter crystallised support for the reform from the financial community. Similarly, the House of Lords Economic Affairs Committee advocated CBI. Against these endeavours, Labour's eventual scheme for CBI confronted the issues that previously stalled implementation (see Brown 1997).

In order to achieve political credibility it was important for Labour to improve the quality of evidence in policy-making. A prominent feature of Labour's plan for BoE independence was the scrutiny of other central bank systems. Policy-makers swiftly narrowed down the models that corresponded with their economic objectives. 'Many forms of independent central banks were ruled out almost immediately' (Treasury official, personal interview, 7 May 2003). The structure and functions of the BoE were contemplated by policy-makers in the context of not only other exemplar models of independent central banks, but also the British political environment. 'Labour found a solution that existed somewhere else in the world and fitted with our parliamentary system' (Treasury official, personal interview, 27 September 2004). Since Britain traditionally placed a high value on democratic control, this was something the BoE would have to reflect. *Ergo*, it was a priority for policy-makers to incorporate mechanisms in their plans for the central bank to be transparent and accountable to the electorate via parliament.

Political developments made CBI possible. While the Conservatives would not implement it, Labour was bolstered by substantial electoral support and its strong mandate provided greater scope over the programme of reforms it could institute. In this setting, BoE independence was legitimised and moved up the agenda as an item for consideration. The economic gains were important for implementation but the political gains in terms of anti-inflationary credibility were crucial for policy change. Brown was certain he got the timing of the policy right: 'It was the only time you could have done it without there being huge allegations about political manipulation ... if you had done it at two months people would have said, "He's got a problem here, hasn't he, he's trying to get out of it"' (cited Pym and Kochan 1998, p. 16). The sequence of events showed that the decision was made before Labour knew the extent of its electoral majority.

Analysis: applying models of policy change

The utilisation of theoretical models can assist us in explaining the policy process leading to the reforms. In both cases, the period which set the policies in motion was piecemeal in nature. In this vein, the 'incremental model' is useful. It views institutions as sticky and given to inertia, which results in gradual policy change. The approach conveys reliance 'on the record of past experience with small policy steps to predict the consequences of similar steps extended into the future' (Lindblom 1988, p. 172). Like all public policies, monetary policy is not made in a vacuum, without any sense of what has gone before. A policy can evolve from a process of bargaining and negotiation between decision-makers called 'partisan mutual adjustment' (Lindblom 1988, p. 184). With the concept of 'disjointed incrementalism' (Braybrooke and Lindblom 1963), policy-making is said to be underpinned by trial and error methods. The approach has been modified to incorporate issues of power and bias (Lindblom 1977). From a birds-eye perspective, the incremental model captures the step-by-step adjustments in the monetary policy process preceding institutional change.

Foreign systems of central banks influenced the policy process. From this perspective, 'policy transfer' analysis explains how policies utilised in one system emerge in another. The framework investigates how and why decision-makers turn to other systems for alternative ideas, programmes and policies. Adapting the models of Rose (1993, pp. 30–31) and Dolowitz and Marsh (2000, p. 13), Bulmer and Padgett (2004, p. 106) outline a practical typology for evaluating transfer outcomes:

> *Emulation* or copying is the strongest form of transfer, entailing 'borrowing' a policy model more or less intact from another jurisdiction (inevitably there will be some adaptation to accommodate contextual differences). *Synthesis* involves combining elements of policy from two or more different jurisdictions. *Influence* suggests a weak form of transfer in which the external exemplar(s) serve(s) merely as an inspiration for a new policy, but where institutional design occurs either *tabula rasa* or draws on extant domestic policy norms. Finally, the *abortive* variant occurs where a putative transfer is blocked by veto actors in the borrower jurisdiction.

The recognition of particular economic problems clearly concerned decision-makers in both cases. Hence, multiple streams analysis (Kingdon 1995) can be useful in explaining the character of the agenda-setting process. It views the policy process as composed of three streams: problems, policies, and politics. They permeate the government and combine at critical junctures, which produces agenda change. While the problem and policy streams interact due to the presence of 'policy entrepreneurs', the politics stream flows independently. A consensus is achieved in the problem stream through a bargaining process, in contrast to forms of persuasion and 'softening up' in the policy stream. Whereas the policy stream affects the alternative proposals, the government agenda is formed in the problem and politics streams. Changes here produce 'policy windows' and create opportunities for policy entrepreneurs to attach their solutions to problems. Accordingly, an analysis must be made of the background to the schemes for BoE nationalisation and BoE independence, the exogenous basis by which they ensued, and an exploration of the policy agendas of the Labour Party.

Explaining central bank nationalisation

The Labour Party's problem of securing adequate control of the economy was central to the policy for CBN. A broad arrangement of measures was contemplated of which public ownership of the central bank was an essential component. In order to implement its manifesto, Labour required greater monetary authority. With this dilemma the nationalisation of the BoE emanated against a backdrop of sustained review and modification of monetary proposals of the political left. The exit from the gold standard in 1931 redefined the problem. It served as a focusing event on the political agenda and demonstrated the inadequacy of monetary policy. In particular, CBN gained greater exposure as left-wing groups studied how existing monetary strategies could be extended. As Durbin (1985, p. 14) observes:

> At the policy-making level, the issue of control over the economy was decided implicitly in the party's debates over the nationalization of the commercial joint stock banks in addition to the Bank of England. At the more academic level, there was a continuing colloquy among socialist economists on the nature and principles of democratic socialist planning. The major difference of opinion lay between those who wanted to use the market pricing system to allocate resources and those who wanted to use government controls to determine output goals and to plan the physical distribution of resources.

Public policy-making at this time was formulated in a crowded arena as left-wing groups attempted to influence the party agenda. A process of 'partisan mutual adjustment' (Lindblom 1988, p. 184) was manifest in which policy ensued by way of bargaining and negotiation. Several groups or policy entrepreneurs (the Independent Labour Party, New Fabian Research Bureau, and XYZ club) discussed central bank reform. Their interaction, buoyed by the influence of Keynesianism, generated a debate surrounding an appropriate form of monetary control in the economy and shaped alternative proposals. These groups made their case through the publication of reports and pamphlets, enabling them to engage with a wider audience. Through the imposition of leftist ideology, it was their objective to reform the party's policies to assimilate a socialist perspective. They participated in the process of 'softening up', which occurred before the policy window opened in 1945.

The move to incorporate the joint stock banks in Labour's monetary plans in 1932, 1934 and 1944 is explained by the notion that decision-makers lack full political control and are pressured by other agents in the policy process, particularly in the policy implementation stage (Lindblom 1988). While the party's leadership resolved that ownership of the joint stock banks was unnecessary, the reassessment and reversal of policy is once more a product of partisan mutual adjustment. In particular, decision-makers were able to demonstrate to the wider party that CBN was sufficient to meet its monetary objectives. Broadly speaking, as Labour looked for a practical policy position its attitude on the level of monetary control required began to temper. The 'policy primeval soup' evolved with time as proposals were amended and previous variables recombined. Hence, control of the joint stock banks was at times attached to CBN and re-floated to sustain momentum as a suitable scheme in left-wing circles. Significantly, CBN was a constant element of the schemes. At this time Pollard (1979, p. 177) observes that there was very little added to theory or argumentation of the policy to nationalise the BoE. Indeed, the Labour hierarchy dismissed extensive monetary control of the economy.

Inside the party, the plan to nationalise the BoE was based on marginal trial and error interventions, exemplified by the move for and subsequent abandonment of wider monetary control. According to Leruez (1975, p. 43), 'in this crucially important area Labour's policy was cautious, not to say timid'. Eatwell (1979, p. 26) refers to the 'essential continuity after 1931 of the moderate and gradualist attitudes of most of the leadership' and this was reflected in the party programmes. It 'was a less dramatic change than has often been asserted. That said, there is no doubt that government dictated, and monetary policy was completely politicised' (Cappie 2004, p. 71). On this reading, Labour's monetary appraisal can be seen as the emergence of a practical proposal to nationalise the BoE. Giuseppi (1966, p. 188) observes Piercy's statement that: 'Some time hence ... this whole measure will be seen in its proper perspective as a wise and timely step in the evolution of our banking system.' Minor adjustments were made in shaping an appropriate framework for monetary reform, with the successive policy statements utilising the plans of previous programmes.

The growth of CBN overseas validated a similar reform in Britain. Following the decision to abandon the ownership of the joint stock banks in 1937, Pollard (1979, p. 178) comments: 'all that was left was the alignment of the central bank with the practice of other capitalist countries, in the interests of employment'. The leadership was moved by 'the need to follow the rest of the Western world by taking over the central bank, but no other banking institution' (Pollard 1979, pp. 178–179). The argument put forward was that '[t]here is complete public ownership in Australia, Canada, New Zealand, Eire, and three of the Scandinavian countries; there is complete State control of policy in France, Norway and Switzerland; and in all other Central Banks of importance' (Labour Party 1946, p. 15). As Rubenstein (2003, p. 236) confirms, '[m]any of these measures found little opposition and appeared to be inevitable ... it was obviously anomalous that the Bank of England, which set interest rates, should be in private ownership'. Moreover, a memorandum from the Dominions Office to the Treasury on 3 August 1945 outlined the technical composition of several central banks in making the case for BoE nationalisation (PRO 1945).

However, while the status of foreign central bank models was important for Labour, specific arrangements of CBN were not integral to the reform. In this case, what was transferred was the idea of nationalisation but not the specifics of it. It is often the case that actors are confronted with limited information and are faced with institutional and structural constraints (Dolowitz 2000). Policy transfer may therefore be based upon an inaccurate or subjective assessment of the 'real' situation. To this end, transfer is undertaken within the confines of 'bounded rationality' (Simon 1957) or 'disjointed incrementalism' (Lindblom 1988). The policy for BoE nationalisation reflects this line of thought. Labour decision-makers searched for information to substantiate this position, which so happened to be found in abundance overseas. Fundamentally, the fact that many other central banks were government controlled supported the argument for a similar repositioning of the BoE's status.

Political factors also assisted BoE nationalisation. The election of the Attlee government in July 1945 created a policy window following a lengthy period of gradual policy-making. Contrary to Lindblom's incremental model, Kingdon (1995, p. 170) stresses the importance of quick action in the short duration of an open window. The notion of policy-making occurring in small steps is countered by the premise that the big steps are always taken very quickly or not at all. Access to Labour leaders was fundamental to the adoption of proposals. While groups such as the NFRB and ILP played a role in advancing socialist thought, they did not dominate the policy process in terms of proposing detailed monetary schemes. Rather, well-connected and persistent policy entrepreneurs are usually more likely to succeed at 'coupling' (Kingdon 1995, pp. 180–181). Here, Labour's unofficial group of financial experts, the XYZ club, came into its own. By its authoritative position, political connections, and wisdom, the XYZ had some claim to a hearing (see Dalton 1957, pp. 23–24, Davenport 1974, pp. 75–76). The group had direct contact with Dalton and channelled the debate towards the significance of CBN (Howson 1993, p. 71).

As the policy window opened, with the support of Labour leaders, the politically expedient proposal emerged at the top of the party's agenda. CBN alone survived the selection process of the policy primeval soup. It was embedded in the party's ideological beliefs and concordant with the values of the policy community. It struck the right balance between the government setting the wider remit of the central bank and the BoE having the necessary apparatus to dictate an appropriate monetary policy to the joint stock banks. Ultimately, political support for CBN and a dearth of opposition facilitated its rise in the public agenda and saw the proposal transform into policy.

Explaining central bank independence

Surrounding the reform for CBI incremental policy-making was evident by a series of gradual not-system-shifting changes to the BoE's operations. Monetary policy-making at this time was somewhat constrained. For Powell (1991, p. 197), 'the self-reinforcing feedback mechanisms that support path dependent processes make it difficult for organisations to explore alternative options'. Given this, it is evident that the organisational make-up of policy-making in the Treasury was not conducive to the idea of CBI in the early 1990s. Monetary policy was split into two entities: Monetary Group 1 and Monetary Group 2. The former were administrators, in charge of policy, and for whom monetary policy was a political decision to be made by those accountable to the electorate. The latter were specialists, who gave advice, and for whom monetary policy was an economic decision, which supported independence. It is easy to see how the debate on CBI was restricted. This is not to say that the conception did not pervade the Treasury. Indeed, 'there were piles of papers on independent central banks. We edged towards it but the decisive step wasn't there' (Treasury official 2004).

Recognition of the vertical Phillips heralded a change in the direction of monetary policy and created conditions in which CBI was scrutinised in a positive light. Indeed, when Brown accepted the monetarist assertion that there was no long-term trade-off between unemployment and inflation, his view on the status of the BoE changed. Political control over monetary policy had no economic benefits. Conversely, delegation would engender political integrity. The credibility deficit was exacerbated for Labour because of its difficult past experiences of economic management. From a theoretical perspective, policy-making inadvertently ensued from the monetarist doctrine and was gradual in nature.

Moreover, the policy primeval soup was soon dominated by this paradigm, which triumphed in the selection process. It was the prevailing alternative to the extant system and received sympathetic media attention. Previous attempts at implementation and coupling the problem, policy and political streams evidently failed in the political stream. Kingdon (1995, p. 109) observes that 'conditions become defined as problems when we believe that we should do something about them'. For the Conservatives the state of monetary policy was a condition but for Labour, intertwined with its pursuit of economic credibility, it was a problem. The plans in the late 1980s and early 1990s were not persuasive. Policy entrepreneurs were unsuccessful at convincing the Conservative leadership of the benefits to CBI. However, this paved the way for the idea to be discussed in a political context.

The key to policy change was the role of the inner circle of advisers in the Labour Party. Specifically, Ed Balls developed the scheme by sounding out experts in the policy community and re-introducing it to the political left. Zahariadis (2003, p. 69) notes that being an adviser to a politician increases the political power of the entrepreneur's ideas. Brown was the principal political actor who needed to be convinced or 'softened up'. As Brown's *eminence grise*, Balls had a claim to a hearing and coupled BoE independence to Labour's problem of economic credibility. Concurrently, Labour reached into the policy stream for an alternative to the monetary regime in place. It devised a 'pick-and-mix' (Keegan 1997, p. 8) or *synthesis* model of CBI (see Bulmer and Padgett 2004, p. 106). Policy-makers met numerous central bankers and studied the institutional arrangements of various models: the German, French, Canadian, and Australian systems were considered along with the ECB model (Treasury official 2003). The idea of a single objective for inflation was utilised from New Zealand, and US practice was followed by adopting a roundtable system to conduct monetary policy transparently. The New Zealand arrangement of a single objective was diffused by policy-makers close to Brown through consultation with insiders. The insight from the US was mainly in the form of advice given on the best practice of conducting monetary policy (Brown 2002). This is something that did not feature in the nationalisation reform.

Policy transfer analysis shows that delegation is based on an informed and calculated decision. Labour policy-makers factored into their proposal the desirable features of central bank systems as they developed a suitable monetary framework for Britain. In part, this explains why the scheme was rebuffed in the 1980s and early 1990s; it did not correlate with local needs as perceived by the Prime Minister. Given that a paramount determinant of CBI in Britain was securing accountability and transparency of monetary policy, policy-makers looked abroad for solutions to ensure that their plans incorporated appropriate lines of answerability. The model formulated in 1997 addressed this concern explicitly.

The movement towards BoE independence is consistent with the depoliticisation thesis (Burnham 2001). One objective of pursuing a depoliticised strategy is to enhance government control. Subtle signs of this were evident in the new framework with the statutory retention of the responsibility to formulate monetary policy (setting the inflation target), the political override provision in the monetary policy committee's decisions, and the opaque system of selection and reselection of government nominees on the committee. Policy-makers established a credible monetary policy notwithstanding these stipulations. With its emphasis on exogenous dynamics, depoliticisation neatly assimilates policy transfer analysis of BoE independence. The internationalisation of economic policy-making certainly aided the reconsideration of CBI in Britain. However, while the reform is to some degree reflective of the broad internationalisation of policy-making it also transcends the pattern of internationalisation. Labour policy-makers were not constrained in their ability to make autonomous policy choices in spite of global policy demands. While the international policy-making environment helped to sustain the idea, this was not by itself enough for implementation. Policy transfer analysis exposes a context in which specific actions were taken in utilising overseas independent central bank frameworks for domestic purposes. The method conveys the significance of strategies adopted in the global domain that prevailed in the reforms and effectively elucidates the exogenous aspect of the reform in light of the endogenous requirements.

The policy window reopened predictably with a change of administration following the May 1997 General Election. There were particular circumstances that made BoE independence propitious. It produced a dramatic turnover of parliamentary seats in favour of Labour. The size of its majority was significant because it overwhelmed the residual 'Old' Labour antipathy towards the BoE. By securing macro-economic credibility, 'New' Labour had more scope to pursue its manifesto commitments.

Conclusions

The post-war institutional reform of the BoE is a story of how the Labour Party surmised that in the right environment, its authority over monetary policy should be adjusted through the creation of an independent central bank. This article has found substantial empirical evidence of incremental policy-making, which accounts for the period of relative stability in the policy process that surrounded the reforms. Yet, significant changes were made through the use of small steps. Broadly speaking, the reforms were not formulated and contemplated in a short timeframe. A path was generated in the political process that culminated in institutional policy change.

This article has established the value of policy transfer analysis in determining the degree to which foreign central bank systems were scrutinised in respect of the two reforms. There are, however, contrasts between the two reform processes as well as parallels. In 1946, the merit of policy transfer was used merely to support the case for institutional policy change, which was achieved through the general symbolism and character that CBN embodied, rather than through a specific model. In 1997, foreign systems were formative factors, more intensely evaluated, and tailored to address domestic concerns. The scrutiny of foreign systems was nevertheless central to the fulfilment of Labour's objectives. Multiple streams analysis was utilised to examine how the policy agenda was set inside the Labour Party and how alternatives were defined. The alternatives to the monetary system in place (CBN and CBI) emerged gradually. Hence, the reforms were underscored by a careful and measured reconsideration of a mature idea by the political left. However, while the background to the reforms was incremental, the changes themselves were dependent on the conjunction of problems, policies, and politics. The process of coupling was inured by entrepreneurial position and the availability of policy windows. In sum, the explanatory strengths derived from integrating these three theoretical models is self-evident. In combination, they can be utilised to clarify which variables influence and shape policy outcomes from pre-decision-making and agenda-setting through to decision-making and implementation thus providing a holistic understanding of the policy process.

References

Braybrooke, D. and Lindblom, C., 1963. *A strategy of decision: policy evaluation as a social process*. London: Collier-Macmillan.

Brown, G., 1997. *Statement to the House of Commons on the Bank of England*. London: HM Treasury, 20 May.

Brown, G., 2000. *The conditions for high and stable growth and employment: lecture to the Royal Economic Society*. London: HM Treasury, 13 July.

Brown, G., 2002. *Speech by the Chancellor Gordon Brown at the Official Opening of the new Treasury Building*. London: HM Treasury, 25 September.

Bulmer, S. and Padgett, S., 2004. Policy transfer in the European Union: an institutionalist perspective. *British journal of political science*, 35 (1), 103–126.

Burnham, P., 2001. New Labour and the politics of depoliticisation. *British journal of politics and international relations*, 3 (2), 127–149.

Cappie, F., Goodhart, C., and Schnadt, N., 1994. The development of central banking. *In*: F. Cappie, C. Goodhart and N. Schnadt, eds. *The future of central banking: the tercentenary symposium of the Bank of England*. New York: Cambridge University Press, 1–112.

Chester, N., 1975. *The nationalisation of British Industry 1945–51*. London: HMSO.

Dalton, H., 1957. *The fateful years: memoirs 1931–1945*. London: Frederick Muller.

Dalton, H., 1962. *High tide and after: memoirs 1945–1960*. London: Frederick Muller.

Davenport, N., 1974. *Memoirs of a city radical*. London: Weidenfeld and Nicolson.

Dell, E., 1997. *The chancellors: a history of the Chancellors of the Exchequer, 1945–90*. London: Harper Collins.

Dolowitz, D., 2000. Policy transfer: a new framework of policy analysis. *In*: D. Dolowitz, *et al.*, eds. *Policy transfer and British social policy: learning from the USA*. Hulme, Buckingham: Oxford University Press, 9–37.

Dolowitz, D. and Marsh, D., 2000. Learning from abroad: the role of policy transfer in contemporary policy-making. *Governance*, 13 (1), 5–24.

Durbin, E., 1985. *New Jerusalems: the Labour Party and the economics of democratic socialism*. London: Routledge.

Eatwell, R., 1979. *The 1945–1951 Labour governments*. London: Batsford.

Giuseppi, J., 1966. *The Bank of England: a history from its foundation in 1694*. London: Evans Brother.

Goodhart, C., 2003. Whither central banking? *In*: D. Altig and B. Smith, eds. *Evolution and procedures in central banking*. Cambridge: Cambridge University Press, 65–81.

Hennessy, E., 1992. *A domestic history of the Bank of England 1930–1960*. Cambridge: Cambridge University Press.

HM Treasury, 1988. *File of an independent Bank of England. Autumn. Freedom of Information disclosure. 7 March 2005*. London: HM Treasury. Available from: www.hm-treasury.gov.uk

HM Treasury, 1991. *File of an independent Bank of England. 28 March. Freedom of Information disclosure. 7 March 2005*. London: HM Treasury. Available from: www.hm-treasury.gov.uk

HM Treasury, 1992a. *File of independence of the Bank of England. 30 June. Freedom of Information Act disclosure. 7 March 2005*. London: HM Treasury. Available from: www.hm-treasury.gov.uk

HM Treasury, 1992b. *File of inflation objectives. 24 September. Freedom of Information disclosure. 6 October 2005*. London: HM Treasury. Available from: www.hm-treasury.gov.uk

HM Treasury, 1992c. *File of the government's inflation objective: should we target inflation directly? 29 September. Freedom of Information disclosure. 6 October 2005.* London: HM Treasury. Available from: www.hm-treasury.gov.uk

HM Treasury, 1993. *File of possible arrangements for an independent monetary authority. 18 January. Freedom of Information disclosure. 7 March 2005.* London: HM Treasury. Available from: www.hm-treasury.gov.uk

Howson, S., 1993. *British monetary policy 1945–51.* Oxford: Clarendon Press.

Keegan, W., 1997. Bright smile that hid the sadness of 'King' George. *Observer,* 11 May, p. 8.

Kingdon, J., 1995. *Agendas, alternatives, and public policies.* 2nd ed. New York: Longman.

Labour Party, 1926. *Socialism in our time: Labour's road in power, the policy of the living income.* London: ILP publication Department.

Labour Party, 1928a. *Labour and the nation.* London: Labour Party.

Labour Party, 1928b. *Labour and the nation: banking and currency policy.* London: Labour Party.

Labour Party, 1931. *Labour's call to action: the nation's opportunity. General Election Manifesto 1931.* London: Labour Party.

Labour Party, 1932. *Currency, banking and finance.* London: Labour Party.

Labour Party, 1934. *For socialism and peace.* London: Labour Party.

Labour Party, 1937. *Labour's immediate programme.* London: Labour Party.

Labour Party, 1946. *The Bank of England and the nation.* Labour Discussion Series. London: Labour Party.

Leruez, J., 1975. *Economic planning and politics in Britain.* London: Martin Robertson.

Lindblom, C., 1977. *Politics and markets: the world's political and economic systems.* New York: Basic Books.

Lindblom, C., 1988. *Democracy and market system.* Oslo: NUP.

Morgan, K., 1984. *Labour in power: 1945–51.* Oxford: Clarendon Press.

Patel, S., 2008. An independent Bank of England: the political process in historical perspective. *Public policy and administration,* 23 (1), 27–41.

Pollard, S., 1979. The nationalisation of the banks: the chequered history of a socialist proposal. *In*: D. Martin and D. Rubinstein, eds. *Ideology and the Labour movement.* London: Croom Helm, 167–190.

Powell, W., 1991. Expanding the scope of institutional analysis. *In*: W. Powell and P. DiMaggio, eds. *The new institutionalism in organizational analysis.* Chicago: Chicago University Press, 183–203.

PRO, 1945. *T 241/5, F. Briefs for second reading, 4. Central banking in the Dominions, 3 August 1945.* London: Public Record Office.

Pym, H. and Kochan, N., 1998. *Gordon Brown: the first year in power.* London: Bloomsbury.

Rose, R., 1993. *Lesson drawing in public policy: a guide to learning across time and space.* Chatham, NJ: Chatham House.

Rubenstein, W., 2003. *Twentieth-century Britain: a political history.* Basingstoke: Palgrave.

Simon, H.A., 1957. *Administrative behaviour: a study of decision-making processes in administrative organizations.* 2nd ed. New York: Macmillan.

Singleton, J., 1995. Labour, the Conservatives and nationalisation. *In*: R. Millward and J. Singleton, eds. *The political economy of nationalisation in Britain 1920–50.* Cambridge: Cambridge University Press, 13–33.

Tomlinson, J., 2004. Labour Party and the city 1945–1970. *In*: R. Michie and P. Williamson, eds. *The British government and the City of London in the twentieth century.* Cambridge: Cambridge University Press, 174–192.

Wood, G., Mills, T., and Capie, F., 1993. *Central bank independence: what is it and what will it do for us?* Current Controversies No. 4. London: IEA.

Zahariadis, N., 2003. *Ambiguity and choice in public policy: political decision making in modern democracies.* Washington, DC: Georgetown University Press.

The uncertain potential of policy-learning: a comparative assessment of three varieties

Katrin Toens[a] and Claudia Landwehr[b]

[a]Institute for Political Science, University of Hamburg, Hamburg, Germany; [b]Institute for Political Science, Goethe-University, Frankfurt, Germany

This article reviews recent conceptual debates on cross-national and cross-sectoral policy-learning in the political science literature. It proceeds from the argument that the existing literature is characterised by the absence of a comparative assessment of the risks and potentials of different strategies of policy learning. This sin of omission does not only have significant implications for the study of policy learning but also for its practice. The authors use the normative concept of improvement-oriented learning to assess the risks and potentials of three learning strategies: imitation, Bayesian updating and deliberation. They observe that the distribution of risks and potentials is most advantageous in deliberative learning strategies, but that imitation is the most risky learning strategy, and Bayesian updating ranges somewhere in-between.

Introduction

Since the mid-1990s, concepts of policy learning have increasingly found their way into research on international relations and European integration where they are frequently used in the analysis of transnational policy transfer and the cross-border diffusion and convergence of policies (see Rose 1991, Dolowitz and Marsh 1996, Goldsmith 2003, Holzinger *et al.* 2007, Bandelow 2008). With the shift in research interest from domestic learning processes to the issues of when and how states learn from one another, less self-referential forms of learning have suddenly come to the fore. Learning is no longer seen as the result of reflections on one's own experiences. Instead, the experiences of other actors in other political contexts form the basis for policy learning. This goes to the extent that no longer experiences as such, but rather the orientation towards others is identified as the main factor behind learning, for example when the adaptive behaviour of states reacting to social pressure for assimilation and bandwagoning effects is described as social learning (see also Levi-Faur 2002, e.g. Chamley 2004).

Altogether this literature has led to a broadening of the conceptual and empirical basis of social science debates on the topic of learning. Policy analysis can profit from this, provided that it succeeds in more clearly identifying the learning advancements associated with policy change. From an analytical standpoint, it often remains unclear with regard to the described adaptation phenomena to what extent they are motivated by learning advancements or mere ideational trends, the formation of ideational hegemony or cognitive diffusion without learning advancements (see also Walt 2000, Nullmeier 2003).

However, uncertainties concerning the range and potentials of individual learning strategies cannot only be traced back to the inflationary use of the concept of learning. The conceptual shortcomings of previous learning theory debates have also contributed to this. In the past the focus was placed not so much on the actual core question *how* individuals and other political actors learn from one another; the identification of material levels of learning as well as various forms of learning success instead pertained to *what* is learned (see Bandelow 2003b, p. 304).[1] As a result, attention was seldom paid to the 'respectively taken "paths of learning", the differences between various processes or forms of learning as well as the learning-promoting (or -impeding) strategies and "learning figures" selected by the involved individual actors' (Maier *et al.* 2003, p. 12).

Against this background, we place the focus of our article on the comparative analysis of the risks and potentials of different strategies and processes of learning. We begin with imitation. Imitation is a particularly frequently discussed concept of transnational policy learning, which in part has to do with the fact that it is actively promoted as a learning strategy associated with soft governance instruments of the EU. We assume that imitation can stimulate policy learning at a very basic level of trial and error. However, these learning effects are far from self-evident and require further explanation. Learning by imitation like all learning strategies bears not only potentials but also risks. This raises questions with regard to the specific form and scope of this strategy of learning. It is therefore useful to contrast imitation with other learning strategies, which can be described as more advanced with regard to specified procedural and quality criteria for learning. To this end, imitation will be compared with two other concepts of policy learning, Bayesian updating and deliberation.

Our article proceeds in three steps. First, we will explain the concept of learning, upon which our analysis is based. A comparison of the risks and potentials of different learning strategies needs to draw on an underlying understanding of learning, which functions as a kind of conceptual bracket for the different concepts of learning. This function will be assumed by the concept of improvement-oriented learning, which highlights the cognitive as well as evaluative and judgemental components of learning. After this clarification of the concept of learning, we will introduce quality criteria for policy learning, which enable us to define the risks and potentials of distinct learning strategies and processes. The main emphasis is then placed on the systematic comparison of the three learning strategies, the results of which we discuss in a summary. The conclusion seeks to highlight the theoretical contribution of our distinction to the study of policy learning and deliberative policy-making.

Policy learning as improvement-oriented learning

The various concepts of policy learning discussed in the policy literature generally assume that all learning has a strong cognitive dimension. Learning is based on gaining knowledge, which is manifested in the capacity to draw lessons from the experiences and problems associated with certain policy content, goals, and interventions (see May 1992, p. 333). To the extent that learning marks a form of policy change, which comes about as an expression of cognitive abilities, a minimum degree of intention and the political will for self-modification are required.

By contrast, the evaluative-judgemental component of learning involved in the concept of improvement-oriented learning is less self-explanatory. The concept of learning is not always used in a normative sense in policy research. The relevant policy analysis literature on learning (e.g. Heclo 1974, Hall 1993, Sabatier 1993) precisely does not require learning to trigger an improvement (see Bandelow 2003a, p. 108). For example, Heclo defines social learning as a relatively stable change in behaviour, which results from previous experiences (1974, p. 306). Sabatier describes policy-oriented learning 'as a relatively stable change in thought or in behavioural intentions ... which results from experiences and has to do with the realisation or the modification of policy goals' (Sabatier 1993, pp. 121–122). Finally, Hall's concept of social learning, too, targets the cognitive dimension of learning, disregarding its evaluative-judgemental components. Social learning is defined as 'a deliberative attempt to adjust the goals or techniques of policy in response to past experience and new information' (Hall 1993, p. 278).

It therefore makes sense to distinguish a concept of improvement-oriented learning from the nominal concept of learning which focuses on mere change (also change-oriented learning). Improvement-oriented learning is learning which can be designated as an improvement on the basis of a certain criteria (Nullmeier 2003). Such an understanding of learning is analytically and normatively demanding. It is analytically demanding because, in contrast to merely change-oriented concepts of learning, it cannot be used in a general manner. Instead it is an evaluation and specification-based concept that can be refused as a description of certain kinds of policy change. Normatively speaking it must specify standards for evaluation, on the basis of which policy change can be defined as better or worse. Such an evaluation is notoriously difficult for reasons to be elaborated on below. At the same time, we cannot simply elude the difficulties posed by the evaluative-judgemental components of the concept of learning, as the evaluative component, which primarily comes to bear in the everyday usage of the concept of learning[2] cannot be neutralised for science. Political science in particular cannot shun it, as the evaluative component is also always an integrative element of democratic politics, in which decision-makers compete for political support and are put under learning pressure by voters when they promise policy-related improvements. Hence, the concept of improvement-oriented learning can at least gain standards for evaluation from the field of inquiry by adopting the goals of certain political actors. Things become more complicated when a specific standard of scientific observation is set or presupposed as generally applicable. Here, the question arises whether and to what extent the concept of policy learning can elude such a standard. As long as the term 'policy learning' gives rise positive associations, it is only consequential to make the standards for an evaluation of policy change explicit.

Seen from this angle, the concept of improvement-oriented learning requires policy analysis research on learning to revert to normative political theory. However, the strong material evaluation of learning always bears a component of irrevocability. It is therefore to some degree incompatible with the inevitable incompleteness and context-dependence of learning, which is always of a preliminary character due to the epistemic boundaries of all knowledge. Information and opinions are potentially false and hence uncertain, even when they suggest certainty in the short-term. Policy learning is additionally bound to contextual circumstances, which are not guaranteed in every actual situation and learning environment. This concerns, above all, the fact that policy change is adaptable and customisable. The smaller the creative capacity of political actors, the smaller the probability that learning advancements will be made and/or be reflected in policy outcomes. One must also mention here that the involved actors' trust in the willingness to learn and change and their ability to compromise in view of the goals and strategies of learning are additional contextual conditions which facilitate learning. The contribution of normative learning theory to empirical policy research is limited, where such contextual conditions presupposed or demanded without consideration of the actual circumstances of policy learning. Its ideational claim may appear to be beside the point; especially when one brings to mind that normatively unaspiring concepts of change-oriented learning are already confronted with the accusation of being unrealistic assumptions, because they practically neglect conflicts of interest by conceiving 'politics as a cognitively harmonisable dispute, in which change is to be given priority over non-change' (Maier *et al.* 2003, p. 14).

This problem is particularly evident when we consider all the learning-impeding factors states are confronted with under the conditions of globalisation. These factors span from the limited state capacity to shape policy change, to increased uncertainty and lack of knowledge and the resulting inability to estimate consequences of political actions on to problems with regard to effective intercultural communication and trust. If the concept of learning is not to be reduced to change-oriented learning or even entirely dispelled from policy analysis, it should at least be freed from the normative claims of the ideal learning theory.[3]

Paradoxically, the deterioration of the conditions for policy learning leads to an increase in the pressure on policy-makers to learn, because learning can become a means of assertion or even survival for policy-makers when faced with a loss of power.[4] The current fascination with benchmarking, best practices, evaluation, and 'learning through international comparisons of achievements' in politics reflects this dilemma. By more or less voluntarily exposing themselves to continual surveillance and regularly displaying their learning results in comparative assessments, rankings and other result-oriented comparative rituals, governments can demonstrate their permanent willingness to learn and thereby conceal their actual lack of capacity for self-determination and self-regulation (which is also signalled by these less self-referential forms of learning).

Policy learning is context-dependent for a second reason that has to do with the orientation towards the common good democratic political decisions need to display. To the extent that politics is aimed at producing collectively binding decisions, it (sometimes more and sometimes less explicitly) asserts to produce decisions which are oriented towards the common good or at least compatible with the community's welfare. However, the claim to a *single* common good is difficult to justify. Whenever decisions aimed at a common good are addressed, touchy issues are broached, for example the social relevance and the planning horizon of policies and the substantial features and goods and values which are to be achieved or fulfilled by means of actions aimed at the common good (Offe 2001). In a strict sense, learning policy-makers are also faced with definition problems, which are aggravated to the extent that they are dealing less and less with culturally homogenous and introverted societies: a development to which normative theories of democracy typically react by proceduralising the concept of a common good.

Against this background, we advocate the middle ground of a thin normative learning theory. Instead of seeking a thorough material evaluation of levels of learning and advancements in learning, the normative dimension of policy learning is accommodated by the procedural theory of learning, which evaluates strategies of policy change under the assumption 'that policy outcomes, which are the results of a certain procedure, are more likely to produce positive results ... than policy outcomes which were not subject to such a process' (Nullmeier 2003, p. 339). This raises questions about the quality criteria of learning processes.

Quality criteria of learning processes

In the following we assume that the learning potential of policy-makers varies according to the applied learning strategies. The different potentials for learning we assume are based on two quality criteria of learning processes: the incorporation of information and of difference, a relationship that is to be elaborated on.

The incorporation of information

We prefer the concept of information to that of knowledge, at least insofar as the latter is associated with the truth in philosophical terms. The spread of new information relevant to learning targets increases learning potential, because it potentially can correct previous (mis-)information. However, the spread of information also bears risks. Not only the experience of contingency and lacking knowledge increase with it, but also the risk of a strategically simulated information deficit. Examples are the dealing with information in a deliberately selective manner, the targeted downplaying and/or discrediting of certain information, or the denial of access to information relevant to learning goals (nondisclosure). There are thus at least two risk factors which can impede or prevent learning processes: (non-intended) misinformation and the risk of non-learning by strategically simulated information deficits.

The masking of conflicts of interest and power constitutes a weakness in learning theory, to which policy research with a strong cognitive focus appears particularly vulnerable (Maier 2001, Maier *et al.* 2003, p. 13). Thus one of the challenges of research on learning is to avoid the dichotomisation between policy learning as knowledge-driven policy change and knowledge and information-independent interest and power games. The particularity of the democratically legitimated will-formation process in the national framework for action consists precisely in the fact that the institutions of representative democracy are aimed at subverting the rigid distinction between power- and idea-based politics. In Halls terms: 'most of the time, "powering" and "puzzling" (i.e. problem-solving) go together. Both are dimensions of the process whereby policy changes, especially in democratic polities, whose institutions tend to combine the two endeavors' (Hall 1993, p. 289). To this extent, international learning processes, which play out beyond the established democratically legitimated procedures of political will formation in the national framework of action, must be examined with regard to whether they have corrective mechanisms which can ensure that the spread of information leads to 'puzzling' rather than 'powering'.

Incorporation of difference

The incorporation of difference means that various sources of information are taken into consideration. The more information from sources which exist independently of one another is incorporated, the greater the likelihood that the corrective function of the spread of information is guaranteed. Information is not neutral and the production and spread of information is a social process which is influenced by different cultures of information dissemination. Just like interpretations of problems and proposed solutions, the processing and filtering of information is to a considerable extent culturally determined. As a quality criterion, the incorporation of difference emphasises the fact that one can always view and interpret things differently. It aims to ensure the social and thematic openness of strategies for policy learning, which is significant in particular with regard to the responsibility of policy-makers to promote the community's welfare. Viewed from this angle, the incorporation of difference increases the welfare-enhancing potential of policy learning.

Using both quality criteria, observed policy changes can be compared with the status quo and evaluated. We suggest to distinguish learning strategies which bear different potentials and risks. The greater the risk minimisation through the incorporation of information and the greater the potential for enhancing a common good through the incorporation of difference, the greater the learning potential is. We ideal-typically define three learning strategies (imitation, Bayesian updating and deliberation) and discuss their learning risks and potentials. For reasons elaborated on in the following, we believe that imitation is the riskiest strategy of policy learning with the lowest potential for enhancing common welfare, while deliberative learning is a clearly less risky form of policy learning with a higher potential for enhancing common welfare and Bayesian updating can be found somewhere in-between.

Imitation, Bayesian updating and deliberative learning

In the following section, the three learning strategies will be presented and discussed with regard to their respective potentials and risks.

Policy learning by copying strategies for action: imitation

Policy learning by copying strategies for action is currently a particularly popular theme in policy research, which deals with learning by international comparison. Thus studies examine diffusion and convergence processes in which countries learn from the experiences of other, so-called model countries by imitating particularly promising strategies of achieving goals (best practices). In consequence, policies become more similar. Lesson-drawing, model learning (Rose 1991), social learning (Chamley 2004), cascading or bandwagoning (Lohmann 1994, Levi-Faur 2002) are terms used quite frequently to describe such processes of adaptation and convergence. Here we choose the superordinate concept of imitation, because it describes a process which is implicit to all these forms of learning.[5]

Policy learning through benchmarking and comparative assessments was already introduced in the early 1980s as a new source of legitimacy for public reforms. During the 1990s this learning strategy was discovered as a new form of communication-driven cooperation, for example within the EU or OECD framework (Holzinger and Knill 2005, Martens and Wolf 2006). By developing performance indicators, declarations of intent to achieve goals, time constraints as well as public recognition and disdain rituals (shaming and blaming) countries voluntarily and mutually expose themselves to pressures for adaptation. Examples of this are the *open method of coordination* in European employment and social policy (see Büchs 2007), the Bologna Process to create a European Higher Education Area (Heinze and Knill 2007), the orientation towards Finnish secondary education policy as a reaction to the so-called PISA shock (Toots 2007) or the emulation of American workfare programs (Dolowitz 1998).

One positive aspect is that such imitation processes can trigger strong impetuses for innovation. From the perspective of individual countries the constructive potentials of imitation span from increased willingness to take risks to testing entirely new strategies on to uprooting structurally pre-established political anomalies by the so-called path leap (Pierson 2000, p. 262). Learning obstacles rooted in routinised patterns of behaviour, rituals and routines, cultural path dependencies and established power structures can be subverted in this manner. One example is the paradigm change in German higher education policy from the extremely bureaucratic state authorised instrument of curriculum framework orders, which were frequently reprimanded as being inefficient, to the institutionalisation of a decentralised semi-private accreditation system. This radical change of direction was substantially triggered by the domestically advocated orientation towards developments of quality assurance in other countries (Toens 2007).

However, the radical nature of the aspired reforms goes hand in hand with problems of adjustment. Whenever policy change is based on experience that gained was at other points in time, in other policy areas and/or other countries, it is particularly risky because wrong conclusions can be drawn from adopting ideas without deeper insights into the original contexts. Strictly speaking, the actual learning only begins when implementation problems are overcome, which result from the necessity of adjusting external policy models to local contexts (Rose 1991, May 1992, p. 333). Learning then becomes a time-consuming trial and error process, which to a certain extent contradicts the artificially produced time pressure under which international benchmarking processes are frequently carried out.

Empirical analyses of political benchmarking processes (e.g. Cox 1999, Stone 1999, 2000, Strassheim 2003, Büchs 2007, Toots 2007) reveal that the learning strategy of imitation bears more risks than potentials. We will highlight three problems here. The first is the problem of context oblivion. In his frequently quoted essay on lesson-drawing, Richard Rose already warned about the call of the siren (1991, p. 27). The more successful a measure, the greater the likelihood that other countries will be seduced into imitating it, even if undesired side-effects in their own social context and policy area are foreseeable. The probability of political shipwreck increases under conditions of high uncertainty and intense reform pressure (Strassheim 2003, p. 229). This problem can be exemplified by Estonian secondary education policy (Toots 2007). The seductive impact of Finnish school policy, which was ranked at the very top in the comparative PISA study, triggered the Estonian government to imitate Finnish decentralisation policies. However, copying these policies, which granted schools more freedom in the development of curricula and in dealing with school students, proved to be extremely counterproductive, because it increased the social disadvantages of slow learners. The reason for this was a misfit in context. Unlike in Finland, slow learners in Estonia were often transferred to schools for mentally handicapped children instead of being given special support in regular schools. Given this, the increase in interschool competition gave an incentive to Estonian schools to get rid of slow learners instead of improving their learning conditions. The counterproductive effects of policy imitation would have been foreseeable if policy-makers had more thoroughly incorporated their own context and experiences into the decision-making process. Thus, this example also shows that imitation can lead to the neglect of one's own experiences (Toots 2007, p. 16).

Context oblivion can culminate in a kind of fixation on abstract points of reference, which promotes the filtering of information. By drawing on the example of American workfare programs, Strassheim (2003) argues that benchmarking is a policy style which encourages the neutralisation of certain information instead of neutrality in dealing with information. Decisive for this development was the fixation of individual American states on the so-called caseload reduction. In the race for the lowest number of cases the actual policy goal of fighting poverty was neglected. Instead the only issue that counted anymore was whether they could succeed in getting people off welfare programs as quickly as possible. The policy thus created necessities, which were difficult to challenge in political discourse.

Third and finally, there is the danger of denial of learning results as a consequence of the pressure for conformity and prestige. Politicians are subject to constant observation. They tend to adapt and adjust to the expectations of others where it serves to protect their own reputation (Kuran 1989). The result of this is frequently (self-) delusion with regard to what is actually achieved. An example of this is the so-called stocktaking approach in European higher education policy (see Toens 2008). A part of the Bologna process to reform national higher education policies is the agreement by the (meanwhile) 46 participating countries to regularly put the results of national reform efforts up to debate. Based on the data from national stocktaking reports, the country-specific policy results are compared with one another and designated by the colours of a traffic light as green (for good), yellow (for medium) and red (for bad) (Working Group on Stocktaking 2005). This resulted in a striking accumulation of good practices, which meanwhile are drawing lapidary remarks in Brussels such as 'too much green'. Thus, doubts have been cast with regard to the credibility of the results of the stocktaking reports of national governments.[6] The country reports on the state of implementation can only be regarded as reasonably informative in combination with the stocktaking reports of non-state actors. Altogether, we therefore must bear in mind that the learning strategy of imitation bears clearly more risks and problems than potentials.

Policy learning as adaptation to assessments of probability: Bayesian updating

A more demanding form of learning than pure imitation is the adaptation of probability assumptions in reaction to new experiences and information. The updating theorem stated by Thomas Bayes (1702–1761) constitutes an abstraction of belief-formation, which can also be assumed to exist in reality as a form of learning. While the imitation of policies is ultimately the testing of strategies according to the trial and error principle, Bayesian updating may be applied to the premises of decisions and strategies. Even if the Bayesian theorem can, in principle, also be applied to the adjustment of strategies, we are concerned here with updating as a way of forming premises for decision-making.

The classical model by Bayes assumes that actors begin a process of belief formation with a prior probability, which is assigned to a given proposition. This probability can assume a value between 0.0 (i.e. the proposition is regarded as definitely not true) and 1.0 (i.e. the proposition is regarded as definitely true). In cases of great uncertainty and little information a value of 0.5 appears realistic, which means that the proposition is held equally likely to be true or false. However, the prior probabilities people assign to propositions can vary for different reasons such as traditions, taboos or biased information.

The formula according to which actors update the probability assigned to a proposition is as follows:

$$p_{\phi/X} = [(p_{X/\phi})(p_\phi)] / [(p_{X/\phi})(p_\phi) + (p_{X/\neg\phi})(p_{\neg\phi})].$$

$p_\varnothing$ is the prior probability, x is the experience or information, in reaction to which it is updated, and $p_{x/\varnothing}$ is the conditional probability that x occurs, given that the proposition ø is true. $p_{\varnothing/x}$ is the accordingly updated probability, or the probability assignment adapted to new experience or information (see Goodin 2003, p. 113).

When transferring the Bayesian model from individual to collective actors, thus to governments or even states, various problems arise. For example, what should one assume to be the collective prior probability: an average of individual probability assignments or that of a pivotal decision-maker? In addition, how does the impact of new information differ depending on how many members of the collective it is accessible to? Despite these difficulties, the Bayesian model can be useful as an approximation to real processes of collective belief formation. If one understands updating as a learning strategy, it consists in the targeted gathering and examination of information and in the systematic updating of existing beliefs and consequently of policies. However, Bayesian updating must be seen as a purely cognitive process of assessing probabilities assigned to claims about facts. Normative-evaluative attitudes, which can also be the subject of learning, do not play a role in this form of learning.

An empirical example of a policy area in which decisions are based on updating processes that may be seen as coming close to the Bayesian model are decisions over the financing of specific medical services. Here policy-makers are increasingly drawing on the results of so-called 'evidence-based medicine'. Evidence-based medicine compiles Health Technology Assessment (HTA) reports, which incorporate research results published in international journals and give evidence of the effectiveness and efficiency of treatment methods. Such HTA reports, which are generally compiled by commissioned expert institutes, increasingly serve as a basis for financing decisions. It is noteworthy here that the reports are all based on the same information: research findings published in top-ranking journals.

The obvious gain from learning in terms of adjustments of probability assignments by Bayesian updating lies in the optimised incorporation and evaluation of information. While in imitation, the success or failure of a strategy alone is decisive, a much larger basis of information can be employed in updating. It makes sense to assume that improvements in the premises for decision-making, i.e. beliefs that are more likely to be true, will also lead to better policy choices. Moreover, updating allows clues on the probability of still untested strategies to be successful. Thus, beyond the mere copying of strategies, creativity also becomes a possible result of policy learning.

At the same time, updating also bears risks, although they are smaller than in the case of pure imitation. These risks are primarily associated with the selection and quality of the information. First, there are cases in which the available information is simply insufficient or misleading: updating cannot make beliefs better than the existing evidence (Dietrich and List 2005, p. 187). An additional problem is that information, as a rule, is not based on one's own experiences and observations, but on the reports of other actors. Between such reports, interdependencies must be assumed to exist. This means that similar and compatible pieces of information stemming from the same source may be viewed as separate pieces of evidence: think of the numerous urban legends as an example.

One need not be a conspiracy theorist to be aware of the dangers of distorted communication and hegemonic discourses. Aside from the fact that it can of course be true or false, information is neutral. However, the extent to which dissemination and assessment of information are dependent on actors' material resources should not be underestimated. The example of evidence-based medicine illustrates this. The practice of research funding through the pharmaceutical industry has the effect that certain diseases and treatment methods are researched more frequently than others. Moreover, many methods, for example psychotherapy, are by principle more difficult to assess than others, e.g. oral anti-depressants, because factors of influence partially cannot be controlled for. Finally, negative results are much less frequently published in medical journals than positive results.

The benefit from learning strategies, which focus primarily on the gathering of information and the adjustment of probability assignments, for a (however defined) common good thus remains questionable in several respects. Under certain circumstances, updating strategies can help to avoid mistakes and improve the selection of strategies, but policy goals themselves are hardly critically assessed. In consequence, policy choices are unlikely to do justice to the plurality and variety of interests, values and perspectives. The concentration on a purely epistemic concept of learning and a respective understanding of democracy frequently go hand and hand with the unjustified assumption of a consensus over particular policy objectives, to which all decisions are subordinate. An example of this is the purported consensus over the necessity to reduce employers' social insurance contributions in Germany. This frequently blurs out conflicts over objectives, frequently to the disadvantage of already underprivileged groups.

Policy learning as a means of reflecting on goals and decision-making premises: deliberation

In policy analysis and political rhetoric, the theory of deliberative democracy has come to enjoy great popularity beyond democratic theory in the narrow sense.[7] Here we are concerned not so much with our own independent definition of what deliberation means and requires or with a discussion of the democratic legitimacy of deliberative procedures of decision-making. Instead, we wish to demonstrate the potential of deliberation as a learning strategy and explain to what extent deliberative learning is superior to both the pure imitation of strategies for action and the updating of beliefs by means of information. Even if deliberative learning results in decisions that are better informed or more just, by whatever set of standards, questions still arise with regard to their democratic (input) legitimacy. However, we are here only concerned with the learning potential of deliberation.

Deliberation is to be understood, first, as a form of interaction, which either occurs spontaneously or is purposefully brought about by respective means of institutional design. The aim is for the group to engage in an exchange of ideas on what should be done collectively, i.e. drawing up and assessing strategies for action. Even if complex and normatively demanding concepts dominate in the literature, two features of interaction can be argued to be constitutive for deliberation: publicity and reciprocity (see Landwehr 2009, ch. 2). Publicity requires not so much a mass media public as the general accessibility of forums for outsiders. In interaction, this ensures the generalisability of arguments and the justification of decision-making premises. By reciprocity we mean that actors acknowledge one another as rational decision-makers and assume that the reasons named by the respective other could in principle reasons for oneself, too.

Deliberation is frequently equated with arguing and contrasted with bargaining as a mode of interaction (Saretzki 1996). Even if the focus on generalisable arguments and transferable reasons for action is crucial for deliberation, it is not sufficiently defined by the simple distinction between arguing and negotiating. Situations can arise in which people do argue but the condition of reciprocity is not fulfilled, because actors do not recognise the motivating reasons of their inter-locutors as potentially relevant. Many public debates are examples of this. Conversely, there are cases where institutional design seems to aim at bargaining but where interaction can in fact take on deliberative qualities, for example mediation. What is crucial for deliberation is that actors reflect on and question their own goals.

In the examples from social, education and health policy discussed above, a deliberative form of policy learning could therefore have had entirely different ramifications than imitation or the pure updating of beliefs. Instead of simply copying the school systems of the most successful countries in the PISA study, decision-makers could have addressed the question of whether to give priority to the advancement of underprivileged or highly-talented pupils. It would of course have been ideal if both could have been achieved with the same strategy. However, at the latest when resources have to be allocated concretely, conflicts between goals arise and should be made explicit. In decisions over the financing of medical services, deliberative procedures have repeatedly shown that cost-benefit evaluations alone are not sufficient for setting priorities and that conflicting goals like equal opportunity, help for the neediest, and personal responsibility are equally crucial.[8]

From a normative standpoint, the theory of deliberative democracy calls not only for public participation and reciprocity, but also for broad and equal inclusion in deliberation. Precisely here is where the risks of deliberative learning lie. The most important problem in this regard is the self-selection of the participants, which is a prerequisite for policy area-specific stakeholder processes and is continuously lamented in citizen participation projects. In the former case, questions arise with regard to the general legitimacy and significance of decisions. In the latter, the problem is that the socially privileged are more likely to participate and also exert more influence in the procedures.

In this way, deliberative learning can lead to a biased consideration of information and reasons for action. Unlike the updating of beliefs though, the basis of deliberative learning processes consists not only of experiences and accounts of experiences, but also of arguments about more complex relationships. While in the cases of both imitation and updating, the learning mechanism takes place in an automated fashion, reasons for action and arguments are systematically scrutinised and justified in deliberation. Scrutinising and justification only require a sufficient number and variety of different positions and perspectives to exist within a forum (Dryzek and Niemeyer 2008). Insofar as at least one participant questions any argument that is named and demands justification, majorities in the forum are of subordinate importance for scrutinising it.

With regard to the promotion of a common good, the great strength of deliberative learning strategies is precisely that they do not assume or require a consensus on goals. Instead, the interactive process of reaching understanding on values and interests and the creative definition of shared goals and a common good are the great potential benefits from deliberative learning. To achieve them, it is crucial to appropriately deal with differences: by incorporating the broadest possible range of interests and perspectives and by considering and scrutinising them argumentatively. Under conditions of value and interest pluralism, the results of such scrutiny will be not so much consensuses on goals as compromises *between* goals. Compromises between conflicting fundamental values and interests always remain contingent to a certain degree insofar as they cannot be derived from subordinate principles. Nevertheless, they must be justified and their premises scrutinised.

Thus, in an ideal scenario deliberative learning processes and learning strategies not only promise the broader incorporation of information, but also the broader incorporation of difference in terms of contrasting interests, values and beliefs systems. Consequently, we would hope to find compromises based on legitimate values and interests. In some cases, however, a fundamental understanding of the inevitability of conflicts over and between policy objectives and of the necessity to reach compromises can already be regarded as learning achievements.

Potentials and risks of learning strategies compared

Based on the identified quality criteria for learning processes, the comparison of the three selected learning strategies leads to the following results (see Figure 1). Imitation is the riskiest strategy of policy learning. Although this form of learning bears a particularly high potential for innovation, it also bears the risk of producing latent power potential and a kind of soft power (Stone 2000), which can limit or even hinder learning in terms of improvement-oriented learning. Empirical examples of policy change by means of imitation demonstrate the dangers of context oblivion and shutting out diverging realms of experience and different perspectives on the same political program. The selection of imitation as a learning strategy thus does not necessarily lead to better policy decisions.

Moreover, imitation frequently is aimed not so much at promoting a common good, but in practice often serves to increase the prestige of governments seeking quick success amid competition for best practices. This tendency is further abetted by the fact that international benchmarking processes promote the informalisation of policy-making (see Greven 2005). Therefore, we can no longer automatically

Assessment / Strategy	Potential	Risk
Imitation	▪ Innovation by path leap ▪ Breaking down learning obstacles	▪ Context oblivion ▪ Downgrading one's own experiences ▪ Shrugging off and neutralisation of certain information ▪ Denial of learning results under pressure for reputation
Bayesian Updating	▪ Better cognitive decision-making premises ▪ Creativity: testing entirely new strategies becomes possible	▪ One-sided or misleading information ▪ Assumption of a non-existent consensus over goals
Deliberation	▪ Orientation of decision-making processes to common welfare ▪ Rethinking targets and admitting conflicts over goals ▪ Taking different interests and perspectives seriously	▪ Distorted communication ▪ Exclusion of the socially disadvantaged

Figure 1.   Potential and risks of selected learning strategies.

presume that the balanced relationship between 'powering' and 'puzzling'. that is assumed to obtain in the institutions of representative democracy at the national level, still exists (Hall 1993).

Learning strategies and learning processes oriented towards the model of Bayesian updating potentially optimise decision-making premises. Comprehensively scrutinising available information also makes it possible to probe entirely new political strategies, because worthwhile predictions on their potential for success can be made on the basis of rationally motivated assessments of probability. However, strategies based on Bayesian updating also bear the risk that misjudgements will occur due to one-sided or misleading information. Above all though, a prerequisite for the purely instrumental use of information is a consensus on goals, which can seldom be assumed to exist in politics. The greatest problem with this learning strategy thus consists in the insufficient incorporation of differences in terms of conflicting interests and perspectives on problems. However, since this strategy is aimed not so much at adaptation as at the improvement of decision-making premises, the learning risks are altogether smaller than in cases of pure imitation.

Finally, deliberation is the most promising learning strategy in several ways. Here, too, risks of distorted communication and problems regarding the appropriate incorporation of socially underprivileged groups do exist. However, the superiority of deliberation over the other two learning strategies consists in the better consideration to differences in the form of conflicting interests, perspectives and value systems, in a political decision-making process oriented more towards a common good, and in the transparent management of conflicts over goals.

Conclusions

We believe that the understanding of learning as improvement-oriented learning and the distinction between imitation, updating and deliberation as different strategies of learning makes an important theoretical contribution to the study of policy transfer and policy learning in three different ways. First, it can help to organise the growing body of literature on policy learning/transfer. Very different processes and strategies are currently being described as learning, and these also require different explanations and evaluations. Terminological and conceptual clarity and differentiation are a first prerequisite for a better understanding of policy-learning (and by implication policy transfer) and its potential. The evidence provided by the already large number of empirical analyses could be better assessed if the types of learning authors refer to were more clearly distinguished.

Our distinction between the three learning strategies is of course not the only possibility, but we believe that it could, second, provide a useful guide for future empirical investigation. If observed instances of policy transfer are more adequately categorised, this also opens up the possibility for a better explanation of their success or failure. Far from claiming that what we have sketched in this article is exhaustive in this regard, we hope to have shown some useful points of departure for analysis and explanation. If, for example, as in the case of Estonian school policy, learning leads to apparently inferior results, this may be accounted for by the selection of the least sophisticated learning strategy, namely imitation. In addition, the selection of learning strategies itself should be accounted for by reference to institutional context conditions and constraints actors are faced with. Here lies a promising route for further research beyond the limited scope of this article.

Finally, our distinction could provide guidance for the evaluation of instances of policy learning/transfer and thus constitute a contribution to normative policy-analysis. While we join in the ubiquitous call for more deliberative policy-making, we also want to make clear that while deliberation is the most promising learning strategy, it is also the one with the most demanding contextual preconditions. In terms of non-ideal theory, it is therefore essential to ask which learning strategies are in fact available to actors and weigh their risks and potentials for the given situation. Moreover, since each strategy promises different gains, it might under certain circumstances be possible to combine them in political practice. Our comparison is summarized in Figure 1 and provides an important reference point for an evaluation of which combinations bear the most promise.

Notes

1. See for example the distinction between simple learning (change in strategy in view of reaching goals), complex learning (modification of goals and target hierarchies) and reflexive learning (change in strategy in view of learning), which dates back to the organisation sociology of Argyris and Schön (1978). See also Hall's (1993) reference to first, second and third-order change, which is illustrated in the distinction between change in policy instruments, techniques, and goals.
2. For example, when it is claimed that learning cannot be wrong or learning is better than not learning.
3. See also the proposal for a differentiated use of the concept of learning, e.g. 'Policy learning is concerned with lessons about policy content–problems, goals, instruments, and implementation designs. Political learning is concerned with lessons about manoeuvering within and manipulation of policy processes in order to advance an idea or problem' (May 1992, p. 340).
4. In the words of K.W. Deutsch (1966) power means not to learn, if one can afford it. Conversely, pressures to learn increase with powerlessness.

5. We cannot do justice to the diverse forms of imitation here, which span from copying a policy to emulating selected elements on to inspiration by an idea (for details see Rose 1991).
6. See the counter-initiative of national students' associations who point out the bad practices in individual member states in their so-called *Bologna black book* (European Students Union 2005).
7. Examples of classic texts are Gutmann and Thompson 1996, Dryzek 2000, as well as the volumes by Bohman and Rehg 1997 and Elster 1998.
8. The best-known example of this kind of citizen involvement in health care priority-setting took place in the US state of Oregon (Fleck 1994).

References

Argyris, C. and Schön, D.A., 1978. *Organisational learning. A theory of action perspective.* Reading, MA: Addison-Wesley.

Bandelow, N.C., 2003a. Lerntheoretische Ansätze in der Policy-Forschung. *In:* L.M. Maier, *et al.*, ed. *In Politik als Lernprozess?.* Opladen: Leske + Budrich, 98–121.

Bandelow, N.C., 2003b. Policy-Lernen und politische Veränderungen. *In:* K. Schubert and N. Bandelow, eds. *In Lehrbuch der Politikfeldanalyse.* München: Oldenbourg, 289–330.

Bandelow, N.C., 2008. Government learning in German and British European politics. *Journal of common market studies*, 46 (4), 743–764.

Bohman, J. and Rehg, W., 1997. *Deliberative democracy.* Cambridge, MA: MIT Press.

Büchs, M., 2007. *New governance of European social policy. The open method of coordination.* Basingstoke: MacMillan.

Chamley, C.P., 2004. *Rational herds. Economic models of social learning.* Cambridge: Cambridge University Press.

Cox, R.H., 1999. Ideas, policy borrowing and welfare reform. *In:* R.H. Cox and J. Schmid, eds. *Reformen in westeuropäischen Wohlfahrtsstaaten – Potentiale und Trends.* Tübingen: WIP Occasional Paper Nr. 5, 14–27.

Deutsch, K.W., 1966. *The nerves of government. Models of political communication and control.* New York/London: The Free Press.

Dietrich, F. and List, C., 2005. A model of jury decisions where all jurors have the same evidence. *Synthese*, 142, 175–202.

Dolowitz, D.P., 1998. *Learning from America: policy transfer and the development of the British workfare state.* Portland: Sussex Academic Press.

Dolowitz, D.P. and Marsh, D., 1996. Who learns what from whom: a review of the policy transfer literature. *Political studies*, 44, 343–357.

Dryzek, J., 2000. *Deliberative democracy and beyond.* Oxford: Oxford University Press.

Dryzek, J.S. and Niemeyer, S., 2008. Discursive representation. *American political science review*, 102 (4), 481–493.

Elster, J., ed., 1998. *Deliberative democracy.* Cambridge: Cambridge University Press.

European Students Union, 2005. *The black book of the Bologna process.* Brussels: The National Unions of Students in Europe.

Fleck, L.M., 1994. Just caring: Oregon, health-care rationing, and informed democratic deliberation. *Journal of medicine and philosophy*, 19, 367–388.

Goldsmith, B.E., 2003. Imitation in international relations: analogies, vicarious learning, and foreign policy. *International interactions*, 29, 273–277.

Goodin, R.E., 2003. *Reflective democracy.* Oxford: Oxford University Press.

Greven, M.T., 2005. The informalisation of transnational governance: a threat to democratic government. *In*: E. Grande and L.W. Pauly, eds. *Complex sovereignty: reconstructing political authority in the twenty-first century.* Toronto: Toronto University Press.

Gutmann, A. and Thompson, D., 1996. *Democracy and disagreement.* Cambridge: Cambridge University Press.

Hall, P.A., 1993. Policy paradigms, social learning, and the state. The case of economic policymaking in Britain. *Comparative politics*, 25, 275–296.

Heclo, H., 1974. *Modern social politics in Britain and Sweden.* New Haven: Yale University Press.

Heinze, T. and Knill, C., 2007. *Analysing the differential impact of the Bologna Process: theoretical and methodological considerations on transnational communication and cross-national policy convergence. ECPR joint sessions of workshops.* Helsinki: University of Helsinki.

Holzinger, K., Jörgens, H. and Knill, C., eds., 2007. *Transfer, Diffusion und Konvergenz von Politiken.* Wiesbaden: VS Verlag für Sozialwissenschaften.

Holzinger, K. and Knill, C., 2005. Causes and conditions of transnational policy convergence. *European public policy*, 12, 775–796.

Kuran, T., 1989. Sparks and prairie fires: a theory of unanticipated political revolution. *Public choice*, 61, 41–47.

Landwehr, C., 2009. *Political conflict and political preferences. Decision-making between facts, norms and interests.* Colchester: ECPR Press.

Levi-Faur, D., 2002. *Herding towards a new convention: on herds, shepherds and lost sheep in the liberalisation of the telecommunications and electricity industries.* University of Oxford: Nuffield College Working Papers in Politics, 2002–W6.

Lohmann, S., 1994. The dynamics of informational cascades. The Monday demonstration in Leipzig, East Germany, 1989–1991. *World politics*, 47, 42–101.

Maier, L.M., 2001. Sammelrezension: Ideen und Policies. *Politische Vierteljahresschrift*, 42, 523–548.

Maier, L.M., et al., eds., 2003. *Politik als Lernprozess? Wissenszentrierte Ansätze der Politikanalyse.* Opladen: Leske + Buderich.

Martens, K. and Wolf, K.D., 2006. Paradoxien der Neuen Staatsräson. Die Internationalisierung der Bildungspolitik in der EU und der OECD. *Zeitschrift für Internationale Beziehungen*, 13, 145–176.

May, P.J., 1992. Policy learning and failure. *Journal of public policy*, 12, 331–354.

Nullmeier, F., 2003. Zur Normativität des Lernbegriffs. *In*: L.M. Maier, *et al.*, eds. *Politik als Lernprozess?* Opladen: Leske + Budrich, 329–342.

Offe, C., 2001. Wessen Wohl ist das Gemeinwohl? In Die Öffentlichkeit der Vernunft und die Vernunft der Öffentlichkeit. *In*: L. Wingert and K. Günther, eds. *Die Öffentlichkeit der Vernunft und die Vernunft der Öffentlichkeit.* Frankfurt: Suhrkamp, 459–489.

Pierson, P., 2000. Increasing returns, path dependence, and the study of politics. *American political science review*, 94, 251–267.

Rose, R., 1991. What is lesson-drawing? *Journal of public policy*, 11, 3–30.

Sabatier, P.A., 1993. Advocacy-Koalitionen, Policy-Wandel und Policy-Lernen: Eine Alternative zur Phasenheuristik. *In*: A. Héritier, ed. *In Policy-Analyse: Kritik und Neuorientierung.* Opladen: Westdeutscher Verlag.

Saretzki, T., 1996. Wie unterscheiden sich Argumentieren und Verhandeln? Definitionsprobleme, funktionale Bezüge und strukturelle Differenzen von zwei verschiedenen Kommunikationsmodi. *In*: V.V. Prittwitz, ed. *Verhandeln und Argumentieren. Dialog, Interessen und Macht in der Umweltpolitik.* Opladen: Leske und Buderich.

Stone, D., 1999. Learning lessons and transferring policy across time, space and disciplines. *Politics*, 19, 51–59.

Stone, D., 2000. Non-governmental policy-transfer: the strategies of independent policy institutes. *Governance*, 13, 45–62.

Strassheim, H., 2003. Der Ruf der Sirenen – Zur Dynamik politischen Benchmarkings. Eine Analyse anhand der US Sozialreform. *In*: L.M. Maier, *et al.*, eds. *Politik als Lernprozess?*. Opladen: Leske + Buderich, 227–244.

Toens, K., 2007. Curricular governance in Germany. A historical institutionalist perspective. *ECPR joint sessions of workshops*. University of Helsinki.

Toens, K., 2008. Hochschulpolitische Interessenvertretung im Bologna Prozess. Akteure, Strategien und machtpolitische Auswirkungen auf die nationalen Verbände. *In*: U. Willems, T.V. Winter and B. Rehder, eds. *Interessenvermittlung im Wandel*. Wiesbaden: VS Verlag.

Toots, A., 2007. How the EU and Finland affect Estonian educational policy. The policy learning approach. *ECPR Joint Session*. University of Helsinki.

Walt, S.M., 2000. Fads, fevers, and firestorms. *Foreign policy*, 121, 34–41.

Working Group on Stocktaking, 2005. *Bologna process stocktaking report 2005*. Bergen: Norwegian Ministry of Education and Culture and European Commission.

Lesson-drawing and public policy: secondhand smoking restrictions in Scotland and England

Bossman E. Asare[a] and Donley T. Studlar[b]

[a]Division of Social Science, Graceland University, Lamoni, IA, USA; [b]Department of Political Science, West Virginia University, Morgantown, WV 26506-6317, USA

The dangers associated with the use of tobacco products have been documented extensively in the literature on public health and tobacco control. As a result, various countries, including subcentral units in federations and other devolved political systems, have adopted policies to control tobacco consumption. This article examines the effects lesson-drawing had on the adoption of restrictive secondhand smoke policies in Scotland and England in 2006 and 2007. Using elite interviews and documentary sources, the study finds that in both countries secondhand smoke policies were influenced by the adoption of similar policies in other English-speaking jurisdictions, especially the nearby Republic of Ireland. In turn, the adoption of a non-smoking policy in Scotland influenced England. This confirms Castles' (1993) claim of similar policies developing in the English-speaking 'family of nations' even at different levels of government. Policy transfer from Ireland to the United Kingdom is highly unusual, as is lesson-drawing from another jurisdiction within the United Kingdom to England. This may have occurred because the policy is fundamentally declaratory but with some need for compliance checks that are not resource-intensive. This path of lesson-drawing may be rare in the United Kingdom, but it may have broader implications for different types of lesson-drawing in multilevel governance.

Britain is an extreme example of policymakers ignoring geographical propinquity in favour of social psychological proximity. Ireland and France are each less than 25 miles from Great Britain, yet policymakers in London never think of looking there for lessons in public policy. British policymakers often look across the ocean to the United States or Canada, or even farther away to Australia (Rose 1993, p. 107).

Certainly, the ban on smoking in public places in Ireland was close enough to provide very good evidence that it should be copied in the UK; 'If they can do it, we certainly can' (Dr. Andy McEwen, personal communication, 2007).[1]

Introduction

Lesson-drawing across jurisdictions in tobacco control is well established (Studlar 2002, 2004, 2007, Farquharson 2003, Shipan and Volden 2006). One of the latest policy instruments being diffused is bans on secondhand smoke in restaurants and bars. Previously these venues had been subject to restrictions rather than prohibition because of resistance from their owners and patrons, backed by the tobacco industry, who argued that smoking after drinking was necessary to their success. Furthermore, they contended that bans in some jurisdictions would cause a loss of smokers' business to nearby locales lacking such prohibitions. Even these last redoubts for indoor smoking have increasingly been subject to challenge in recent years.

Ireland's 2004 introduction of a comprehensive countrywide indoor smoking ban, including restaurants and bars, surprised the rest of the world because of the long-standing 'pub culture' in that country. Soon thereafter, jurisdictions in the United Kingdom, first Scotland, followed by Northern Ireland, Wales, and England through the Westminster parliament, adopted similar sweeping non-smoking legislation after years of using 'voluntary agreements' with the hospitality industry to try to limit indoor smoking. This rapid adoption of similar polices in two nearby countries, with five separate jurisdictions, deserves closer scrutiny as to the significance of diffusion of policy in the process. Focusing on the policy process in Scotland and England, this article examines the adoption of secondhand smoke policies and the role of lesson-drawing from other jurisdictions.

The genesis of policies to control secondhand smoke is traceable to studies and reports in the early 1980s that concluded that environmental tobacco smoke (ETS) or secondhand smoke was responsible for the increases in certain diseases, such as cancer. Generally, policies to control secondhand smoking are premised on the idea that, even if smokers have voluntarily decided to assume the risks of incurring certain deadly diseases, they should not be allowed to increase the risk of others to these diseases. This has influenced the adoption of a number of restrictive tobacco control policies, including smoking restrictions in public places in several jurisdictions. The formation of the Framework Convention on Tobacco Control (FCTC) in 2003 under the leadership of the World Health Organization (WHO) underscored the commitment of countries and the European Union (EU) to address tobacco consumption. As the first global treaty on tobacco control, the WHO FCTC requires that parties to the agreement adopt appropriate policies to protect all persons from exposure to tobacco smoke.[2]

This article examines lesson-drawing as an independent variable. It explores how the drawing of policy lessons from other jurisdictions with restrictive policies on indoor smoking influenced policy development in British jurisdictions. Data for the study were collected through interviews and documents on tobacco control policy in British jurisdictions especially Scotland and England, as well as sources abroad. Interviewees are leading experts in tobacco control in public health institutions, tobacco control advocacy organizations, and academic institutions. Several individuals representing different departments were interviewed on questions related to the role of these jurisdictions, the effects of devolution, the activities of anti-tobacco groups, and the effects of lesson-drawing on the adoption of secondhand smoking policies. The study employed a purposive sampling method in order to identify the persons who have firsthand information about how lesson-drawing has shaped tobacco control policy in Scotland and England. The interviews were conducted through telephone and email from November 2006 to April 2007. Other sources included published academic books and articles and documents from governments, interest groups, and the World Health Organization.

Examining lesson-drawing as a possible influence on the adoption of secondhand smoking restrictions in England and Scotland poses a number of questions. First, how did lesson-drawing affect the adoption of policies in these two jurisdictions? Second, were there also lesson-drawing influences on the secondhand smoke policies chosen by the two other jurisdictions, Wales and Northern Ireland? Third, what was the source of the lessons: traditional English-speaking 'loaners', to the EU, such as the United States, Canada, Australia, and the European Union, or nearby Ireland, rarely consulted by the UK for policy transfer?

Lesson-drawing in public policy

Lesson-drawing is associated with several similar concepts such as policy diffusion, policy borrowing, policy transfer, emulation, policy copying, policy bandwagoning, policy shopping, and systematically pinching ideas (Schneider and Ingram 1988, Ikenberry 1990, Bennett 1991, Cox 1999, Dolowitz and Marsh 2000, Studlar 2002). Stone (2000) has noted that these various terms indicate that the transfer of policies, or action-oriented programs of governments (Rose 2005) to other jurisdictions, is a voluntary activity. This is based on a rational attempt to understand the most suitable programme for the home jurisdiction based on a study of one or more other jurisdictions, either those on the same level or on multiple levels (Evans 2004). These are unlike concepts such as penetration or external inducement (Ikenberry 1990), negotiated transfer (Evans 2004), direct-coercive transfer (Dolowitz and Marsh 2000), and exporting ideas or 'policy pusher' (Nedley 2004), which indicate some degree of compulsion by jurisdictions to follow the policies of others (Stone 2000).

Lesson-drawing can occur in different forms. Rose (2005) denotes seven different ways in which countries draw public policy lessons from abroad, ranging from 'photocopying' to 'selective imitation'. Other analysts (Dolowitz and Marsh 2000, Evans 2004, Ladi 2005) prefer a more parsimonious synthesis: (1) copying without modification, which is rare; (2) emulation, acceptance of a policy as the best practice to be followed closely; (3) hybridization/synthesis, combining elements of policies from different settings to make them more sensitive to domestic conditions; and (4) inspiration, borrowing an idea to stimulate fresh thinking and to facilitate policy change. These lessons can be drawn across policy sectors as well as across different jurisdictions such as countries. Tobacco control policies usually take the form of emulation or hybridisation.

Lesson-drawing studies generally have stressed how policies transfer horizontally from some jurisdictions to others, often countries or provinces. Vertical lesson-drawing can also occur, but especially when it is top-down, this may involve some amount of coercion or negotiated transfer, such as through financial incentives (Welch and Thompson 1980, Mossberger 2000). Within the broader literature on policy transfer, lesson-drawing indicates that policy-makers look elsewhere, especially to jurisdictions with best practices in certain policy sectors, for ideas on how to address public policy problems. Typically, these are ideas that have proven to be successful at addressing public policy problems in those jurisdictions and, consequently, they become benchmarks for countries looking for policy lessons. Policy-makers do this because they want to achieve similar, if not the same, goals as the countries from which the policies were adopted. The key policy and political actors involved in networks for lesson drawing or policy transfer include elected officials, political parties, bureaucrats, non-governmental advocacy groups, policy entrepreneurs and experts/consultants, transnational corporations, think-tanks, and intergovernmental institutions (Dolowitz and Marsh 2000).

Rose (2005, p. 22) has posited that lesson-drawing is a 'distinctive type of program, because it draws on foreign experience to propose a programme that can deal with a problem confronting national policy-makers in their home environments'. Policy-makers have to develop a cause-and-effect model of how particular programme elements produce a desired goal. According to Studlar (2002), lesson-drawing is complicated because those searching for lessons must have a comprehensive knowledge about the content of policy and policy development in two or more jurisdictions. Normal procedure is for policy-makers to travel to other jurisdictions to observe the operation of policies of interest as well as reading about such policies and receiving testimony about them from informed sources.

Rose (1993) contends that lesson-drawing has both normative (desirability) and empirical (practicality) components, which are integral to the process of learning from different jurisdictions. Empirically, policy-makers seeking to draw policy lessons from other places draw models of how policies work, what policy elements could be adopted and how, and the possible consequences of drawing policy lessons from other places. Normatively, policy-makers look for lessons that are consistent and compatible with their values. This suggests that lesson-drawing will mostly occur among countries with similar levels of economic and political development.

Castles (1993) takes this idea further, arguing that there are policy linkages based on cultural influences and historical ties among countries, what he calls 'families of nations'. Although the transmission belts for these influences are left somewhat vague, lesson-drawing is a distinct possibility. Both Castles (1993) and Rose (1993) stress that less internationally powerful and populous countries are more likely to draw lessons from more internationally powerful and populous countries than the reverse. In other words, while there may be policy-specific borrowing, there is a general international hierarchy of policy lenders and borrowers (Leichter 1983, see also Evans 2004). While this may involve some amount of coercion, at least historically, it can also be based on learning through selective information flow, even within epistemic communities, advocacy coalitions, and policy transfer networks (Ladi 2005). In Castles' schema, countries from particular families of nations, such as the English, Nordic, or Germanic, are more likely to look to culturally, historically, and linguistically-related countries to draw policy lessons. There is some empirical confirmation of this (Evans 2004).

On the basis of the discussions above, lesson-drawing is most likely to occur when policy-makers in some jurisdictions become convinced that others have policy practices worth examining and possibly adopting, in whole or in part, for their own jurisdictions. Diplomatically and economically powerful countries and provinces within countries that have excelled in particular areas of policy are more likely sources for lesson-drawing. For instance, several studies have demonstrated that Canadians are particularly attentive to the United States as a source of policy ideas (Hoberg 1991, Studlar 2002).

Such lesson-drawing is not necessarily easy, however, as resistance to new ideas may occur based on tradition, vested interests, inapplicability of others' experiences, or different values (Rose 2005). In addition to positive lessons being offered from other jurisdictions' policy experiences, negative lessons also may be drawn (Evans 2004). Some jurisdictions will be centres for lesson-drawing in tobacco control based on individual best practices or their overall ranking in benchmarking (league tables) for policies that have been proven effective in addressing the problem over time. For instance, Canada and the US state of California have been cited as playing this role (Smoking: just say no 2000, Studlar 2005).

Best practices in tobacco control are evidence-based policies and programs that have been proven effective in one or more jurisdictions and therefore are attractive to others desiring similar results (Centers for Disease Control and Prevention 1999, World Conference on Tobacco Or Health 2000, Nathan 2004). For instance, the Centers for Disease Control and Prevention (1999) document draws upon best practices in comprehensive tobacco control programs and policies in the US states. The WHO publication *Tools for advancing tobacco control in the XXIst century: success stories and lessons learned* (2003) performs a similar function for Europe.

More broadly, contributors to *World's best practices in tobacco control* (World Conference on Tobacco Or Health 2000) observe that evidence-based policies from various countries across the globe are essential for addressing the tobacco problem in other jurisdictions. The contributors cited countries with best practices in particular tobacco control instruments, including New Zealand, Australia, the United Kingdom, the United States, Ireland, Singapore, Canada, and Sweden, as well as subcentral jurisdictions such as Victoria and Tasmania in Australia and California and Massachusetts in the USA. However, what has influenced the adoption of tobacco control policies, especially on secondhand smoke, in the United Kingdom?

A brief history of tobacco control policy in the United Kingdom, 1997 to 2007

Recent studies have noted that the United Kingdom has some of the most comprehensive tobacco control policies in the European Union and the world (Joossens 2004, Joossens and Raw 2006, 2007, Asare 2007, Cairney 2007b). More specifically, these studies have argued that the United Kingdom has adopted best or comprehensive practices in tobacco control policy, including high taxation, a tobacco advertising ban, policies to combat tobacco smuggling, the use of publicly-financed Nicotine Replacement Therapy (NRT) to help smokers quit, public health education, restrictions on smoking in public places, age limits on cigarette purchases, and forthcoming graphic health warnings on cigarette packs, among others. Also, the United Kingdom has the highest government spending directed at tobacco reduction among EU member countries, along with one of the largest reductions in smoking over the past 30+ years (European Commission 2004). Even though most of these policies were adopted by the central government, the constituent countries have been responsible for controlling cigarette smoking in public places (Asare 2007, Cairney 2007a,b).

Before 1997, preserving the individual choice to smoke and the economic profitability of the tobacco industry were more important than public health reasons in influencing tobacco control policy (Cairney 2007b). High cigarette taxes were good for the British treasury, which was more dependent on such revenue than other

European countries (Berridge 2004, European Commission 2004). Numerous studies documented the influence that the tobacco industry exerted in the country (Friedman 1975, Daube 1979, Calnan 1984, Cox 1984, Taylor 1985, Baggott 1988, Read 1996, Berridge 2004). Voluntary agreements on advertising and sponsorship, health warning labels on packages, and cigarette contents largely allowed the tobacco industry to regulate itself, even against the increasingly vehement anti-tobacco stance of tobacco control groups such as the Action on Smoking and Health (ASH), the British Medical Association (BMA), the Royal College of Physicians (RCP) and others (Berridge 2004). Although the EU forced the government to adopt mandatory rotating health warnings and rules on cigarette contents, the UK resisted an advertising ban in EU deliberations (European Commission 2004). With the central government refusing to take comprehensive action against smoking, there remained wide scope for the tobacco industry to promote its products and few restrictions on smoking venues. While smoking rates had declined in the United Kingdom, government policies were far from comprehensive (Baggott 1988, Berridge 2004).

The new Labour government in 1997 was committed in its campaign documents to a stronger tobacco control agenda, including changing the traditional British practice of voluntary agreements with the tobacco industry to control advertising. However, initially it continued voluntary agreements with the hospitality industry for secondhand smoke restrictions (Asare 2007, Cairney 2009). After attaining office, it appointed the first Minister for Public Health in the UK. Policies were based on two Health Department White Papers that laid emphasis on public health issues, including greater tobacco control restrictions. These were *Smoking kills* (1998) and *Choosing health* (2004). The latter was influenced by the Treasury-commissioned Wanless Report (2004) on long-term public health trends, which urged firmer action on smoking. In both Health documents, the government set targets to reduce the smoking prevalence rate. The 2004 paper set a target of 21% or less by 2010, with a specific reduction in prevalence among routine and manual groups in England to 26% or less. The Scottish Executive also announced plans to reduce the smoking prevalence rate.[3]

Already in 1999, the British government had made a substantial investment in smoking cessation through a pilot programme of free treatment for smokers under the National Health Service (NHS). Eventually this became a more general programme for the NHS. This commitment was recognized as a 'best practice' (Raw and McNeil 2003, European Commission 2004). Later the government approved £60 million for local areas to undertake smoking cessation programs for pregnant women.

On tobacco advertising, the government decided to follow the first EU *Tobacco Advertising Directive 1* (TAD1), which required the banning of tobacco product advertisements on billboards and in the print media. This directive also gave sports and arts agencies a 5-year period to look for alternative sponsors for their programs.[4] Nonetheless, by 2001, no definitive UK action had been taken, which prompted several anti-tobacco groups to question the commitment of government towards tobacco control. Tobacco control groups also were critical of government intentions to exempt Formula One Racing from the ban, possibly because of the financial support Labour received from the company (Berridge 2004). However, Germany and some tobacco companies successfully petitioned the European Court of Justice to overturn the EU ban in 2000 (Berridge 2004).

Table 1.   Chronology of tobacco control in the United Kingdom, 1997–2007.

1997	Labour manifesto promises to ban tobacco advertising Labour government announces it would take action on cigarette smoking. First Minister for Public Health appointed.
1998	White Paper, *Smoking kills*; Government-subsidized cessation services begin
1999	Higher taxes, anti-smuggling enforcement improved; Scientific Committee on Tobacco and Health official government report on dangers of secondhand smoke; New voluntary code on non-smoking indoors
2000	Introduction of Tobacco Advertising and Promotion Bill to ban advertising
2002	*Tobacco Advertising and Promotion Act* passed, implemented 2003
2003	National Assembly for Wales requests legislative power on secondhand smoke
2004	Wanless Report, *Securing good health for the whole population*; White Paper, *Choosing health* Scottish Executive proposes indoor smoking ban, after a Private Member's bill
2005	Scottish Parliament passes the *Smoking, Health and Social Care (Scotland) Act* for ban in workplaces and public places, implemented in March 2006. Labour election manifesto promises partial smoking ban. In October, Northern Ireland Minister announces smoking ban in workplaces for 17 April 2007.
2006	House of Commons votes to introduce indoor non-smoking ban in England, implemented 1 July 2007; also allows National Assembly for Wales authority to make decision for Wales. Wales bans smoking indoors as of 1 April 2007.

Source: Berridge (2004), Cairney (2007a, 2007b), Asare (2007), ASH-UK www.ash.org

In 2002, the EU responded with a more limited directive, TAD2, banning advertising in print, radio and over the Internet, but not indirect advertising, brand stretching and advertising in non-EU-based media (Hervey 2001, Khanna 2001, Duina and Kurzer 2004, Strünck 2005). By that time, the Labour government had finally introduced its own domestic legislation, closely mirroring the defunct TAD1. The *Tobacco Advertising and Promotion Act 2002* came into effect in 2003 (Berridge 2004).[5] This ban has put an end to almost all forms of tobacco advertising and sponsorship in the country, including Internet advertising.[6] Policies have also been adopted to control tobacco advertising at point of sale (Asare 2007).

The government also introduced a 5% annual increase in real terms on tobacco taxes as a means to make cigarettes less affordable. Since poor smokers would be affected more by the higher taxes, the government offset this by broadening cessation services, including the provision of NRT free of charge to poor people by the NHS (Berridge 2004, Asare 2007).[7] That left secondhand smoke as the major issue left unresolved, with anti-tobacco groups clamouring for a ban. In 1998, an authoritative report by the Scientific Committee on Tobacco and Health confirmed the dangers of secondhand smoke. The adoption of devolution by the Labour government in 1997 provided an opportunity for a venue change through which anti-tobacco groups could overcome central government's reluctance to act (Cairney 2007b).

Secondhand smoking legislation: lesson-drawing in Scotland

Scotland's role in tobacco control policy, particularly policies to control cigarette smoking in public places and work places, began in 1999. Scotland had the highest smoking prevalence rate in the United Kingdom (Office for National Statistics 2004). Ironically, Scotland also has a strong tradition of health research and innovation (Berridge 2004). The Scottish Executive endorsed the UK *Smoking kills* White Paper of 1998 and vowed to adopt policies with a Scottish perspective to address cigarette smoking. The Executive arrived at this decision against the backdrop of tobacco control advocacy and research groups' complaints that *Smoking kills* did not envision strict government regulation of secondhand smoke (ASH Scotland 2005).

The government's stance on being tough on tobacco consumption was also spurred by anti-tobacco groups' propagation of numerous studies that concluded secondhand smoke was harmful to non-smokers. The groups called on the Scottish Parliament to pass legislation to restrict tobacco smoking in certain public places and workplaces within the shortest possible time. Additionally, two leading public officials in Scotland issued warnings about the public health situation. For instance, in his 1999 annual report the chief medical officer, Sir David Carter, pressed for a ban on smoking in public places in order to limit significantly the health hazards associated with tobacco smoking (ASH Scotland 2005).

Consequently, in response to media, public and anti-tobacco groups' concern about the negative effects of smoking in public places and workplaces on the health of the Scottish people, the Scottish Executive first adopted a voluntary agreement with the hospitality industry (pubs, bars, restaurants, hotels, etc) in May 2000 called the *Scottish Voluntary Charter*. Under this agreement, the hospitality industry was required to guarantee smoke-free areas in their premises. The Minister of Health for Scotland told the hospitality industry that if they failed to comply with the agreement, the government would introduce legislation to ban smoking in the hospitality industry. Nevertheless, even after reaffirming this commitment in *A breath of fresh air for Scotland* (2004), few hospitality companies complied with the agreement.

This convinced some senior public officials and anti-tobacco groups that the hospitality industry did not want to protect their workers and the public from the hazards of secondhand smoke (ASH Scotland 2005).[8] Pressured by bills introduced by backbenchers, in 2005 the Scottish Labour government through the Minister of Health, Andy Kerr,[9] introduced its own legislation to control cigarette smoking in public places and workplaces (Cairney 2009). Anti-tobacco groups in the country had evidence from Ireland that its 2004 legislation restricting smoking in public places and workplaces was effective in addressing secondhand smoking (Asare 2007).

The Scottish Parliament passed legislation in the same year prohibiting smoking in almost all workplaces and public places. The legislation, the *Smoking, Health and Social Care Act 2005*, entered into force on 26 March 2006. In addition to the Irish smoking ban, the Scottish Executive also was influenced by policy lessons on smoking restrictions from other places such as New York City, Canada, and Australia (Asare 2007). Knowledge of effective smoking restrictions in other jurisdictions allowed policy-makers in Scotland to adopt similar policies. The compliance rate of the legislation has been estimated to be high. Until April 2007, Scotland was the only constituent country in the UK with a comprehensive ban on smoking in public places and workplaces. This legislation partly contributed to the adoption of comprehensive secondhand smoking policies in the other three constituent countries (ASH Scotland 2005, Asare 2007).

Along with lesson-drawing, the granting of some policy autonomy to the Scottish Parliament was responsible for its decision to adopt comprehensive smoking bans in public places and workplaces. An interviewee even observed that:

> This devolved political system has enabled Scotland to adopt tobacco control measures ahead of other regions, notably the ban on smoking in public places. Wales and Northern Ireland have subsequently adopted this policy, while England eventually did last year (to be introduced in 2007) (Dr. Kelley Lee, personal communication, 2007).[10]

As Cairney (2009) points out, however, the central UK Health Ministry was closely involved in the legislative processes in all of these jurisdictions.

Secondhand smoking restrictions in England

Following concerns by anti-tobacco groups on the negative effects of secondhand smoking, in the 2005 election campaign the Labour party leadership made a manifesto commitment for legislation for a partial ban on smoking in public places and workplaces (Cairney 2007b). Nevertheless, after winning the election, some Members of Parliament (MPs) from the governing party considered that a partial ban of smoking in public places would lead to confusion and be impractical. About 89 MPs, 60 of them Labour backbenchers and the remaining 29 from other parties in the House of Commons, opposed the partial ban and called for a total ban of smoking in all public places. The MPs stressed that smoking should be banned in public buildings, restaurants and pubs. This was supported by the chief medical officer for England, who had been calling for such a ban in his annual reports since 2002, often citing other countries favourably (Cairney 2007b, 2009).

When the Labour leadership realized that it would be politically risky to ignore the concerns of its backbenchers, the government agreed to a free vote in the House of Commons for MPs to choose between a complete ban and partial ban of smoking in public places and workplaces (Templeton 2005). The chair of the Commons Health Select Committee (HSC), Kevin Barron, argued that a complete ban would help re-establish some leadership credibility after a series of backbench revolts on other issues (Cairney 2007b). It was highly unusual for a free vote to be allowed on a government-sponsored bill. Unlike most votes in the Commons, voting on this health bill would be based on individual MPs' views and popular opinion rather than strict partisanship (Webster and Charter 2006).

Accordingly, in February 2006, the House of Commons voted twice to make smoking in public places and workplaces illegal. In the initial vote, which required that smoking be banned in public places, including licensed premises was passed by 454 to 127. The last vote passed by 384 to 184 for a ban on smoking in public places, including private pubs, clubs and workplaces (Cowley and Stuart 2006, Cairney 2007b). Because of the free vote, 91% of MPs in the governing party, including 84% of cabinet ministers, voted in favour of comprehensive smoking bans. Cabinet members such as former Health Minister John Reid, who voted against the comprehensive smoking ban, argued that the government had to stick to its manifesto pledge of a partial smoking ban (Cowley and Stuart 2006). Even though the main opposition party, the Conservatives, opposed a complete ban, the level of support from the Labour party MPs was exceptional. This was partly because ASH and the BMA lobbied MPs directly while local health practitioners pressured MPs at the constituency level to support total smoking ban in public places (Cairney 2007b).

The bill came into force on 1 July 2007 in England, with fines for noncompliance (Webster and Charter 2006, Asare 2007). Later the government ran a public information notice in England on the dangers of secondhand smoke on television, online, in the press and on posters. This was another step to make cigarette smoking a socially unacceptable behaviour in the interests of general public health.

In the wake of the Irish and Scottish laws, the political authorities of other jurisdictions in the United Kingdom also passed regulations banning tobacco use in public places and workplaces. In Northern Ireland, self-government had been suspended, and the Minister for Health for that country, Shaun Woodward, was part of the UK central government. He visited Ireland and New York City in search of usable lessons. After public consultations and extensive media coverage of the Irish smoking ban, in 2005 Woodward prohibited smoking in enclosed public places and workplaces in Northern Ireland as of 30 April 2007 (Asare 2007, Cairney 2009).[11] In Wales, passage of the *Health Act 2006* by Westminster enabled the National Assembly of Wales (NAW) to regulate secondhand smoke policy for that country, something that had been on the agenda there since 2003. The grant of authority, combined with the examples of Ireland, Scotland, and Northern Ireland, spurred the NAW promptly to ban smoking in enclosed public places in Wales (Asare 2007, Cairney 2009). Thus, with the implementation of the *Health Act* in England in mid-2007, all four parts of the UK effectively had banned indoor smoking within a period of two years. This rapidity was all the more remarkable in view of the longstanding reluctance in the UK to confront this issue.

Effects of lesson-drawing in England

Interviews with knowledgeable informants indicate that lesson-drawing from Scotland and Ireland propelled England's decision to adopt similarly restrictive policies on secondhand smoking. An interviewee indicated that the central government took action on smoking in public places for England because Scotland had showed in the 2005 legislation that it was possible to have a smoke-free society (Julia Hurst, personal communication, 2007). Although only a minority of the interviewees supported this position, there is still considerable evidence that the central government followed the leadership of a unit under its authority.

The Irish smoking ban, announced in 2003 and begun in March 2004, made it the first country in Europe to adopt legislation that prohibited cigarette smoking in enclosed public places and workplaces, including restaurants and bars (Howell 2004, Allwright *et al.* 2005). The adoption of the legislation led to a significant reduction in respiratory symptoms as well as protecting workers from exposure to secondhand smoke (Allwright *et al.* 2005). Three annual reviews from 2004 through 2006 by the Irish Office of Tobacco Control have indicated that the success of the legislation has been remarkable; in 2006 the compliance rate by enclosed workplaces was about 95% (Office of Tobacco Control 2006). The public also showed overwhelming support for the policy by reporting violators of the legislation (Office of Tobacco Control 2006).

The question for Westminster became whether to leap ahead to the desired goal of banning indoor smoking, as the Irish and subsequently Scottish legislation had done, or to pursue a step-by-step approach. A Department of Health (DOH) report acknowledged that the government considered developments in tobacco control policy in other jurisdictions before adopting smoke-free public places and workplaces legislation for England. These included, however, experiences in the federal system of the United States, which provided international precedents for the more incremental approach favoured by the government (Cairney 2009). Members of the House of Commons, dominated by Labour, visited Ireland in 2004 and decided that the enhanced Irish version of tobacco control would be more effective for public health in England than what was on offer in the government bill (Templeton 2005, Cairney 2007a).

Interviewees were unanimous in their submission that the Irish smoking ban became the deciding factor for England to adopt comprehensive secondhand smoking policies. They pointed out that since the adoption of the ban on smoking in public places and workplaces in 2004 in Ireland, there were incessant demands on the central government from various segments of society for legislation to control smoking in public places and workplaces. Many of these submissions specifically cited the Irish precedent (see ASH 2004, n.d.).

Over the years, public health campaigners had promoted more stringent tobacco control policies for the UK, often citing foreign examples, especially from English-speaking Commonwealth countries. Another, more coercive, influence on British policy has been the European Union, which has harmonized member states' on taxation, health warnings on packages, advertising bans, cigarette contents, and also advocated member action on other tobacco control issues, such as secondhand smoke (European Commission 2004). In fact, the EU health warnings were stimulated by the example of Ireland, which did not want to compromise its mid-1980s mandatory rotating warnings under EU free trade rules (European Commission 2004). Despite earlier British resistance to some of these measures, especially mandatory health warnings and advertising, eventually the UK became reconciled to

Table 2.   Two smoking votes in House of Commons, February 2006.

	Ban on public licensed premises				Ban to include private clubs			
	Yes		No		Yes		No	
	N	%	N	%	N	%	N	%
Labour	304	91	29	9	278	84	52	16
Conservative	81	46	94	54	47	27	125	73
Liberal Democrats	55	95	3	5	47	85	8	15
Plaid Cymru	2	67	1	33	2	67	1	33
Democratic Unionist	8	100	0	0	8	100	0	0
Party SDLP	2	100	0	0	2	100	0	0
Ulster Unionist Party	1	100	0	0	1	100	0	0
Others	1	100	0	0	1	100	0	0
Total	454		127		384		184	

N = number of MPs.
SDLP = Social Democratic and Liberal Party.
Source: Cowley and Stuart (2006).

them. The EU actions were influenced by lessons drawn from other jurisdictions, notably Australia and Canada (European Commission 2004). While drawing a major tobacco control lesson directly from Ireland was unprecedented, the activities of epistemic communities and internationally-oriented advocacy groups had prepared the way.

Conclusions

The preceding analysis finds that lesson drawing has been instrumental in the adoption of secondhand smoking restrictions policy in both England and Scotland. The process of lesson drawing in these two jurisdictions involved a policy transfer network made up of civil servants, politicians, and anti-tobacco advocacy groups, supported by a broader epistemic community of scientists as well as favourable media coverage, and a more willing public. The causal model employed had a relatively simple, inexpensive design: reducing the damaging health effects of smoking by limiting where people could smoke. Secondhand smoke policies in England and Scotland as well as in Ireland have converged by using the same policy instrument, a ban on almost all indoor smoking. Cairney (2009) argues that the dramatic Irish ban was both popular and considered effective, providing a model for a non-incremental approach. The initial response to the Scottish legislation was similarly positive.

While lesson-drawing has largely been used to study policies cross-nationally, it is also essential for understanding public policies within countries, such as the United Kingdom, that have devolved powers to constituent jurisdictions. In this instance, anti-tobacco groups in England were able to use the Scottish secondhand smoking restrictions, as well as the Irish ones, as a precedent for similar legislation. Moreover, lesson-drawing fits with the family of nations conceptualization of Castles (1993), because both England and Scotland learned, either directly or indirectly, from the experiences of other English speaking countries, especially Ireland and the United States. Other jurisdictions in the English-speaking world, including New Zealand, provinces in Canada, states in Australia, and cities and states in the United States as well as some elsewhere, were considering the adoption of indoor smoking bans at approximately the same time (Gilmore 2005). Although Ireland had one of the longest experiences of implementation, British interest there began earlier. The geographical propinquity of Ireland to England and Scotland, as well as a shared language and the dramatic change in Irish government policy extensively covered by the British media, help explain why jurisdictions in the United Kingdom became familiar with the Irish secondhand smoking legislation.

Emulation of policies from Scotland to England is further indication that, in federal and quasi-federal polities, innovative policies can begin from lower level jurisdictions and then be adopted by a higher level. The division of authority over secondhand smoke regulations, even in centralized polities, may make this policy instrument particularly susceptible to such bottom-up policy diffusion. In addition to the United Kingdom, such lesson-drawing has been documented in countries ranging from New Zealand and Australia (Studlar 2005, 2007) to the United States (Shipan and Volden 2006).

More generally, tobacco control is an issue of multi-level governance, ranging from the local to the international, and needs to be analysed as such. The question of venue change and diffusion across jurisdictions are important ones for this policy and can illuminate more general processes in a world of shared governance (see Evans 2004, Cairney 2007b, Asare *et al.* 2009, Mamudu and Studlar 2009). In multi-level governance, there is more opportunity for 'polydiffusion' (Mossberger 2000) from multiple and unfamiliar sources (Evans and Davies 1999, Ladi 2005). This may help account for the counterintuitive finding that Ireland, of all places, was a preeminent source of policy, not only for Scotland but also for England through the central government at Westminster.

As Cairney (2007b) points out, it is highly unusual to have policy transfer move from the rest of the UK to England; usually it is the reverse. Since the United Kingdom is now a quasi-federal polity, older preferences about lesson-drawing developed when policy was exclusively a central choice, may no longer apply. Even if administrative devolution in the United Kingdom still largely relies on informal coordination between the central and devolved levels, such cooperation is no longer necessarily dominated by the centre.

It is perhaps as unusual to have a policy move from Ireland to England as from a devolved legislature to the central one in the United Kingdom. The United Kingdom has transferred many policies to its former colonies all over the world. Less frequently, but perhaps more often in the post-World War II period, it has searched abroad for lessons or incorporated them into domestic legislation (Heclo 1976, Leichter 1983). Documented cases of policy transfer to the United Kingdom typically find the lessons learned emerging from the United States and Canada, larger, more complex countries (Wolman 1992, Rose 1993, Studlar 1993, Dolowitz 1997, Mossberger 2000, Evans 2004, Waltman 2009). Thus the non-smoking legislation may be unprecedented for policy transfer to the United Kingdom from Ireland, a much smaller country more accustomed to taking policies from the UK, either from their common historical heritage or more deliberately. There is, however, more interaction on possible policy lessons between lower level jurisdictions in the United Kingdom and Ireland since they are similar in population (Cairney 2009).

Secondhand smoke bans are a type of policy that could be emulated 'up the hierarchy' from a smaller, younger country to a more populous, older one as well as from a devolved institution to the central government. This is largely what Dolowitz and Marsh (2000) call a voluntary policy, driven by perceived necessity for domestic or international prestige reasons, and a declaratory policy needing relatively little resource-intensive enforcement in money, personnel, or complex legislation. In short, it is largely self-enforcing and, on such policies, larger jurisdictions have no particular advantages although this did not prevent those opposed to a complete ban that it had never been tried on such a large and diverse population (Cairney 2009). In fact, Ireland's legislation acted, in effect, as a quasi-experiment for other countries. Its' small and relatively ethnically and cultural homogeneous population, lack of urban areas, and centralized authority allowed it to serve as a laboratory for a near-prohibition of indoor smoking. Other jurisdictions could wait, observe, and consider whether they wanted to follow. Because of the good initial reports, anti-tobacco activists inside and outside government were able to offer Ireland as a nearby, understandable example of what was possible. Then Scotland, Northern Ireland, Wales, and England followed.

In general, tobacco control is an issue that is very susceptible to lesson drawing across jurisdictions and countries, as many studies over the years have demonstrated

(Studlar 2002, 2005, 2007, Farquharson 2003). This is based on epistemic communities agreeing on the scientific evidence of harm from cigarette smoking, international and domestic advocacy groups who campaign against tobacco through publications, conferences, and travelling experts shrewd in garnering favourable media coverage. The policy transfer network also includes government officials and politically-based policy entrepreneurs in different jurisdictions. The latter groups are critical in convincing their counterparts who may be lukewarm, indifferent, or even opposed to lessons drawn from other jurisdictions because 'they cannot work here'. The more evidence that exists of successful adoption and implementation of policies elsewhere, the more persuasive the case that the anti-tobacco network can make in a particular jurisdiction.

While the conditions for some restrictions on secondhand smoke in Scotland and England had been developed from international lesson-drawing processes as well as domestic sources (Cairney 2007a), what pushed the Scottish and Westminster governments (and also the Welsh and Northern Ireland governments, according to Cairney 2009) to adopt a comprehensive ban was the Irish experience: dramatic, apparently successful in implementation, and well-publicized through anti-tobacco group advocacy. In Scotland, this encouraged a Labour government seeking significant policy action eventually to adopt a 'maximalist' position. Without the push from Ireland and then Scotland, all of the contemporary political problems at Westminster probably would have been insufficient to overcome the position of the government. Anti-tobacco advocacy groups were also unusually publicly active on the issue (Cairney 2007a), in a similar pattern to what occurred in Canada during the passage of the comprehensive tobacco control legislation from 1987–1988 (Studlar 2002). Lacking support from the Conservatives as the major opposition party, sufficiently numerous votes from Labour backbenchers on a whipped bill would have been unlikely to overcome the formidable barriers protecting governing party unity. The fact, however, that tobacco control was not a significant voting issue for the public allowed the government to allow a free vote without too much embarrassment.

One would not expect these findings to have universal application. Public health issues, while often developing a strong scientific base, tend to generate political controversy because they involve governments attempting to alter individual behaviour (Leichter 1991). Nevertheless, actions taken by governments to combat the tobacco epidemic could be applied to other public health issues such as obesity. While there has been increased concern about this issue, obesity is a more complicated issue; scientific as well as political consensus is more difficult to obtain. Even with the strong, globalized anti-tobacco groups operating since the 1980s, it has taken time for action beyond voluntary agreements on secondhand smoke to be taken in the United Kingdom.

Nor is it likely that jurisdictions in the United Kingdom will continue to look to Ireland for lessons to draw for public policies. In the case of secondhand smoke policy, the debate was over how fast and thoroughly to proceed with increased restrictions; in short, it was a controversy over calibration of policy instruments. Ireland provided a critical evidentiary base in this case, but it is likely to remain a 'one-off' case in jurisdictional terms. Similarly, as Cairney (2007a) points out, the vertical policy process in the United Kingdom is normally 'top-down' rather than 'bottom-up'. Thus while this case fits with more general findings for tobacco control policy processes across countries, it is unlikely to diffuse to other policy issues within the United Kingdom.

Notes

1. Department of Epidemiology, University College of London.
2. Article 4(1)-Guiding Principles of WHO FCTC.
3. Government Public Health White Paper, 2004.
4. From 1998 White Paper, *Smoking kills.*
5. Tobacco Advertising and Promotion Act 2002 from the Office of Public Archives http://www.opsi.gov.uk/acts/acts2002/ukpga_20020036_en_1 The Government set different effective dates for the full implementation of the various parts of the advertising ban.
6. ASH Briefing: The UK ban on Tobacco Advertising.
7. From 1998 White Paper, *Smoking kills.*
8. The Scottish Executive (2004) A Breath of Fresh Air for Scotland, Improving Scotland's Health: The Challenge.
9. He was named the Scottish politician of the year in 2006 for spearheading the banning of smoking in public places and workplaces in Scotland http://news.bbc.co.uk/2/hi/uk_news/scotland/north_east/6156548.stm
10. London School of Hygiene & Tropical Medicine, University of London United Kingdom.
11. The Smoking (Northern Ireland) Order 2006 No. 2957 (N.I.20) http://www.opsi.gov.uk/si/si2006/uksi_20062957_en.pdf [Accessed 23 September 2008].

References

Allwright, S., *et al.*, 2005. Legislation for smoke-free workplaces and health of bar workers in Ireland: before and after study paper. *British medical journal*, 331, 1117. Available from: http://www.bmj.com/cgi/content/full/331/7525/1117 [Accessed 20 January 2007].

Asare, B., 2007. *Tobacco control: comparative public policy in the United Kingdom and South Africa.* Saarbrücken, Germany: VDM Verlag.

Asare, B., Cairney, P., and Studlar, D., 2009. Federalism and multilevel governance in tobacco policy: the European Union, the United Kingdom, and UK devolved institutions. *Journal of public policy,* 29 (1), 79–102.

ASH, 2004. All party group of politicians urges Health Secretary to adopt Irish smokefree model. ASH News Release, 20 October. Available from: http://www.ash.org.uk/ashb127ac49.htm [Accessed 27 November 2006].

ASH, n.d. Lessons learned from Ireland's smoke-free law: the case for similar UK-wide legislation. Available from: http://www.nosmokinglaw.co.uk/smokingbaneireexperience.htm [Accessed 27 November 2006].

ASH Scotland, 2005. *The unwelcome guest: how Scotland invited the tobacco industry to smoke outside.* Edinburgh, Scotland.

Baggott, R., 1988. Health vs. wealth: the politics of smoking in Norway and the UK. *Strathclyde Papers on Government and Politics,* No. 57.

Bennett, C., 1991. Review article: what is policy convergence and what causes it? *British journal of political science,* 21 (2), 215–233.

Berridge, V., 2004. Militants, manufacturers, and governments: postwar smoking policy in the United Kingdom. *In*: R. Bayer and E. Feldman, eds. *Unfiltered: conflicts over tobacco policy and public health.* Cambridge: Harvard University Press, 89–113.

Cairney, P., 2007a. A 'multiple lenses' approach to policy change: the case of tobacco policy in the UK. *British politics*, 2 (1), 45–68.

Cairney, P., 2007b. Using devolution to set the agenda? Venue shift and the smoking ban in Scotland. *British journal of politics and international relations*, 9 (1), 73–89.

Cairney, P., 2009. The role of ideas in policy transfer: the case of UK smoking bans since devolution. *Journal of european public policy*, 16 (3), 471–488.

Calnan, M., 1984. The politics of health: the case of smoking control. *Journal of social policy*, 3 (13), 278–296.

Castles, F., ed., 1993. *Families of nations: patterns of public policy in Western democracies.* Aldershot: Dartmouth.

Centers for Disease Control and Prevention, 1999. *Best practices for comprehensive tobacco control programs.* Atlanta, GA: US Department of Health and Human Services.

Cowley, P. and Stuart, M., 2006. *The St Valentine's day manifesto massacre: the smoking votes.* Available from: http://www.revolts.co.uk/smoking%20vote%2014%20Feb%2006.pdf [Accessed 20 January 2007].

Cox, H., 1984. Smoking, tobacco promotion and the voluntary agreements. *British medical journal*, 288, 303–305.

Cox, R., 1999. Ideas, international policy transfer and 'models' of welfare reform. Paper presented to the *Conference on Global Trajectories.* The Robert Schuman Centre, European University Institute, Florence, Italy 25–26 March.

Daube, M., 1979. The politics of smoking: thoughts on the Labour record. *Community Medicine*, 1 (4), 306–314.

Dolowitz, D., 1997. British employment policy in the 1980s: learning from the American experience. *Governance*, 10 (1), 23–42.

Dolowitz, D. and Marsh, D., 2000. Learning from abroad: the role of policy transfer in contemporary policy-making. *Governance*, 13 (1), 5–23.

Duina, F. and Kurzer, P., 2004. Smoke in your eyes: the struggle over tobacco control in the European Union. *Journal of european public policy*, 11 (1), 57–77.

European Commission, 2004. *Tobacco or health in the European Union: past, present and future.* Luxembourg: Office for Official Publications of the European Commission.

Evans, M., ed., 2004. *Policy transfer in global perspective.* London: Ashgate.

Evans, M. and Davies, J., 1999. Understanding policy transfer: a multi-level, multi-disciplinary perspective. *Public administration*, 77 (2), 361–385.

Farquharson, K., 2003. Influencing policy transnationally: pro- and anti-tobacco global advocacy networks. *Australian journal of public administration*, 62 (4), 80–92.

Friedman, K., 1975. *Public policy and the smoking-health controversy.* London: Lexington Books.

Gilmore, N., 2005. *Clearing the air: the battle over the smoking ban.* Dublin: Liberties Press.

Heclo, H., 1976. *Modern social politics in Britain and Sweden.* New Haven: Yale University Press.

Hervey, T., 2001. Up in smoke? Community (anti)-tobacco law and policy. *European law review*, 26 (2), 101–125.

Hoberg, G., 1991. Sleeping with an elephant: the American influence on Canadian environmental legislation. *Journal of public policy*, 11 (1), 107–132.

Howell, F., 2004. Ireland's workplaces, going smoke free: Editorial. *British Medical Journal*, 328, 847–848.

Hurst, J., 2007. Responses on interview questions on tobacco control in Scotland [telephone]. (Personal communication, 12 February 2007).

Ikenberry, J., 1990. The international spread of privatization policies: inducements, learning and 'policy bandwagoning. *In*: E. Suleiman and J. Waterbury, eds. *The political economy of public sector reform and privatization.* Boulder: Westview Press, 99–106.

Joossens, L., 2004. *Effective tobacco control policies in 28 European countries.* Brussels: European Network for Smoking Prevention.

Joossens, L. and Raw, M., 2006. The tobacco control scale: a new scale to measure a country activity. *Tobacco control*, 15, 247–253.

Joossens, L. and Raw, M., 2007. *Progress in tobacco control in 30 European countries, 2005–2007.* Presented at 4th European Conference on Tobacco or Health, Basil.

Khanna, D., 2001. The defeat of the European Tobacco Advertising Directive. *In*: P. Eeckhout and T. Tridimas, eds. *Yearbook of European law: volume 20*. Oxford: Oxford University Press, 113–138.

Ladi, S., 2005. *Globalisation, policy transfer and policy research institutes*. Northampton, MA: Edward Elgar.

Lee, K., 2006. Responses to interview questions on UK tobacco control. [e-mail]. (Personal communication, 25 October 2006).

Leichter, H.M., 1983. The patterns and origins of policy diffusion: the case of the Commonwealth. *Comparative politics*, 15, 223–233.

Leichter, H.M., 1991. *Free to be foolish: politics and health promotion in the United States and Britain*. Princeton: Princeton University Press.

Mamudu, H. and Studlar, D., 2009. Multilevel governance and shared sovereignty: European Union, member states, and the FCTC. *Governance*, 22 (1), 73–97.

McEwan, A., 2006. Responses on interview questions on tobacco control in the United Kingdom [e-mail]. (Personal communication, 19 October 2006).

Mossberger, K., 2000. *The politics of ideas and the spread of enterprise zone*. Washington: Georgetown University Press.

Nathan, R., 2004. *Model legislation for tobacco control: a policy development and legislative drafting manual*. France: International Union for Health Promotion and Education.

Nedley, A., 2004. Policy transfer and the developing-country experience gap: taking a southern perspective. *In*: M. Evans, ed. *Policy transfer in global perspective*. Aldershot, Hampshire: Ashgate, 165–189.

Office for National Statistics, 2004. *Living in Britain: results from the 2002 general household survey*. London: The Stationery Office.

Office of Tobacco Control, 2006. *Annual report*. Ireland: Office of Tobacco Control.

Raw, M. and McNeil, A., 2003. Tobacco dependence treatment in England. *In*: *Tools for advancing tobacco control in the XXIst Century: success stories and lessons learned*. Geneva: World Health Organization.

Read, M., 1996. *The politics of tobacco: policy networks and the cigarette industry*. Aldershot, Hampshire: Avebury.

Rose, R., 1993. *Lesson drawing in public policy: a guide to learning across time and space*. Chatham, NJ: Chatham House.

Rose, R., 2005. *Learning from comparative public policy: a practical guide*. London: Routledge.

Schneider, A. and Ingram, H., 1988. Systematically pinching ideas: a comparative approach to policy design. *Journal of public policy*, 8 (1), 61–80.

Shipan, C. and Volden, C., 2006. Bottom-up federalism: the diffusion of antismoking policies from US cities to states. *American journal of political science*, 50 (4), 825–843.

Smoking: just say no, 2000. *The Economist*, 9 December, p. 72.

Stone, D., 2000. Learning lessons, policy transfer and the international diffusion of policy ideas. *Centre for the Study of Globalization and Regionalization*, 9th February 2000.

Strünck, C., 2005. Mix-up: models of governance and framing opportunities in US and EU consumer policy. *Journal of consumer policy*, 28 (2), 203–230.

Studlar, D., 1993. Ethnic minority groups, agenda setting and policy borrowing in Britain. *In*: P. McClain, ed. *Minority group influence: agenda setting, formulation and public policy*. New York: Greenwood Press, 15–32.

Studlar, D., 2002. *Tobacco control: comparative politics in the United States and Canada*. New York: Broadview Press.

Studlar, D., 2004. Tobacco control policy in a shrinking world: how much policy learning? *In*: E. Vigoda-Gadot and D. Levi-Faur, eds. *International public policy and management: policy learning and policy beyond regional, cultural and political boundaries*. New York: Marcel Dekker, 189–209.

Studlar, D., 2005. The political dynamics of tobacco control in Australia and New Zealand: explaining policy problems, instruments, and patterns of adoption. *Australian journal of political science*, 40 (2), 255–274.

Studlar, D., 2007. Ideas, institutions and diffusion: what explains tobacco control policy in Australia, Canada and New Zealand? *Commonwealth and comparative politics*, 45 (2), 164–184.

Taylor, P., 1985. *The smoke ring: tobacco, money and multinational politics.* New York: New American Library.

Templeton, S., 2005. The renewed pressure to introduce total smoking ban. *The Sunday Times,* 18 Dec, A. Available from: http://www.timesonline.co.uk/article/0, 2087-1938184,00.html. [Accessed 30 December 2006].

Waltman, J., 2009. Reformulating social policy: the minimum wage, the New Deal, and the working families tax credit. *In*: T. Casey, ed. *The Blair legacy: politics, policy, governance, and foreign affairs.* London: Palgrave, 112–134.

Webster, P. and Charter, D., 2006. Britain gives up smoking. *The Times,* 15 February,. Available from: http://www.timesonline.co.uk/article/0,,2-2041159,00.html [Accessed 1 February 2007].

Welch, S. and Thompson, K., 1980. The impact of federal incentives on state policy innovation. *American journal of political science,* 24 (4), 715–729.

Wolman, H., 1992. Understanding cross-national policy transfer: the United Kingdom and the United States. *Governance,* 5 (1), 27–45.

World Conference on Tobacco Or Health, 2000. World's best practices in tobacco control. *Tobacco control,* 9, 228–236.

Policy mimesis in the context of global governance

Andrew Massey

Department of Politics, University of Exeter, Amory Building, Rennes Drive, Exeter EX4 4RJ, UK

The concept of 'policy transfer' is contested. Earlier work has discussed the defining traits, but generally concluded that the dissimilarities of regional and local implementation ensure a simple transfer in the form of a generic template remains elusive (Common 2001). The argument of this article is that it is more accurate to refer to policy mimesis, the imitation or reproduction of a policy in another context, rather.than a simple transposition across geographical and political boundaries. There are levels of isomorphism within a given public administration. Both coercive and mimetic isomorphism, as well as professionalization, act as intrinsic dynamics to successful policy mimesis and its impact within policy networks to effect isomorphic recombination. The importance of locating policy analysis within its proper context includes giving due cognisance to *time*, chronologically and historically, as well as social culture, political culture, economics and geographical location (Pollitt 2008). This article is not an attempt to apply any one theoretical perspective, but a discussion as to why each attempted transfer of a policy is unique. Reference is made to a case study, the successful privatization of Kenya Airways (KQ) which is explored in more detail elsewhere (Massey 2010), as an example of policy mimesis and an explanation of the role of different 'triggers' and dynamics that drove the process forward as part of the global advance of New Public Management, an adjunct to many aspects of global governance.

Introduction

The concept of 'policy transfer', as this volume demonstrates, is a contested one. Earlier work has discussed the defining traits, but generally concluded that the dissimilarities of regional and local implementation ensure that a simple transfer in the form of a transportable generic template remains elusive (Common 2001). The argument of this article is that it is more accurate to refer to policy mimesis, the imitation or reproduction of a policy in another context, rather than a simple transposition across geographical and political boundaries. The historical, geographical, economic, social and political context within which a policy is located informs the dynamics that determine the way in which policy is made and implemented. They also structure its effectiveness, in relation to its stated goals. It may be that there is no such thing as a simple policy transfer, or indeed a transfer at all, rather there are levels of isomorphism within a given public administration. Both coercive and mimetic isomorphism may be observed, a concept mostly applied to the debate on Europeanization, but it is a perspective that has wider application (Lodge 2002, pp. 48–49, Carr and Massey 2006, p. 25). Professionalization is also an intrinsic dynamic to successful policy mimesis and its impact within policy networks to effect isomorphic recombination is a key to understanding 'policy transfer' in areas such as privatization, regulatory reform and marketization (Lodge 2002, Massey 2010).

The importance of locating policy analysis within its proper context includes giving due cognisance to *time*, chronologically and historically, as well as social and political culture (Pollitt 2008). The policy process exists within a narrative informed by the theoretical and practical context in which it is situated. Pollitt explores the use of several theoretical perspectives to explain this phenomenon and demonstrates the value of the Path Dependency Model amongst others (2008). This article is not an attempt to apply any one theoretical perspective, but a discussion as to why each attempted transfer of a policy is unique. Reference is made to a case study, the successful privatization of Kenya Airways (KQ) which is explored in more detail elsewhere (Massey 2010), as an example of policy mimesis and an explanation of the role of different 'triggers' and dynamics that drove the process forward as part of the global advance of New Public Management, an adjunct to many aspects of global governance.

The privatization of KQ, as with many others, illustrates the importance of context, of people and of place. It demonstrates the need to structure institutions and procedures in such a way that the desired results may be attained, but it is the personnel that staff them that are important (Massey 2010). KQ's example demonstrates the need to secure a constellation of factors in order to effect change; a punctuation point within the daily administration of an institution in order to move away from current practice and break the cycle of decline (Pollitt 2008, p. 46). The methodology involved interviewing several senior British and Kenyan public and private sector officials (Massey 2010). The remainder of this article explores in turn the concept of global governance; the nature of public goods; the context and purpose of public administration; and the applicability of the concept of policy mimesis.

Global governance

Governance refers to the inclusion of civil society and the economic, professional and social interest groups into the process of governing though that inclusion is neither comprehensive or on an equal basis (Anyang'Nyong'O 2002). Some groups and networks are exclusive and dominant and it is these that civil society struggle to hold to account. It follows therefore that there may exist both *good* governance and *bad* governance, with the latter falling short of those elements such as accountability and transparency (Massey 2010). Governance is, 'rules, processes and behaviour that affect the way in which powers are exercised ... particularly as regards openness, participation, accountability, effectiveness and coherence' (Massey and Pyper 2005, p. 8 cited EU White Paper). A more global perspective views the concept of governance as a description of the realization that with few exceptions hierarchical and bureaucratically centralized government is no longer the dominant form of political system, in most states a more pluralistic concept of power and service delivery now holds sway, albeit in a series of structures often dominated by powerful coalitions of interests (Massey 2010). It is necessary, however, to recognize the disparity of power and influence that exists between different polities and the weakness of some national powers and groups of powers to address wider issues of crime, economic exploitation and environmental degradation. *Good* governance begins with transparency and democratic accountability. Not only government institutions, but also civil society institutions involved in governance, NGOs and others, according to some observers, may (or perhaps 'should') aspire to be transparent, accountable for their actions, operate ethically beyond the boundaries of race, ethnicity, religion, culture and politics and respect, and support individual human rights (Omelicheva 2004, p.8 cited Massey 2010).

New Public Management tools such as privatization can contribute to good or bad governance depending on the context in which they are located; they are simply means and not ends. If located within a context of low corruption and independent civil society institutions that include an independent judiciary and a clear regulatory framework that is enforced, then it may contribute positively; if not then it may contribute to continuing corruption (Massey 2010). The state can ensure good governance by becoming more engaged in certain areas, not less, for example by protecting citizens through an effective regulatory framework, as well as ensuring basic political and social order, that is personal security, political legitimacy, popular participation and the rule of law (Anyang'Nyong'O 2001, p. 8). There needs to be a functioning civil society replete with a complexity of institutions to entrench these important aspects.

Although there are aspects of 'global governance' observable from the time of the classical empires, the modern concern with globalization (an essentially economic phenomenon) and global governance (a political and administrative phenomenon) dates from 1945 and the establishment of the institution and organizations of the United Nations. Obviously global governance is distinct from 'world government', and indeed in many ways conflicts with that concept. It is also distinct from, though related to, the many private governance arrangements involving transnational corporations and business associations in the international arena (Ruggie 2004, pp. 502–503). The sudden end to the Cold War and the dissolution of the Soviet Union accelerated the liberalization and globalization process (Putzel 2005, Thynne and Massey 2009). Calls for the democratization and accountability of global governance coming as a response to the actions of NGOs, especially the Bretton Woods Institutions of the World Bank and International Monetary Fund, need to be linked to a 'detailed consideration of governance mechanisms' (Whitman 2002, p. 47). It may be argued that:

> The nation state, empires through colonisation, national self-determination through decolonisation, economic globalisation, and the possibility of global civil society are all appreciated as being the products of significant, and often oscillating, forces in national and international arenas particularly over the last 250–300 years. Also appreciated as being of great importance nationally and internationally, but over a much shorter period of time, has been the progress made in the recognition and protection of human rights and justice, in respect of which much more remains to be achieved (Thynne and Massey 2009, p. 14).

The premise behind the hollowing-out of the state thesis (Rhodes 1997) has not meant that power has gone away, but that it is no longer located exclusively in terms of national sovereignty. As such, policy making takes place within the economic context of globalization and the political context of global governance.

The study of global governance involves exploring collective international action in many forms in the public sphere, especially that concerned with global public goods, with consequences for human rights, humanity and the quality of life. It focuses on the nature and extent of state power in relation to the power of markets and civil society, both nationally and internationally. Global governance is related to the organization of the role of transnational corporations (TNCs) and NGOs, especially those that are becoming institution-defining entities in international arenas such as GATT and the WTO (Thynne and Massey 2009, pp. 13–27). Governance without government (or more accurately beyond, or outside of government) is in danger of transferring control over important global (and national) public goods to powerful TNCs and NGOs: organizations operating within institutions that may lack locatable accountability, as such the means of ensuring coherent and equitable action require the existence of a coherent and equitable system of global governance (Thynne and Massey 2009).

Archibugi's belief that the concept of national sovereignty itself has declined to the extent it is merely 'a dogma to overcome', has led him to argue that, 'the belief that a political or institutional body should be exempted from justifying its actions is incompatible with the essence of democracy' and therefore that, 'we must face up to the challenge of finding an effective replacement', for national sovereignty, 'since the formal claim of sovereignty is still needed today to curb the dominance of the strong over the weak' (2004, p. 452). His (and others) call for some kind of global constitutionalism, including a World Court, however, infers some kind of world government. Such a prospect has amongst its critics those who have already criticized the political role adopted by the European Court in the EU and the US Supreme Court. For an accountable ordering of global public goods, it is preferable to retain a major role for traditional politics (and policy makers) and avoid a further move towards the juridicalization of political life as constitutionalizing issues out of the political domain reduces the likelihood of positive political change (Thynne and Massey 2009).

In the national arena, public goods are those that are available for all to consume. Economic theory suggests that in their pure form their enjoyment by one or more groups do not detract from their utility for other groups and that they are non-exclusive (Kaul 2005, p. 137 cited Thynne and Massey 2009, pp. 13–27). Examples of national public goods include law and order, health-care and education. Universal rights may assume the role of global public goods, alongside more traditional items such as the atmosphere, the sea and other global 'commons'. In the case of the atmosphere, for example, it has been used globally as a sink for depositing greenhouse gas emissions and the sea has been exploited for its 'free' food resources and also as a dump for human waste (Kaul 2005, pp. 137–139 cited Thynne and Massey 2009). Kaul argues there is a need to, 'rethink notions of "public" and "private"'. Individual firms and households pursue self-interests; and states can provide incentives for them to jump over their hurdles of self-interest and contribute more to the provision of global public goods (Kaul 2005, pp. 139–140 cited Thynne and Massey 2009). In terms of the notion of policy mimesis, the use of concepts such as the UN's Millennium Goals and the Bretton Woods institutions' drive for modernization through NPM, act as dynamics to achieve public sector modernization and civic society growth. These *de facto* global governance pressures lead to isomorphic tendencies in many states. However, the formal structures these take will vary over time and place. The complexity of the global policy process means that the distinction between public and private, and between national state institutions, is blurred often in practice, if not in law. Global civic politics are located within a context of overlapping and constantly shifting boundaries. The old national certainties and structures are removed from much of global governance, which is often a kind of private governance. As Ruggie argues:

> Non-state actors in world politics may be animated by universal values or factional greed, by profit and efficiency considerations, or the search for salvation. They include transnational corporations and financial institutions; civil society organizations; faith-based movements; private military contractors that in some respects resemble the mercenaries of yore; and such illicit entities as transnational terrorists and criminal networks. Whatever their other differences, this much they have in common – increasingly, they think and act globally (Ruggie 2004, pp. 509–510 cited Thynne and Massey 2009, p. 17).

The emergence of significant forms of private governance in the global arena, as recognized here by Ruggie, is also addressed, for example, by Pattberg (2005). He argues (Pattberg 2005, pp. 591–592) that private governance embraces 'at least three substantive shifts within world politics'. Thus:

> First, the locus of authoritative problem solving does not rest with governments and their international organizations alone. Authority is indeed relocated in many different settings, involving public-private as well as purely private actor constellations. Second, the predominantly confrontational relation between companies, governments, and civil society has been complemented by partnership as one possible mode of interaction. And third, cooperation is getting more and more institutionalized, resulting in social practices that effectively govern specific issue areas (Thynne and Massey 2009).

Institutions of 'good' global governance need to come to terms with these issues and realities. It is the interplay between 'civil society organizations and transnational corporations that is engendering and instituting new expectations concerning the global social responsibility' of companies, individuals and NGOs (Ruggie 2004, p. 510). Global governance will need to develop legitimate institutions for addressing these issues. This will require attention to accountability, transparency, social capacity building and ethics in novel but democratic ways. These values are important because in recent years in the context of rapid global change and 'significant social, economic, and political crises, some communities and polities have broken down, even to the point of violent conflict' (Putzel 2005, p. 6). It should be remembered that what is often referred to using the brief term 'globalization' is liberal globalization based upon the three pillars of the Washington consensus: fiscal austerity, privatization and market liberalization (Putzel 2005, p. 7).

Joseph Stiglitz, the former chief economist of the World Bank has criticized this view for the negative impact it has had on many impoverished communities (Putzel 2005, p. 7 cited Thynne and Massey 2009, pp. 13–20). Partly as a result of this, some commentators are moving towards a new model of public management which Stoker (2006, p. 46) identifies as the 'public value management' model. He argues that for 'the advocates of public value management, there is a strong sense that the public realm is different from that of the commercial sector' and that governing 'is not the same as shopping or more broadly buying and selling goods in a market economy. As a result, some of the prescriptions of New Public Management drawn from private sector experience may not be appropriate' (Stoker 2006). Analysts need to be aware that 'in the public value model, politics is not confined to some specific space, and this characteristic makes for a considerable contrast' with 'traditional public administration and New Public Management' (Stoker 2006). He argues that 'in the public value paradigm, politics is the process that breathes life into the whole process' (Stoker 2006). This approach allows for the forceful introduction of politics as an integral part of policy analysis and (more importantly) as the driving dynamic in global governance in respect of scarce, or limited and valuable global public goods. The process and procedures of politics are important as a means of coping publicly with complexities and uncertainties in national and international policy alike (Thynne and Massey 2009, pp. 14–17, 25–26).

Public administration

Within the discipline of public administration, the concern regarding the applicability of NPM techniques by the Bretton Woods institutions, as noted in the preceding section, became more widespread as some of their effects became a cause for concern. An adherence to privatization by the World Bank and International Monetary Fund (IMF) throughout the 1990s led some writers to discern a comprehensive and undifferentiated approach to public sector reform in Africa, Asia and the former Soviet Union; reform informed by an economic determinist view of society (Anyang'Nyong'O 2002, Mwaura 2007 cited Massey 2010). A state's public administration reflects the political and social values and practices of a country and is an essential element in maintaining a society's cohesion and prosperity. A properly functioning democracy and the development of good governance are dependent upon an effective and ethical public administration (Pichardo Pagaza and Argyriades 2009, Massey 2010). Public institutions, 'are always means and never ends; they represent "tradeoffs": Improvements in one or more performance measures are realised only at the sacrifice of others' and the resulting institutional structures reflect this (Williamson 1985, p. 408). Policy-makers are constrained by the decisions taken by their predecessors (in the form of laws, custom and practice, sunk investments in plant and machinery, budgetary commitments) by the historical legacy they inherit and by their own biases (Pollitt 2008). Everything in terms of policy decisions takes place in the way it does because of what has gone on before and what is going on around and nothing can be entirely replicated when it crosses geographical and cultural boundaries. All policy transfer is in reality policy mimesis.

Policy mimesis

In former colonial countries, the concern (indeed the search) for good governance as a tool to assist in ameliorating poverty can be traced to their independence struggles. Colonial governments established parastatals 'on the understanding that they would be the most appropriate mechanism for providing services that were not provided by the private sector' (Mwaura 2007, p. 42). The governments of the newly-independent states built on this, developing public enterprises in order to 'maintain a high degree of public control over national resources as a means of facilitating national growth' and promote social justice (Ikiara 2000, pp. 44–45). Simultaneous to this was a growth in the work of many NGOs in these countries in areas as diverse as health care, famine relief and economic development. Substantial state directed resources were used to develop the provision of education, health and physical infrastructure in Africa in the immediate post-independence period (Anyang'Nyong'O 2001, p. 7). A proportion of this was given by donor nations, the amount varying from country to country. Many emergent states considered 'nationalization' an essential element of economic survival and there was sustained, if uneven, development in the first decades of independence. In many states 'it became clear that state intervention in the economy was not necessarily leading to sustained wealth creation that could improve the lives of the poor' (Anyang'Nyong'O 2001, p. 7). Too often, it seemed, an interventionist state and growing public sector led to 'wealth being concentrated within small and corrupt privileged elite. In such countries, politics also remained the preserve of this elite, with the state assuming an increasingly authoritarian character' (Anyang'Nyong'O 2001, p. 7).

During the 1980s and 1990s, many Western countries were implementing the principles of NPM, the IMF and World Bank tried to impose a consensus on how to develop and run emergent countries. They took the view that the policy of privatization had been 'good' for those economies that had taken it the furthest, the US, UK, Australasia and the Tiger economies of the Far East; the reasoning followed it would also be 'good' for the former Soviet Union and Africa (Massey 2010). African governments were persuaded and sometimes coerced into copying Western patterns of liberalization and state restructuring, with loans, aid and favourable trading agreements being contingent upon such reforms (Kwama 2008). As noted elsewhere, this approach was overly simplistic in that the successful policy transfer of liberalization and NPM to East Asian countries reflected different socio-political constructions and relationships between the political elite and civil society, even then the transfer took place *mutatis mutandis* and was not a straight copy but an interpretation of the Western approach (Common 2001, Massey 2010). Privatization worked in those countries because it was done in a way that integrated it with the prevailing social, economic and political institutions, without challenging those institutions. The attempt to simply 'transfer' these policies to the former Soviet Union and Africa missed this essential point.

Many African observers were highly critical of the simplistic 'one-size-fits-all' approach adopted in the former Soviet Union under IMF and World Bank pressure. For thoughtful African observers Russia illustrated many of the problems of privatization and was identified with the demise of major industries and the collapse of important parts of civil society (Anyang'Nyong'O 2001, p. 8, Massey 2010). The IMF and WB view that 'good economic performance required liberalized trade, macroeconomic stability' and getting prices right, meant they pushed for less government intervention in the economy and the use of markets to allocate resources efficiently. NPM also meant the importation of private sector managers and techniques into the remaining governmental institutions (Anyang'Nyong'O *et al.* 2000, p. 2). There remained a significant problem with this for African observers in that it presupposed an independent judiciary, fully functioning civil society and a largely incorrupt public service. In much of Africa these do not exist and what occurred was similar to that which was inflicted upon the former Soviet Union in that public monopolies became private monopolies and there occurred state-sanctioned robbery on a large scale (Murray 2006).

The context for the pressure from the Bretton Woods institutions to privatize lies in the historical context of privatization as it was implemented in the US and UK. The privatization of public assets as a key policy commitment got underway in earnest in the 1980s, under the governments of Margaret Thatcher and Ronald Reagan (Massey and Pyper 2005). British privatization took place in a climate that sought to reduce the burden on the Treasury and 'set free' over-staffed and undercapitalized industries. In those cases, such as the utilities that were a natural monopoly, a complex regulatory regime was established by the privatizing statute. By contrast, in Kenya (along with much of Africa) the process really got under way in the early 1990s and was described as 'half-hearted' secretive and a process used to hand over large parts of the public sector to corrupt elites with the collusion of the NGOs involved (Anyang'Nyong'O *et al.* 2000, pp. vii–ix, Massey 2010). The belief that there could be a simple 'copy' of privatization across the board was both naïve and false. But it did not rule out one-off successes and this is what those involved with Kenya Airways were seeking; it may also have shown the way for future successes (interviews with Kenyan officials; Mwaura 2007). It is interesting to understand how and why some of these successes occurred as this explains the way in which we should see them not as policy transfer, but as policy mimesis.

Case study: privatizing Kenya Airways

Given the earlier points regarding privatization (the lack of a comprehensive legal framework for privatization in Kenya in the early 1990s, the prevalence of corruption and the problems of a lack of effective civic society institutions), the prospect of privatizing Kenya Airways (KQ) was problematic. In 1990, the Kenyan vice-president, Professor George Saitoti appointed a 'probe' committee under the chairmanship of Isaac Omolo Okero. The committee was to:

(1) evaluate the qualifications, experience and appropriateness of the staff of Kenya Airways and to recommend optimum staffing levels;
(2) to look into the financial management and capital sources of the Airline and to recommend improvements in general revenue generation;
(3) to examine the management and operations of the Airline and recommend improvements to enable the Airline to operate at optimum level;
(4) to examine the fleet of aircraft and recommend the proper level of equipment and type of aircraft; and
(5) to investigate the affairs of KQ and make recommendations regarding strategic development (Omolo Okero 1990, p. 8, Massey 2010).

The report was presented to the Minister in September 1990; it was devastating in its critique of the *status quo*. It placed KQ within its global context; aviation being a 'highly complicated, competitive, and dynamic industry and no measure of Government protection can enable a National Carrier to compete unless the Airline adopts the same standards of the industry', that Kenya is a desirable destination and suitable for becoming a regional hub (Omolo Okero 1990, p. 3). The problem, however, was that:

> Kenya Airways is presently insolvent, and poorly managed. It has no Corporate Plan, or effective management organisation. There is a lack of communication, discipline and training. The staff is ineffective, poorly remunerated, and lack motivation. In its present form, it is totally uncompetitive within the industry (Omolo Okero 1990, p. 3).

The report recommended the restructuring of the airline and its privatization. KQ was typical of parastatals in Kenya, where the appointment of directors and managers by powerful politicians politicized the process, with appointees acting in the corrupt interests of those individuals who appointed them (Mwaura 2007, p. 49).

Given its position as part of the global airline industry, beyond the boundaries of Kenya and Africa, a privatization of KQ required inward investment. There were insufficient Kenyan resources for a normal 'sell-off'. In order to tempt investors the airline first had to be modernized. To do this, it was necessary to control the corruption and begin to apply industry standard 'best practice'. This meant it was necessary to isolate KQ from the general Kenyan political situation and link it firmly in the global setting of international airlines, thereby protecting it. At the same time, the benefits of this global positioning were to be used for Kenya's advantage, training Kenyans up to international standards to occupy all positions within the airline and to pay them internationally competitive salaries, thereby leveraging in Western standards of pay, conditions and service for East Africa. The benefits to the nation from possessing a modern profitable national airline were summarized by Okero as being a major source of employment in a high-technology field, including the opportunity for significant technology transfer to Kenya (Omolo Okero 1990, pp. 17–18, Massey 2010).

Major world airlines strove for fleet commonality to reduce costs and make strategic savings in terms of spare parts and staff training and expertise and use market research to decide the type of aircraft according to the routes flown, KQ had not completed this basic management activity. Consequently the fleet 'composition was at no time based on cost and market analysis. Similar weaknesses were systematically revealed in terms of scheduling, route statistics, marketing, passenger yields, financial management and capital resources, strategic planning, cash accounting, cargo handling, passenger handling, debt scheduling, revenue enhancement, pay and progression planning and promotion strategy' (Omolo Okero 1990, pp. 37–90, Massey 2010). The Committee noted that, 'it is to the credit of the airline that it still operates at all' (Omolo Okero 1990, p. 93). The Kenyan government largely accepted the report's recommendations. Although the global positioning of the airline made this a logical decision, it was also surprising in its Kenyan context as successive Kenyan governments had apparently ignored pressure by Western donor nations to modernize their public administration and reduce corruption, pressure that led to a British High Commissioner publicly berating ministers in 2004 (Phombeah 2004).

It is possible KQ was treated differently to other parastatal privatizations because the individuals concerned with leading the process took charge in a way not repeated elsewhere. Certainly, the dissipation of the nation's resources could be traced to a great extent to the corruption and mismanagement of the public sector. Although parastatals accounted for 11% of GDP between 1986 and 1990, they were 'responsible for a net outflow of three billion Kenyan shillings, equivalent to 0.9% of GDP from central government' (Mwaura 2007, p. 41). The privatization of KQ began to resemble (to borrow from Pollitt) a punctuation point, a fork in the road, or even a transformation (Pollitt 2008, p. 46), for the airline industry, but not, perhaps, for the public sector as a whole (cited Massey 2010).

In 1991, a new board was appointed to 'commercialize and prepare the airline for privatization' (interview with Kenyan official). The new chairman was Philip Ndegwa, one of Kenya's richest people and a power-broker of renown. Ndegwa did not have extensive knowledge of the airline industry and was a reluctant presidential appointee (interviews with officials cited Massey 2010). Isaac Omolo Okero was appointed as deputy chairman determined to oversee the implementation of his report. The third member of the team to make a major contribution to restructuring KQ was Brian Davies. Davies was appointed as a result of Ndegwa's concern that neither he nor any senior KQ manager knew how to run an airline. Given this concern he approached Colin Marshall, the CEO of British Airways for advice. The result was the appointment of Davies who had worked for BA for 25 years, finishing as chief engineer (interviews with UK and Kenyan officials).

Davies appointed a team of managers and engineers with global experience and set about modernizing KQ in the image of the world's leading airlines. He was given political protection by Ndegwa, his reluctant chairman, who saw that only a privatization that copied the best practice of the West would be successful and promised the riches of major international investment, leading to potentially large profits. Ndegwa became *de facto* non-executive chairman, leaving the day-to-day management decisions to Davies and his new team of senior managers. This signalled a clear break with the past, putting technical experts in charge and removing the Kenyan elite to the side-lines was unprecedented. From that point, Davies was to explicitly use the UK model for privatization:

> he built the company into a structure that knew its market, reacted to that market, that delivered good service and made a profit. He focussed on the business case and building up technical competence. Ndegwa concentrated on providing political 'cover' for the Board and the management team, keeping ministers and civil servants at bay while the re-structuring was carried out. Given his power and influence with the President and other senior ministers few other people could have performed this role at such a crucial stage (Massey 2010).

As such this was clearly not a policy transfer, so much as inchoate industrial and political transformation.

KQ was freed from cumbersome bureaucracy and given a trading-fund, modelled on successful UK privatizations. It then sought to remove executives who were ministerial appointees and their henchmen. Large numbers were sacked and where they were replaced in the leaner modern structures Davies created it was by professional experts recruited internationally. Midway through the process of modernization and on the cusp of the privatization, Ndegwa died and was replaced as chairman by Omolo Okero. He and Davies continued the modernization, seeing through the privatization process by selling 26% of KQ to KLM, a major world airline. In return for its share, KLM delivered significant amounts of investment in new technology, both IT and aero-engineering, as well as further managerial reform. Fourteen percent of KQ was then sold to foreign investors, mainly fund managers in

London and 3% was given to KQ staff, via a KQ Shareholders' Trust established on behalf of the staff. The rest, 34%, was floated on the Nairobi Stock Exchange. One year later the World Bank awarded the KQ privatization a certificate of merit; it was the most successful World Bank project globally that year (Massey 2010). The tie-in with KLM was a major success and in addition to the other benefits to KQ established Nairobi as a hub airport, an essential pre-requisite to delivering substantial profits. These profits began to grow and Okero used the money to invest in new equipment, especially new aircraft to replace the inappropriate fleet his report had identified. No dividends or low dividends were paid in these years. In 1999 it was voted African Airline of the year, and again in several subsequent years, also recording record profits up to 2006, the year Omolo Okero retired as chairman.

The fourth remarkable leader in this study is Monica Oyas, who completed the process of modernization by implementing modern Western notions of management best practice. Oyas joined KQ in 2002 and set to work implementing an ambitious restructuring plan that included appointment on merit, management appraisals and the setting of target driven management, all the paraphernalia of modern corporate governance (Massey 2010). The number of Directorates was reduced, from 14 to 7, freeing up the senior managers and the new CEO, Titus Naikuni, to concentrate on strategy. Functions were grouped according to their relationship, replacing the old KQ structures with a competency-based approach appointing people to post, based entirely on company need and individual merit. It was transformatory for East African parastatals (although commonplace in international banks and other global players), but was essential in ensuring success for the company and convincing partners and rivals alike that KQ was a modern company able to compete globally on equal terms (Massey 2010).

Conclusions

This case study illustrates the role and importance of individuals and of context in the process of leading change and making strategic decisions. The privatization of KQ came after decades of decline and was set within two contexts: Kenyan and global. It was the insertion of global rules and benchmarks that enabled the constraints of the local context to be overcome, but the process could only proceed by playing to the different power-brokers within that local regional setting. The policy makers copied the best practice of Western examples, but adjusted them to take account of local realities. The privatization of KQ was an example not of policy transfer, but of policy mimesis, cajoled, prodded and lead via a constellation of dynamics, not least of which were many of the institutions embedded in the workings of 'global governance'.

The broader conclusion of the article reflects the importance of the overall context of a policy decision and the way in which that context, which must include the history of the previous decisions can lock in decision-makers. But that at certain junctures a punctuation point can occur or be manufactured that allows change to take place (Pollitt 2008). Within the context of global governance this kind of change will occur when dominant elites and groups seize the resources offered by aligning themselves with transnational institutions and networks, structures that often lack a focal point of accountability or legitimacy. In these terms policy transfer is often a misnomer and it would be more accurate to refer to the concept of policy mimesis. There are clear problems with notions of democratic accountability in this analysis. One way of addressing these is to explore the recommendations of the Pagaza–Argyriades group and note their call to recognize that global governance be recognized 'to mean a democratic system of multilateral governance' that should be located within the global system of international law and administration, ensuring governments make effective use of existing governmental machinery for addressing pressing issues of resource allocation and global goods. An aid to this would include the establishment of a core of public servants placed under UN auspices and trained in accountable, ethical and professional behaviour to internationally recognised standards overseen by a global public services academy' (Thynne and Massey 2009, pp. 212–215). Such a set of institutions may allow the change from policy mimesis to policy transfer proper and reassert a locus of accountability and democratic control.

References

Anyang'Nyong'O, P., 2001. *Governance and poverty reduction in Africa. Economic Research Papers, No. 68.* Abidjan: The African Development Bank.

Anyang'Nyong'O, P., 2002. Democracy and political leadership in Africa in the context of NEPAD. *Japan Institute for International Affairs Conference at the World Summit on Development,* August 31, 2002. Johannesburg, South Africa.

Anyang'Nyong'O, P., *et al.,* 2000. *The context of privatisation in Kenya.* Nairobi: African Academy of Sciences.

Archibugi, D., 2004. Cosmopolitan democracy and its critics. A review. *European journal of international relations,* 10 (3), 437–473.

Carr, F. and Massey, A., eds, 2006. *Public policy and the new European agendas.* Cheltenham: Edward Elgar.

Common, R., 2001. *Public management and policy transfer in South East Asia.* Aldershot: Ashgate.

Ikiara, G.K., 2000. A review of Kenya's public sector. *In:* P. Anyang'Nyong'O *et al.,* eds. *The context of privatisation in Kenya.* Nairobi: African Academy of Sciences.

Kaul, I., 2005. Private provision and global public goods: do the two go together? *Global social policy,* 5, 137–140.

Lodge, M., 2002. Varieties of Europeanisation and the national regulatory state. *Public policy and administration,* 17 (2), 43–67.

Massey, A., 1993. Managing the public sector: a comparative analysis of the United Kingdom and the United States. Cheltenham: Edward Elgar.

Massey, A. and Pyper, R., 2005. *Public management and modernization in Britain.* Basingstoke: Palgrave.

Murray, C., 2006. *Murder in Samarkand: a British ambassador's controversial defiance of tyranny in the war on terror.* London: Mainstream Publishing.

Mwaura, K., 2007. The failure of corperate governance in state-owned enterprises and the need for restructural governance in fully and partially privatised enterprises: the case of Kenya. *Fordhan international law journal,* 31, 134–175.

Omelicheva, M., Global civil society: an empirical portrayal. Paper presented at the annual meeting of the American Political Science Association, Hilton, Chicago and the Palmer House Hilton, Chicago, IL, 2 September, 2004.

Omolo Okero, I.E., 1990. *Report of the committee investigating the management and operations of Kenya Airways* (Chairman I.E. Omolo Okero). Nairobi: Ministry of Finance [this is an unpublished and confidential document].

Pattberg, P., 2005. The institutionalization of private governance: how business and nonprofit organizations agree on transnational rules. *Governance*, 18 (4), 589–610.

Phombeah, G., 2004. *Profile: Edward Clay*. London: BBC.

Pichardo Pagaza, I. and Argyriades, D., *Winning the needed change: saving our planet Earth – a global public service*. Institute of Administrative Science Monographs Volume 30. Amsterdam: IOS Press.

Pollitt, C., 2008. *Time, policy, management: governing with the past*. Oxford: Oxford University Press.

Putzel, J., 2005. Globalization, liberalization, and prospects for the state. *International political science review*, 26 (1), 5–16.

Rhodes, R.A.W., 1997. *Understanding governance*. Buckingham and Philadelphia: Open University Press.

Ruggie, J., 2004. Reconstructing the global public domain: issues, actors, and practices. *European journal of international relations*, 10 (4), 499–530.

Stoker, G., 2006. Public value management: a new narrative for networked governance? *The american review of public administration*, 36, 41–57.

Thynne, I. and Massey, A., 2009. Global governance: prospects and challenges. *In*: I. Pichardo Pagaza and D. Argyriades, eds. *Winning the needed change: saving planet earth – a global public service*. Amsterdam: IOS/IIAS.

Whitman, J., 2002. Global governance as the friendly face of unaccountable power. *Security dialogue*, 33 (1), 4–50.

Williamson, O., 1985. *The economic institutions of capitalism*. New York: The Free Press.

World Bank, 1981. *Accelerated development in sub-Saharan Africa: an agenda for action*. Washington: World Bank.

IN CONCLUSION

Parting shots

This special issue's main concern has been with evaluating how useful policy transfer analysis is as a descriptive, explanatory and prescriptive theory of policy change. With this aim in mind, it has provided both a response to its critics and a variety of new directions for studying processes of policy transfer. It was hoped that this would allow for the development of a better understanding of the phenomenon of policy transfer and its relationship with global and domestic processes of economic, social and political change. It therefore remains to draw some general conclusions on the implications of our case study findings for the broader study of policy transfer.

The domain of enquiry

The study of policy transfer can only be distinctive from the analysis of normal forms of policy-making if its focuses on the remarkable movement of ideas between systems of governance in different countries. Policy transfer and by implication policy learning or lesson-drawing is therefore best concerned with the study of discernible and remarkable features of contemporary policy change not otherwise explained. The daily diffusion of knowledge, intentional or otherwise, at the micro level within organizations or between organizations in a system of governance is not remarkable either in terms of process or of fact. These processes are best the subject of normal policy studies.

Nonetheless, policy transfer analysis undoubtedly contributes a great deal to the study of policy-making. It presents an intellectual context for integrating common research concerns of scholars of domestic, comparative and international politics as it provides a lens for observing both the changing nature of the nation state and the role of state actors and institutions in promoting new forms of political globalization. It demonstrates both the weakness and the strength of the state in the process of policy formulation depending on the form of transfer you are looking at. For example, in indirectly coercive or negotiated forms of transfer, where one agent compels another state to adopt a policy, idea or institution in return for inward investment or aid, it clearly demonstrates the weakness of the state in decision processes. Conversely, the deployment of tactical models of transfer by states illustrates their autonomy from societal and international forces.

Policy transfer analysis also proves useful in helping us to understand how decision-makers acquire knowledge and how they can act as agents of transfer themselves. It exposes the development of inner circles of policy-making participants who promote new forms of complex globalization in the attempt to adapt state action to cope more effectively with what they see as global 'realities'. And, it illustrates that the timescale which is established to search for policy ideas informs the scope of enquiry and almost inevitably draws policy-makers to easily accessible exemplars who share similar ideological commitments and normally a common language. Hence a multi-level search activity creates a pathology for hybrid forms of cross-national and cross sectoral policy transfer and consequently policy and programme copying is very rare.

Theory and method

Policy transfer analysis is a useful heuristic model of policy-making employed for cognitive purposes to suggest something about the properties and relations understood to exist within cross cultural processes of policy-oriented learning. It has *additionality,* because policy transfer analysis does tell us something that we did not know before. We now have a good idea about the domestic and international circumstances which are likely to bring about policy transfer, the scope and dimensions of policy transfer and which aspects of the framework should and should not be pursued in empirical work.

However, up until recently much policy transfer analysis did exhibit an inability to determine with *precision* the phenomenon it was trying to explain. This argument does not negate the importance of the policy transfer approach. As Brian Barry (1975, p. 86) argues, '[o]ur understanding of a subject may be advanced if concepts and processes can be translated into other terms more readily grasped and fruitful analogy will suggest new lines of enquiry by provoking the speculation that relationships found in the one field may hold, mutatis mutandis, in the other as well.' It therefore follows that we should be able to extract novel hypotheses from studies of policy transfer, which must then be articulated in a systematic fashion in order to provide the basis for future empirical research. The articles in this issue followed Barry's prompt in proceeding from the underlying assumption that policy transfer analysis alone cannot provide a general explanatory theory of policy change but when combined with other approaches an empirically grounded account of policy change can be developed. The adoption of a methodological pluralism through the deployment of complementary theories of policy development have been combined effectively to develop a theory of policy change that accounts for the role of particular agents of policy transfer in forging policy change. However, there remain three areas where policy transfer analysis continues to be underdeveloped: validating knowledge claims about the increase of policy transfer activity in an era of globalization; the availability of methods for demonstrating policy transfer; and issues relating to the practice of policy transfer.

Globalization and policy transfer

The first is that policy scientists continue to make the non-falsifiable claim that processes of globalization have increased the opportunities for policy transfer to take place. It remains impossible to disprove this claim one way or another but it does suggest the need to establish a base-line for measuring such claims in the future. This will inevitably involve the application of quantitative methods in the study of policy transfer to measure the frequency of policy transfer innovation.

Demonstrating policy transfer

The second area of underdevelopment lies in the weakness of existing methods for demonstrating policy transfer. David Dolowitz and David Marsh (1996) rightly argue for a clear scheme for measuring the occurrence of policy transfer. To achieve this, they identify five sources through which the existence of policy transfer might be observed: the media, reports, conferences, visits and government statements. However, these categories should be treated more as sources of learning than as sources of evidence that policy transfer has occurred. Unfortunately, much of the existing literature does not provide adequate techniques for demonstrating policy transfer. Indeed, given adequate standards of validation, proof of policy transfer may be more difficult than is commonly assumed by those arguing that it is on the increase. This is because rigorous validation would demand excellent access to key informants, which is often beyond the reach of policy scientists. Consequently, much of the existing literature rests too much on abstracting perfect fit cases of policy transfer. This' is why greater attention must be paid to investigating cases of non-transfer and in-process transfer in order to improve our understanding of the process of policy development. The following five steps can be used as a safeguard against exaggerated claims about the nature and extent of policy transfer.

1. The subject of analysis

At the outset, it is important to be clear about the phenomenon under study. In primary empirical work, a range of possibility exists. One might consider attempts to facilitate/enforce policy transfer, the process of transfer, as it is occurring, or a claim that policy transfer has occurred in the past.

2. Who or what is identified as the agent(s) of transfer: who wants it, what do they want from it, how are they going about effecting it, to whose benefit, and why?

An agent is essential to the voluntary and coercive dimensions of policy transfer given that policy transfer involves action oriented intentional learning. Hence, transfer must be a conscious process, whether this is undertaken voluntarily or whether the subject of coercion.

3. Is there evidence of non-transfer?

There are two potential dimensions of non-transfer to be taken into account in any validation exercise. Elements of an idea or a programme which are borrowed from domestic antecedents or which are innovative can be described as non-transfers. Parts of an original idea or programme discarded or filtered out by the subject/agent are also non-transfers. Detailed comparison of the subject policy against both domestic and original settings is therefore essential if the real extent of transfer in a particular case is to be discovered.

4. What is the evidence offered to support the claim? How good is it?

Researchers should look for a preponderance of evidence, which demonstrates or refutes a process of policy transfer. Clearly, evidence will differ depending on the nature of the subject. For example, in seeking to demonstrate whether an idea or an attitude has been transferred, a researcher will seek to examine the views and interpretations of the recipient subject(s). If on the other hand it were being argued that a programme has been copied, one would expect to find more concrete 'physical' evidence. One can only say that a programme has been copied by another programme if they have been compared. The question of whether the programme has been carried out might then be subjected to implementation analysis to determine how far the transfer has permeated. A distinction should be made between *soft* transfers (ideas, concepts, attitudes) and *hard* transfers (programmes and implementation).

The question then follows as to how good the evidence on offer is. Of course, this is a problem of empirical analysis in general, but it is of particular importance here, given the different kinds of transfer and different evidence, which might support them.

5. What conclusion can be drawn from the above about the nature and extent of transfer, which has taken place?

Here, answers are given to questions about the subject of analysis: what is the content of the transfer if anything? To what extent has the programme been culturally or organizationally assimilated? What measures were taken to filter out incompatible elements? If policy transfer is found to have occurred this will then allow for a determination of the process of policy-oriented learning as either copying, emulation, hybridization, or inspiration.

Practice

From the perspective of practice, three main shortcomings are evident. The first is that the study of policy transfer would benefit from greater reflection on how traditional organizations can become learning organizations. Rose (2005, pp. 104–105), for example, argues that the strategic direction of public organizations are path dependent and characterized by 'inheritance rather than choice' in the sense that 'past commitments limit current choices'. Hence a set of recommendations on how to break from the 'wicked context' problem would be extremely useful.

Second, a more detailed identification of potential obstacles to successful lesson-drawing would provide important insights for practitioners into how to develop: (1) the type of learning organization conducive to the facilitation of successful lesson-drawing and (2) a model of prospective evaluation to guide effective lesson-drawing. Third, the very existence of elite-driven policy transfer networks presents obstacles to the achievement of representative and responsive government and thus raises normative concerns. Policy transfer networks are often dominated by technocratic elites, subject to interest capture and experience problems of weak democratic control and accountability. There is therefore a profound need to ensure that this mode of networked governance achieves public value. I have argued elsewhere that the emergence of public value management (PVM) is a direct response to the development of networked governance and the limits of NPM in managing the inherent problems in this mode of governance (Evans 2009). The same argument can of course be applied to the process of policy transfer. Mark Moore (1995), who developed the concept, argues that public services can add value to society in the same way that private for-profit organizations create value for their shareholders and other stakeholders. By implication, public intervention should be circumscribed by the need to achieve positive social and economic outcomes for the citizenry. What is and what is not public value should be determined collectively through inclusive deliberation involving elected and appointed government officials, key stakeholders and the public.

Endnote

The application of the concept of public value to policy transfer activity particularly in developing areas could prove particularly far-sighted. Here governments are particularly vulnerable to international policy agendas established through the Post-Washington Consensus and elsewhere. Indeed, the ability of many states to make choices about adopting international policy agendas is largely determined by their state of development in general and their ability to manage knowledge in particular (see Riggirozzi 2007). The latter power resource necessitates the existence of an élan of proficient technocrats in the indigenous bureaucracy that has the capacity to make informed policy choices and provide evidence-based resistance to external sources of ill-conceived policy transfer. However, the existence of proficient technocrats in developing countries is often in short supply. This structural vulnerability is reflected both in conditionality (defined here as the pursuit of international policy agendas) in return for development or humanitarian assistance, inward investment and/or technical assistance. This is often a vicious cycle, as governmental organizations do not often possess the expertise to implement international policy agendas and increasingly look outside the organization for technical assistance. Hence, both the dissemination of 'best practice' and the provision of technical assistance to developing countries by international governmental and non-governmental organizations provide opportunity structures for policy transfer.

These opportunity structures for policy transfer enhance the capacity of non-state international actors to penetrate indigenous decision structures and gain a status of acceptance in policy-making processes; giving rise to the development of inner circles of policy-making participants who often promote new forms of political globalization in the attempt to adapt state action to cope more effectively with what they see as global 'realities'. Moreover, the creation of policy transfer networks provides an opportunity structure for the creation of further policy transfer networks creating a path dependent logic of institutionalization, which is often non-indigenous in origin.

This latter observation has profound implications for how we consider the legitimacy of externally promoted policy change in developing countries. Traditionally, conditionality was the most apparent policy instrument for affecting externally promoted policy change in areas of macroeconomic reform such as trade liberalization, structural adjustment and privatization. In many ways it was naked in its despotism and in its negative impact, particularly in African states and newly democratized former Soviets, self-evident. However, today the sources of externally promoted policy change are far subtler in the ways in which they articulate influence over development agendas. The capacity to generate evidence based development choices by organizations such as the World Bank through the establishment of knowledge banks is now one of the key sources of power in international development.

The final argument in this conclusion therefore is to contend that the key to rational and legitimate policy transfer lies in its ownership by local communities. Indeed the evidence suggests that external sources of policy change are rarely successful unless local people articulate them as the path to development of choice. Nonetheless, 'rational' policy transfer activity which avoids the 'learning paradox' is to be encouraged. In sum, policy transfer can be a rational and progressive learning activity but only if the programme that is transferred is driven by indigenous actors, compatible with the value system of the recipient organization, culturally assimilated through comprehensive evaluation and piloting, builds on existing organizational strengths and delivers *public value* in terms of direct or indirect social or economic benefits.

Professor Mark Evans

Director, Australia-New Zealand School of Government, Institute for Governance, University of Canberra

References

Barry, B., 1975. On analogy. *Political studies*, 23 (2–3), 208–224.
Dolowitz, D. and Marsh, D., 1996. Who learns what from whom: a review of the policy transfer literature. *Political studies*, 44, 343–357.
Evans, M., 2009. Gordon Brown and public management reform: a project in search of a 'big idea.' *Policy studies*, 30 (1), 33–52.
Moore, M., 1995. *Creating public value*. Cambridge, MA: Harvard.
Riggirozzi, M., 2007. The World Bank as a conveyor and broker of knowledge and funds in Argentina's governance reforms. *In*: D. Stone and C. Wright, eds. *The World Bank and governance*. London & New York: Routledge, 207–227.
Rose, R., 2005. *Learning from comparative public policy: a practical guide*. London & New York: Routledge.

Index

Page numbers in *Italics* represent tables.

For Product Safety Concerns and Information please contact our EU
representative GPSR@taylorandfrancis.com
Taylor & Francis Verlag GmbH, Kaufingerstraße 24, 80331 München, Germany